ptation
SOCIAL DEMOCRACY, CAPITALISM, AND COMPETITION

Social Democracy, Capitalism, and Competition

A Manifesto

MARCEL BOYER

McGill-Queen's University Press
Montreal & Kingston • London • Chicago

© McGill-Queen's University Press 2023

ISBN 978-0-2280-1889-6 (cloth)
ISBN 978-0-2280-1943-5 (ePDF)
ISBN 978-0-2280-1944-2 (ePUB)

Legal deposit fourth quarter 2023
Bibliothèque nationale du Québec

Printed in Canada on acid-free paper that is 100% ancient forest free (100% post-consumer recycled), processed chlorine free

We acknowledge the support of the Canada Council for the Arts.

Nous remercions le Conseil des arts du Canada de son soutien.

McGill-Queen's University Press in Montreal is on land which long served as a site of meeting and exchange amongst Indigenous Peoples, including the Haudenosaunee and Anishinabeg nations. In Kingston it is situated on the territory of the Haudenosaunee and Anishinaabek. We acknowledge and thank the diverse Indigenous Peoples whose footsteps have marked these territories on which peoples of the world now gather.

Library and Archives Canada Cataloguing in Publication

Title: Social democracy, capitalism, and competition : a manifesto / Marcel Boyer.
Names: Boyer, Marcel, author.
Description: Includes bibliographical references and index.
Identifiers: Canadiana (print) 20230459269 | Canadiana (ebook) 20230459358 | ISBN 9780228018896 (hardcover) | ISBN 9780228019442 (ePUB) | ISBN 9780228019435 (ePDF)
Subjects: LCSH: Capitalism. | LCSH: Competition. | LCSH: Socialism. | LCSH: Human services. | LCSH: Economic policy.
Classification: LCC HB501 .B69 2023 | DDC 330.12/2—dc23

This book was typeset by True to Type in 10.5/13 Sabon

To my wife, Nicole, for her loving tolerance and support over the past sixty years and counting.

Contents

Preface   ix
Acknowledgments   xix

Introduction   3
1 Basic Socio-economic Concepts Revisited   11
2 Competition-Based Social Democracy   32
3 The New Competition-Based Capitalism   57
4 The "Fab Four" Factors of Growth   85
5 Ethics, Equity, and Socially Responsible Behaviour   94
6 Inequalities   121
7 The Cost of Public Funds and the Governance of Public Projects   136
8 Free Trade and National Security   153
   Conclusion: Sweeping but Not Utopian Reforms   166

Notes   189
Index   221

Preface

This book will argue that a true social democracy requires a clear definition and refocus of the respective roles of the public (governmental) and competitive (private) sectors in the provision of public and social goods and services (PSGS), such as education, health care, and transport infrastructure, as well as regulations of different types and forms, with citizens' best interests in mind. The competition-based social democracy (CSD) and the new competition-based capitalism (NCC) models described and advocated here represent a return to basics, to the foundational characteristics of what social democracy and capitalism are supposed to be. Recent decades have witnessed a shift in both models away from competition and competitive processes, which I argue should be the underlying determinants of their potential contribution to social well-being.

For social democracy, this shift has meant more public bureaucratic control of the provision of public and social goods and services and more ironclad protection of state providers from contestation by potentially competing organizations. The result is a loss of purpose stemming from organizational inefficiency, as outcomes deviate increasingly from objectives and the costs of PSGS become larger than necessary. We have seen a capture of public entities by well-organized and self-interested groups at the expense of the informal assembly of citizens. The result is a deep if subtle form of crony capitalism in which private and public entrepreneurs are increasingly aligned. Pyromaniac firefighters have seized crucial positions of power.

THE NEW CSD AND NCC MODELS

The "new" social democracy and capitalism models proposed here are rooted in the *economic* analysis of organizations. This analysis discusses the efficient coordination of activities and decisions, and the use of incentive mechanisms, both with regard to internal processes of organizations and their presence in value chains. The pervasive conflicts of interest in the political-cum-bureaucratic control of the management of PSGS end up negating the rights of citizens to the delivery of those goods and services, with implications for both quantity and quality.

As to the recently proposed models of stakeholder and ESG (or environmental, social, governance) capitalism,[1] they can be characterized as a mire in which vacuous and meaningless mission statements dominate, raising concern within the stakeholder and ESG movements themselves. This situation opens the door for manipulation as well as regulatory avoidance, resulting in a significant risk of a drop in trust toward and within capitalism.

This book presents and argues for significant reforms of capitalism that go hand in hand with significant reforms of social democracy. Both sets of reforms will of course meet strongly voiced denial of the need for such significant reorganization. But attempting to reform social democracy and capitalism is a necessary if titanic task. The fact that modern societies have become wealthier and generally better educated gives some hope that this discussion may lead to a better world for all.

In the CSD model (discussed in chapter 2), the main roles of the public or governmental sector will be identifying the basket of PSGS in quantity and quality and managing incentive contracts with the (competitive) private sector for the production, distribution, and delivery of those goods and services. The public sector would no longer directly manage schools, hospitals, and other such services. The applications to education and health care and other public and social goods and services will be discussed in the conclusion; they should by then be clear enough in spirit without the need to explicitly describe them. However, one conclusion is that there is no "one size fits all" in the management of such goods and services.

In the NCC model (discussed in chapter 3), reform programs are proposed to encourage firms to commit to refraining from doing business with other firms that are heavily subsidized, whether they be suppliers or customers. Other programs suggested here aim at developing markets, property rights, and carbon levies to induce firms to take into account environmental impacts. I argue for the development of liability rules to raise the incentives for firms and their partners to prevent industrial and environmental accidents. I will also propose the abolition of taxes on corporate profits so as to encourage companies to focus on their core missions of wealth creation, R&D investment, and productivity gains.

OBJECTIVES VERSUS MEANS

Many of the debates currently raging in our societies, both developed and developing, are rooted not in a conflict between the Left and the Right, or between socialists, neoliberals, and conservatives, but rather in a confusion between *objectives* on the one hand and *means* on the other.

Properly separating objectives and means leads me to reassess what social democracy is all about. Social democracy's objectives are typically focused on promoting the availability and accessibility of social services and "goods" such as education, health care, civil infrastructure (roads, bridge, sewers and aqueducts, etc.), public security (police and firefighting services), social insurance (unemployment, health services), pensions, street lightning, local and intercity transportation, etc. The means to attain these objectives include different management systems and financing schemes. *Means* relate to who does what and how, who pays what and how in relation to PSGS: either through government control of operations, or incentive contracts between the public and competitive sectors.

People may disagree on the appropriate objectives for a society. They may differ in their views on how efforts should be allocated between creating and redistributing wealth. They may even argue about the relative efficiency of different means available for pursuing shared objectives. But when there is confusion between the objectives and the means available for achieving them, the debate becomes circular and spurious.

To a large extent, an objective must be socially shared, in that we all agree on it or at least have a way to build a consensus around it. Regarding means, the discussion should be more technical. What resources and technologies are available? How can they be integrated and organized to further the objectives? And how much do those means cost?

Achieving a consensus on objectives requires electoral rules and institutions. The discussion of means is essentially concerned with relative efficiency. Achieving a consensus on means requires a competitive economic process via competitive markets and prices.

IMPORTANT CONCEPTUAL (MIS)UNDERSTANDINGS

In order to shed light on the vision and analytical foundations underlying the CSD and NCC models, I will explore some important concepts that may not be fully familiar to all readers.

In chapter 1, I look at a host of socio-economic concepts, in particular organizational challenges; value, profits, and trust; businesses, entrepreneurs, and competition; the complexity of job creation; and the power of the status quo. The often confused discussions related to the notions of value, profit, and job creation in particular justify our spending some time clarifying those concepts.

It is false to argue that, since private firms must earn profits in addition to covering their costs, the prices of their goods and services will necessarily be higher than the prices that a government-owned enterprise would charge for the same goods and services. This error, which is repeated again and again, lies in the confusion between accounting profit and economic profit. Accounting profit is the difference between revenues and all costs, including interest charges on debt but excluding equity capital costs. Economic profit is the difference between revenues and all costs, including interest charges on debt *and* the costs of equity capital, whether that equity capital is private or public. For example, if a hospital is built and financed by a competitive-sector organization, the (equity) capital invested is compensated through profits. If it is built and financed by a public-sector organization, the public capital invested must be compensated at its *opportunity cost* – that is, the value of foregone activities and projects displaced by the hospital project.

In chapter 4, I present the fabulous four factors of growth: human capital; inventions and innovations; incentive mechanisms promoting social well-being (information, congruence, compatibility); and efficient resource allocation and coordination mechanisms. Of these four key factors, the last one plays a particularly important role as it conditions the development of the other three. The chapter will conclude by stressing the role of exchange and trade, and their underlying determinants, in achieving high levels of social well-being – thereby conditioning the development of civilization itself.

In chapter 5, I discuss the concepts of ethics, equity, and socially responsible behaviour, which are at the heart of social democracy. The economic and ecological understandings of ethics and equity are discussed through the ESG compact and the value of environmental and water resources. The chapter discusses corporate social responsibility via four trains of thought. The first links the new, trendy ESG features with the four factors of quality growth discussed in chapter 4. A second focuses on the respective roles of business and government in the development of ESG policies and actions. A third is the inclusion of human rights, and more specifically child labour, within an ESG policy. Finally, a fourth qualifies the corporate extended liability for industrial and environmental accidents and disasters. In each of these cases, the results of economic analysis may be surprising.

I discuss in some depth the role of competition, with a particular emphasis on the price of carbon emissions (in the form of a carbon levy, more often but wrongfully referred to as a carbon tax) and on extended liability in achieving environmental protection. I also address the challenge of protecting water resources, among other common-pool resources. Protecting against the over-exploitation and depletion of water resources is challenging when individuals, acting independently (in an uncoordinated way) and rationally, end up countering society's best interests. Protection against the under-exploitation of water resources is also challenging when individuals, as rights holders with a capacity for preventing others from using the resources, fail to coordinate (coordination breakdown) and end up frustrating what would be a socially desirable outcome. The chapter concludes by claiming that water protection and sharing, a valued principle of social democracy, can be achieved by water pricing and trading.

I take a fresh look at inequalities of income, wealth, and consumption in chapter 6. As inequalities of income and wealth have been increasing since 1980 (they were decreasing for over sixty years before that), the inequalities of consumption have gone down. This reduction is due to the recognition of social transfers of money (including progressive taxation) and social transfers in kind (STIK). This refers to those goods and services produced by the government or private entities, for which consumers either pay nothing or pay less than the full cost. Examples are education, health care, as well as parks and other free or quasi-free community goods and services. Such social transfers, in money and in kind, are a central element of social democracy.

They have increased over recent decades and represent a particularly significant part of the adjusted household disposable income (household disposable income plus social transfers in kind) of those in the bottom 20 per cent and 40 per cent income brackets.

This implies that the extreme emphasis put on income and wealth inequalities in popular, political, and academic circles is misplaced. It unnecessarily exacerbates social conflicts, whereas a more reasonable emphasis on *consumption* inequality, neglected but socially more important, would tend to bring down such conflicts. In Canada, for example, the ratio of household adjusted final consumption (household final consumption expenditures plus social transfers in kind) of the top 20 per cent over the bottom 20 per cent of income has decreased by 25 per cent over the last two decades. In other words, the gap between what the richest and the poorest actually consume or use has decreased.

The chapter also raises the broad question of the role of inequalities in human society. It concludes that income and wealth inequalities may be understood as means to meet three social goals: ensuring an adequate level of savings and investment, enabling appropriate creative destruction (losing/destroying jobs to create new ones), and fostering the development and acquisition of new skills that are socially desirable but individually costly. I claim that productivity gains, economic growth, and prosperity for all *actually require* a significant level of income and wealth inequality. In other words, low levels of income and wealth inequality may reduce savings, and thus investments, to levels lower than desired to increase future social well-being. Similarly, low levels of inequality may reduce the incentives to exert the necessary effort to acquire new skills. Finally, such low levels of inequality may prevent the transformation of jobs, from old and less productive ones (replaced or destroyed) to new and more productive ones (created).

I consider the true cost of public funds/capital and the governance of public projects in chapter 7, where I take a closer look at a major fallacy in assessing the relative cost of public versus private projects, one that is frequently repeated by officials in both the private (competitive) and public (governmental) sectors. In its simplest form, it appears as follows: since the cost of borrowing or financing is higher in the private sector than in the public sector, the cost of carrying out an activity (production, distribution, provision of goods and services) should be lower in the public sector than in the private one. Although governments can borrow at lower rates than private- or competitive-sector organizations, the error in the above argument is that part of the government's cost of borrowing is hidden from the casual observer of yields or borrowing costs.

It is as if citizens had given the government the right and power (a form of option or insurance) to request more money, if necessary, through taxation or other means (the reduction of services, for instance), in order to reimburse lenders. This right does have a price: it is the price the government would have to pay in competitive financial markets for such an option or insurance. This right allows the government to offer a transaction that is essentially risk-free for lenders, but potentially very risky for taxpayers. This cost is real, but is swept under the carpet, and as such is invisible. I claim that the true cost of capital is the same for both the public and the private sector.

I also discuss in chapter 7 the evaluation and governance of public projects, a central piece of both the CSD and NCC models. Since the production and delivery of PSGS will, under the CSD model, fall under the responsibility of the competitive sector under contract with the public sector, it is essential that we consider the proper setting and challenges underlying those contracts.

Under the public-private partnership (PPP) model, for instance, we have an organization composed of two partners, a public one and a competitive (private) one. Each partner has an essential role to play, in order to attain the ultimate goal of providing a set of PSGS to citizens in both quantity and quality. Similarly, under a traditional or GOC (government operations control) organization, we may consider that two partners are present, the principal (higher elected officials) and the agent (civil servants and workers on the ground), both of them in the public sector. Again, each partner has an essential role to play for the organization to be successful. Similarly, in an IOC (internal operations control) organization, we may consider that two partners are present, the principal or ordering party and the agent or contracting party, both of them in the private sector. And again, each partner has an essential role to play to attain the objective of providing a set of goods and services to customers.

The organizational challenges are similar if not the same in all cases. It is often said that the organizational and contractual challenges are present in PPP contexts but not really in GOC contexts. This is erroneous. The main difference between the two contexts is that the challenges are explicitly considered in the PPP context but hidden in the GOC one, under the false premise that the public-sector principal and agent partners share the same mission.

I discuss international trade and national security in chapter 8. An important characteristic of social democracy and capitalism is their general embrace of free trade. But the globalization of markets is often held responsible for destroying jobs in developed countries through offshoring and imports. It is also seen as undermining food security, environmental security, and national security through multilateral supply chains. These perceptions are (mostly) erroneous. The perceived negative impact of free trade often reflects the combined impacts of correlated causal factors. Insufficient effort has thus far been made to disentangle the effects of those factors.

Countries, and hence individuals, benefit from international trade for the same reason that regions benefit from inter-regional trade and individuals benefit from exchanges among themselves: that is, through specialization of labour and increased productivity. As I will explain, this specialization captures the comparative (or relative) advantages of each party and increases the well-being of all, regardless of their absolute advantages or disadvantages. The chapter concludes with a discussion of the subtle relationships between trade surplus or deficit, foreign investment, and exchange rate.

ALL IN ALL

All in all, the CSD and NCC models derive from a conception of social science, and of economics in particular, as the study of mechanisms of coordination, motivation, specialization, regulation, and rules of exchange that condition the development of collective intelligence in human society.

Collective intelligence refers to the interconnection of human brains in achieving higher levels of productivity and social well-being. It is not the imperceptible evolution of the human brain that can explain the rapid gains in quality of life in recent centuries, but the interconnection of those brains through institutions (laws and social rules), specialization, innovative technologies, markets, and trade.[2] The ability to trade, especially with strangers and over time, is a distinguishing characteristic of humans. This capacity far exceeds the simple reciprocity observed among other animals, which is usually limited to individuals of the same clan or family and with respect to comparable physical "goods" received and consumed within a short time span.

Humanity is a social organism, one whose collective intelligence is constantly evolving thanks to increasingly efficient institutions and mechanisms of resource allocation. The cerebral cortex of this organism, consisting of pro-competition institutions and competitive markets and prices, is itself evolving into increasingly more complex, sophisticated, and resilient forms (for instance the Internet, digital platforms, financial options, etc.). This organism and its cerebral cortex are certainly vulnerable to a variety of illnesses (hacking, fraud, crime) of greater or lesser severity and duration. But those are curable with a better understanding of human behaviour, at both the individual and the social or interactive levels.

In this vision, the advancement of civilization follows a key guiding principle: the ongoing quest – in a progression that is sometimes orderly and stepwise and sometimes random and erratic – of mechanisms of exchange, trade, specialization, coordination, communication, and incentivization that are ever more efficient. This quest relies on the simultaneous development of social institutions that create mutual trust between strangers.

Each of us, focused as we are on our specialized tasks, is literally dependent on a large number of strangers; indeed, to account for the people whose work has contributed to my well-being in the past hour alone would require several days.[3]

The collective intelligence that coordinates the work of millions of cells (us) within a modern society, through competitive markets, enabling institutions, and competitive international trade, bolsters this body's resilience to the inevitable shocks and spells of chaos and dysfunction: pandemics, wars, and economic crises. In this way, our world has become more co-operative, more secure, more resilient, and more innovative.

The primary subject of economics is to study the development of collective intelligence within humanity. In this broad program, economics prides itself on forging enriching interactive links with other disciplines, especially experimental psychology, sociology, political science, business administration, and law, as well as with mathematics, computer science, engineering, accounting, and finance.

SOME CAVEATS

In what follows, I try not to get too bogged down in recent and not-so-recent experiences in reforming the state, the economy, and/or the private sector. Comparing, say, the proposed reforms represented by

CSD and NCC with the reform programs underlying other models of social democracy that were or are in vogue under such names as the social state, the social market society, market socialism, the third way (à la Bill Clinton, Tony Blair, and/or Anthony Giddens), the new centre (in Germany), the Australian Labour Party reforms dubbed "economic rationalism" and "national competition policy," Rogernomics in New Zealand, or even the June 1999 Blair-Schröder manifesto for a modern social democracy, would require too much space and would necessarily remain at the level of a bird's-eye view. This would open the door to criticisms of my account of other planned reforms, as both God and the devil are in the details, and would sidetrack my own proposals. The book is a manifesto;[4] it is neither a political program nor a detailed implementation plan.

I develop CSD and NCC models to prevent as much as possible system failures, in both the public and the competitive sectors. No system will be successful 100 per cent of the time. But numerous characteristics of CSD and NCC models, in particular the newly defined roles of each sector and the emphasis on competition and incentive compensation, are likely to reduce fraud as well as cronyism in the production and delivery of PSGs. Numerous examples of past failures in public monopolistic supply arrangements as well as in public-private contractual agreements are due to blurred definition of roles and implementation rules. There is no place for those in CSD and NCC models. As the saying goes: it takes two to tango. Unless both the public and private partners play their respective roles, there is a risk of failure due to misevaluation or misbehaviour. It is because CSD and NCC models are clearly and specifically demanding for both public and competitive partners that they avoid the naivety of current arrangements in the production and delivery of PSGs. The objective of the CSD model is to trigger a profound restructuring of the governmental sector in order to meet these challenges.

Compensation formulas and levels are often a source of criticism of the competitive sector. Criticisms regarding the profit motive and the "excessive" CEO pay, for instance, are most often due to pervasive analytical errors, which I discuss at length in the book. People accept that a football/soccer or hockey player earns tens of millions of dollars per year for kicking balls or shooting pucks, but not a CEO for being responsible for the success of a firm in meeting customers' needs with thousands of jobs at play throughout supply chains. I discuss those issues later in the book. And of course bad CEOs can be catastrophic for the firm and all its stakeholders.

Acknowledgments

This book would not have been possible without the collaboration of my students and research assistants at the Université de Montréal and CIRANO (the Centre Interuniversitaire de Recherche en Analyse des Organisations), in particular Jean-Martin Aussant, Mélanie Arcand, Dahlia Attia, Andrea Montreuil, Cristina Vochin, Paloma Raggo, Hind Zemmouri, Jasmin Valade, David Jarry, Peuo Tuon, Jingmei Zhu, Weihao Sun, Michael Benitah, and Sandy Mokbel. I also wish to thank my grandson Xavier Boyer for his erudition and his passion for discussing the issues associated with capitalism and social democracy, my long-time friend Pauline Breton, whose criticisms and questions have forced me to bring greater rigour and clarity to my arguments, and, most importantly, Richard Baggaley, whose comments were demanding and challenging but always inspirational. I am also indebted to Nicolas Marchetti and Éric Gravel, who were peerless co-workers during their postgraduate fellowship at CIRANO. I owe special thanks also to my sister Gisèle Boyer and my daughter Julie Boyer for numerous helpful discussions.

I am also very grateful to my colleagues at Université de Montréal (including École Polytechnique and École des Hautes Études Commerciales HEC), CIRANO, Toulouse School of Economics, and École Polytechnique de Paris for the many conversations that helped me define and clarify the ideas developed in this manifesto. More particularly, I want to thank Jean-Jacques Laffont, Michel Moreaux, David Martimort, Claude Crampes, Jean Tirole, Jacques Crémer, Christian Gollier, Philippe Aghion, Marie-Claire Villeval, Bruno Versaevel, Michel Truchon, Michel Poitevin, Claude Montmarquette, Robert Lacroix, Michel Patry, Martin Boyer, Thierry Warin, Pierre

Lasserre, Philippe Mahenc, Armel Jacques, Sébastien Pouget, Catherine Casamatta, Patricia Crifo, Jean-Pierre Ponssard, David Encaoua, Tracy Lewis, Richard Kihlstrom, Donatella Porrini, Jack Mintz, Hélène Desmarais, Henri-Paul Rousseau, Bill Robson, Claude Forget, Pierre Fortin, Michel Kelly-Gagnon, Maria Kouyoumijian, André Valiquette, Marc Trudeau, Maria Lily Shaw, Claude Brunet, and numerous others. I also benefited greatly from discussions and comments during presentations I was invited to make on the subjects covered in this manifesto at Université de Toulouse, Université de Lyon, CIRANO, C.D. Howe Institute, the Montreal Economic Institute, Entretiens Jacques-Cartier, the International Chamber of Commerce (Paris, London, and New York), the Competition and Regulation European Summer School and Conference, and many more.

I also wish to thank Robert E. Lucas Jr of the University of Chicago and laureate of the 1995 Nobel Memorial Prize in Economic Sciences, who urged me to complete this work. In a letter of support written in 2018, he wrote,

> Boyer's Manifesto for a Competitive Social Democracy is a very readable and deeply thought statement of his views on the application of economic principles to political decision making. After I read it, I wrote to him to say that I think his Manifesto is very much in the spirit of Pareto. His efficiency criterion makes it clear that economics is not a comprehensive world view or a social welfare function. It is a partial ordering only. I think this makes economic efficiency a more powerful principle, though it can appear a weaker one, because it is compatible with different values, and it can help to reconcile differences in particular cases. This point is subtle and needs to be illustrated with lots of examples, as you do in your book. I hope people will read it and think about it. In short, I admired this work very much and have given copies to friends.

During my career as a university professor of economics (1971–), I have benefited from the opportunity to visit numerous universities and research centres, where some of the ideas in this book were first presented and discussed. I also published articles, reports, and working papers covering some of the material contained in the following chapters. In a sense, this book is the result of a lifelong project.

Among my own published sources, I would like to mention the following, non-exhaustive list: Marcel Boyer and Richard E. Kihlstrom, eds, *Bayesian Models in Economic Theory* (Amsterdam: North-Holland, 1984); Marcel Boyer and Jean-Jacques Laffont, "Expanding the Informativeness of the Price System with Law," *Canadian Journal of Economics* 22, no. 2 (1989): 217–27; Marcel Boyer and Georges Dionne, "An Empirical Analysis of Moral Hazard and Experience Rating," *Review of Economics and Statistics* 71, no. 1 (1989): 128–34; Marcel Boyer, "The Economics of Technological Flexibility: Financial Evaluation and Growth Potential," in *Management of Technology: The Key to Global Competitiveness*, ed. Tarek M. Khalil and Bulent A. Bayraktar (Norcross, GA: Industrial Engineering and Management Press, 1992), 1123–1132; Marcel Boyer, "L'économie des organisations: Mythes et réalités," Conférence présidentielle, Société canadienne de science économique, St-Sauveur, QC, May 1996, published in *L'Actualité économique* 96, no. 4 (2020): 471–98; Marcel Boyer and Jean-Jacques Laffont, "Environmental Protection, Producer Insolvency and Lender Liability," in *Economic Policy for the Environment and Natural Resources*, ed. Athanasios Xepapadeas (Cheltenham, UK: Edward Elgar Publishing, 1996), 1–29; Marcel Boyer and Jean-Jacques Laffont, "Environmental Risks and Bank Liability," *European Economic Review* 41, no. 8 (1997): 1427–59; Marcel Boyer and Michel Moreaux, "Capacity Commitment versus Flexibility," *Journal of Economics and Management Strategy* 6, no. 1 (1997): 347–76; Marcel Boyer and Séverine Clamens, "Strategic Adoption of a New Technology under Uncertain Implementation," CIRANO Scientific Series 97s-40 (December 1997), https://cirano.qc.ca/files/publications/97s-40.pdf; Marcel Boyer and Jacques Robert, "Competition and Access in Electricity Markets: ECPR, Global Price Cap, and Auctions," *Deregulation of Electric Utilities*, ed. George Zaccour (Amsterdam: Kluwer Academic, 1998), 47–74; Marcel Boyer and Jean-Jacques Laffont, "Toward a Political Theory of the Emergence of Environmental Incentive Regulation," *RAND Journal of Economics* 30, no. 1 (1999): 137–57; Marcel Boyer, Tracy Lewis, and W.L. Liu, "Setting Standards for Credible Compliance and Law Enforcement," *Canadian Journal of Economics* 33, no. 2 (2000): 319–40; Marcel Boyer and Jean-Jacques Laffont, "Competition and the Reform of Incentive Schemes in the Regulated Sector," *Journal of Public Economics* 87, nos 9–10 (2003): 2369–96; Marcel Boyer, "Efficiency Considerations in Copyright Protection," *Review of Economic Research on Copyright Issues* 1, no. 2 (2004): 11–27; Marcel Boyer, Michel Moreaux, and Michel Truchon, *Partage des coûts et tarification des infrastructures* (Montreal: CIRANO, February 2006); Marcel Boyer and Jacques Robert, "Organizational Inertia and Dynamic Incentives," *Journal of Economic Behavior and Organization* 59, no. 3 (March 2006): 324–48; Marcel Boyer, Yolande Hiriart, and David Martimort, eds, *Frontiers in the Economics of Environmental Regulation and Liability* (Aldershot, UK: Ashgate, 2006); Marcel Boyer and Éric Gravel, "Évaluation de projets: La valeur actualisée nette optimisée (VAN-O)," *Assurances et gestion des risques* 74, no. 2 (July 2006): 163–85; Paul Audley and Marcel Boyer, "The 'Competitive' Value of Music to Commercial Radio Stations," *Review of Economic Research on Copyright Issues* 4, no. 1 (December 2007): 29–50; Marcel Boyer, *Manifeste pour une social-démocratie concurrentielle* (Montreal: CIRANO, 2009); Marcel Boyer, Michael J. Trebilcock, and David Vaver, eds, *Competition Policy and Intellectual Property* (Toronto: Irwin Law, April 2009); Marcel Boyer, "The Twelve Principles of Incentive Pay," *Revue d'Économie Politique* 121, no. 3 (2011): 285–306; Marcel Boyer, "The Economics of Fair Use/Dealing: Copyright Protection in a Fair and Efficient Way," *Review of Economic Research on Copyright Issues* 9, no. 1 (2012): 3–46; Marcel Boyer, Pierre Lasserre, and Michel Moreaux, "A Dynamic Duopoly Investment Game without Commitment under Uncertain Market Expansion," *International Journal of Industrial Organization* 30, no. 6 (2012): 663–81; Marcel Boyer, M. Martin Boyer, and René Garcia, "Alleviating Coordination Problems and Regulatory Constraints through Financial Risk Management," *Quarterly Journal of Finance* 3, no. 2 (2013); Marcel Boyer and Nathalie Elgrably-Lévy, *Réinventer le Québec: Douze chantiers à entreprendre* (Montreal: Éditions Stanké, 2014); Marie-Laure Allain, Marcel Boyer, Rachidi Kotchoni, and Jean-Pierre Ponssard, "Are Cartel Fines Optimal: Theory and Evidence from the European Union," *International Review of Law and Economics* 42 (June 2015): 38–47; Marcel Boyer, Thomas W. Ross, and Ralph A. Winter, "The Rise of Economics in Competition Policy: A Canadian Perspective," *Canadian Journal of Economics* 50, no. 5, 50th Anniversary Issue (December 2017): 1489–1524; Marcel Boyer, "The Competitive Market Value of Copyright in Music: A Digital Gordian Knot," *Canadian Public Policy* 44, no. 4 (December 2018): 411–22; Marcel Boyer and Anne Catherine Faye, "Music Royalty Rates for Different Business Models: Lindahl Pricing and Nash Bargaining," in *Encyclopedia of Law and Economics*, ed. Alain Marciano and Giovanni Ramello (New York: Springer, 2018), https://link.springer.com/referenceworkentry/10.1007/978-1-

4614-7883-6_761-1; Marcel Boyer, "Erreurs méthodologiques dans l'évaluation des projets d'investissement," *Revue Française d'Économie* 33, no. 4 (2018): 49–80; Marcel Boyer, "The Three-Legged Stool of Music Value: Hertzian Radio, SiriusXM, Spotify," in *Copyright in Action: International Perspectives on Remedies*, ed. Ysolde Gendreau (Montreal: Éditions Thémis, 2019), 13–40; Marcel Boyer, Anne Catherine Faye, Éric Gravel, and Rachidi Kotchoni, "Guiding Principles in Setting Cartel Sanctions," *Concurrences – Competition Law Review* 3 (2019), https://dx.doi.org/10.2139/ssrn.3722811; Marcel Boyer, "Défis et embûches dans l'évaluation des PPP: Pour un secteur public efficace et efficient," CIRANO Cahier Scientifique 2020s-25 (April 2020), https://cirano.qc.ca/files/publications/2020s-25.pdf; Marcel Boyer, "Inequalities: Income, Wealth, and Consumption," CIRANO Cahier Scientifique 2020s-26 (April 2020), https://www.cirano.qc.ca/files/publications/2020s-26.pdf; Marcel Boyer and Éric Gravel, "Looking at the Management of the COVID-19 Lockdown through the Lens of Real Options Analysis," CIRANO Texte d'opinion 2020PE-17 (May 2020), https://cirano.qc.ca/fr/sommaires/2020PE-17; Marcel Boyer, "Competition, Open Social Democracy, and the COVID-19 Pandemic," *Concurrences – Competition Law Review* 2 (May 2020): 33–8; Marcel Boyer, "L'État providence et la Social-démocratie de l'avenir," *L'ÉNA hors les murs* 500 (October 2020): 72–4; Marcel Boyer and Molivann Panot, "Obamacare: Enjeux économiques et constitutionnels," CIRANO Cahier Scientifique 2020s-60 (November 2020), http://cirano.qc.ca/files/publications/2020s-60.pdf; Marcel Boyer, "Northeast America (NEA) Electricity Profile: Proposal of a Free Trade Area," CIRANO Cahier Scientifique 2020s-65 (December 2020), https://cirano.qc.ca/files/publications/2020s-65.pdf; Marcel Boyer, "Beyond ESG: Reforming Capitalism and Social-Democracy," *Annals of Corporate Governance* 6, nos 2–3 (2021): 90–226; Marcel Boyer, "Au-delà de l'ESG: Réformer le capitalisme et la social-démocratie," CIRANO Cahier Scientifique 2021s-02 (February 2021), https://cirano.qc.ca/fr/sommaires/2021s-02; Marcel Boyer, "CEO Pay in Perspective," *Journal of Leadership, Accountability and Ethics* 18, no. 3 (2021): 36–73; Marcel Boyer, "Prix," in *Dictionnaire de droit de la concurrence*, Concurrences, Art. no. 85327, https://www.concurrences.com/fr/dictionnaire/prix; Marcel Boyer, "Les échanges intégrés d'électricité dans le nord-est de l'Amérique," Ministère des finances du Québec (January 2022), http://surl.li/gtnbm; Marcel Boyer, "A Pervasive Economic Fallacy in Assessing the Cost of Public Funds," *Canadian Public Policy* 48, no. 1 (March 2022): 1–10;

Marcel Boyer, "Challenges and Pitfalls in Revising of the Canadian Copyright Act," *Canadian Intellectual Property Review* 37 (2022): 1–38; Marcel Boyer, "The Retail Gasoline Price-Fixing Cartel in Québec," *Canadian Competition Law Review* 35, no. 1 (2022): 134–63; Marcel Boyer, "Comments on Competition Policy and Labour Markets," CIRANO Working Paper 2022s-21 (December 2021), https://cirano.qc.ca/files/publications/2022s-21.pdf.

Last but not least, I am grateful to my doctoral students, who have significantly pushed my intellectual limits over the years: Raymond Théôret (1977), Georges Dionne (1979), Jelloul El-Mabrouk (1983), Lazare Bela (1986), Athanasios Papailiadis (1991), Tahar Mounsif (1994), Asterie Twizeyemariya (1995), and Gamal Atallah (2000).

At the end of this long journey, I wish to reiterate and make mine the sentiment expressed by John Donne (*Devotions upon Emergent Occasions*, 1624) that no man is an island. To a large extent, we are all the product of our familial, professional, and social contacts. Thus, authorship of this manifesto is that of a much larger network. Thank you all.

Of course, I alone am responsible for the expressed content of this book, and in particular for any shortcomings.

SOCIAL DEMOCRACY, CAPITALISM, AND COMPETITION

Introduction

The ability and desire to identify and commercialize inventions and innovations are the main engines of increased productivity, economic growth, and improvements in social well-being. Nothing drops from the sky as if by magic. The roots of this ability and desire lie first in individuals' attitudes toward change and, second, in the receptiveness of institutions to flexibility and uncertainty.

At present time, social democratic societies and their institutions are under considerable pressure to adapt to a more competitive environment. At the same time, these societies must preserve the foundations of their social security programs, which have supported their economic success and have allowed them to attain high standards of living. By historical standards, these results have been very impressive for well over half a century.

The issues confronting us today spring from interactions between the public sector and other stakeholders. These interactions *should* result in more robust and innovative social democracies and produce societies in which justice, equity, and the entrepreneurial spirit are foundational. It is our hope that the competition-based social democracy (CSD) model proposed here together with that of the new competition-based capitalism (NCC) will make an important and original contribution to an improved society.

THE SOCIAL DEMOCRATIC DARE: FEATURES, CHALLENGES, AND PITFALLS

The CSD model is built on five core observations and ten major programs and generic policy initiatives.

Observation 1. There is pervasive lack of performance in the production and delivery of public and social goods and services (PSGS). The ensuing wastefulness has many sources, but the most important ones can be traced to three factors.

The first of these factors is connected to a confusion between objectives, on the one hand, and means, on the other. This confusion affects many sectors and programs of social democratic societies. This confusion underlies many arguments that are as exasperating as they are futile. It is time to clarify the goals we pursue to ensure that the most efficient and least risky ways and means are deployed to reach them.

The second factor is that a large share of the process of supplying PSGS has been captured by well-organized, deeply entrenched, and heavily protected interest groups that have appropriated the very processes of social democracy. Over the years, these interest groups have succeeded in impeding the development of alternatives and competing ideas, thus permanently undermining productivity gains. The very processes of social democracy have been hijacked by these groups, in particular the bloated bureaucracy of the "civil service" and the monopolistic labour unions of the public sector, to the point that the existence of this bureaucracy and these labour unions have become synonymous with social democracy itself. This has come at the expense of beneficiaries and taxpayers.

The third factor pertains to the conflict of interest that undermines the underperformance of the traditional social democratic model, in which conception, financing, supply, and evaluation typically all fall under the purview of a single organization: the government. This conflict of interest is endemic to the traditional social democratic model and creates a climate conducive to scheming, lack of transparency, kickbacks, and the granting of undue perks at the expense of citizens. Basic principles of good governance require a separation of roles and responsibilities between the ordering authority (or principal), the contractor (or agent), and the evaluator (or auditor). Credible accountability and performance incentives are crucial. But they are at best blurred, subject to manipulation, and at worst non-existent in the current social democratic model.

It is important to specify that this problem is due to neither the "public or governmental" *nature* of the provision of PSGS, nor the level of competence of the people involved. The problem is that the public providers of PSGS have succeeded in creating obstacles and barriers to entry, sometimes economic and sometimes legal, to shut out competition. This reduces the opportunity for greater productivity gains and the systematic identification of best practices.

It is time to reassert the primacy of objectives while giving all citizens the right to contest and, when appropriate, replace failing providers of PSGS. The CSD model seeks to resolve the following dilemma: How is it possible that we have so many problems with the production and distribution of PSGS, considering that our wealth has increased almost every year for the past fifty, even seventy-five, years?

Observation 2. The globalization of markets and internationalization of cultures exercise significant pressures on social democratic programs.

If social democratic societies are determined to improve or simply maintain the social protection and security programs they have developed over the last half century as part of their social landscape (including universal access to high-quality education, training, and health-care services, unemployment benefits, environmental protection, water and sanitation services, recreational activities, etc.), they will have to run these programs in a much more efficient manner. Otherwise, increasing economic pressures arising from both the globalization of markets and the internationalization of cultures will result in these programs being trimmed, curtailed, or even eliminated one way or another – perhaps not officially, but certainly in practice as these goods and services suffer from reduced quality, increased uncertainty, and lower dependability.

The increased pressures on resources, labour, capital, and materials, coming from their additional potential use in international trade, will raise their costs, thereby reducing their use in contexts and sectors that cannot adapt and compete. The sectors concerned include those where innovation and productivity are lagging, which raises their relative costs. This reduction in the quality of PSGS will occur not because we can no longer afford them – indeed, we have never been so rich and powerful and, therefore, capable of affording a large quantity of high-quality PSGS! It will occur because the relative cost of these goods and services will increase, due to an increasingly failing public-sector organization. The resources necessary for their production and distribution are better valued elsewhere, in other fields.

The ongoing policy debate regarding the challenges for health care, education, and infrastructure focuses on the issues of taxation and government budget allocation. Various groups are demanding more resources, sometimes under the guise of "necessary (re)investments" in health care, education, infrastructure, the environment, etc. In the CSD model, the fundamental problem is claimed to be not one of money or budget per se, but rather one of organizational inefficiency.

Observation 3. Social democratic societies have primarily been able to achieve a high level of human and social development because they have excelled in maintaining healthy economic growth rates for sustained periods of time, the *sine qua non* of widespread improvements in living standards.

Economic growth is primarily dependent on the quality of institutions and organizations and their ability to allocate resources efficiently, as well as coordinate individuals' actions and motivate them to contribute to the greater social good to the best of their ability. High-quality institutions and organizations, as resource allocation and incentivization mechanisms, surpass in importance all other factors of growth, such as human capital, technological change, and innovations. This is because the quality of institutions and organizations fundamentally conditions the development of the other factors of growth. Many of the problems social democratic societies face today are attributable to the fact that the institutions and organizations, such as the public school system and the health-care system, that characterize their social democratic core have lost their original efficiency.

Observation 4. Social democratic polities have become well-educated, highly skilled societies with significant entrepreneurial capabilities. They have also acquired a high degree of acceptance of diversity, not with respect to fundamental principles and objectives (justice, equity, inclusion, efficiency), but rather with respect to how those principles and objectives may be applied or realized in different contexts. Old rules and methods, such as top-down managerial styles and monopolistic, one-size-fits-all goods and services, while they may have been desirable at some point in the past, may not be the best policies anymore.

Competition and modularity in the production and distribution of PSGS thus become possible and desirable. Modularity is a broad concept that can be applied to many situations, whether in terms of design, production, and use. The underlying idea is to decompose the final product into several subsystems that can be designed and built independently. These subsystems or components are less complex than the system as a whole. The efficient ways and means by which PSGS should be provided in the future will differ from what we have seen in the past, as they adapt to cultural changes, educational attainment, entrepreneurial capabilities, and technological developments. The CSD model makes this adaptation continuous and explicit through a modular, or diversified, portfolio of ways and means to attain the objectives pursued. Competition and modularity were anathema for the PSGS system till the recent past. Now people, better educated and more affluent, may be ready to take a larger share of the responsibility for the provision of PSGS. The government needs not be responsible for everything relevant to citizens' lives.

Observation 5. Human behaviour can in large part be explained and understood with reference to two primary fears: the fear of competition and the fear of uncertainty, which could be the two most important forces hindering a renewal of social democratic societies.

The CSD model seeks to address these fears at their roots. Both fears can be powerful forces of stagnation and regression, but they can also be potent engines of growth in universal well-being. Misunderstanding the role of competition and the nature of uncertainty and risk can lead to years of sub-optimal growth and even systematic waste in the development and allocation of human, natural, and technological resources. One important goal of the CSD model is to harness the natural fear of competition and of uncertainty and risk to foster efficiency, sustained growth, and improved welfare.

The Model, Its Challenges and Pitfalls

Those who think they can do better than current providers of PSGS must be given the opportunity to challenge them in open and transparent calls for tenders and to replace them if their submissions are deemed credible and better for all stakeholders. For this to be possible, we need to reconsider the organizational model of social democracy.

True social democracy must necessarily be competitive, or more precisely, competition-based. The CSD programs and reforms proposed below are quite ambitious and represent considerable challenges. They make it possible to ensure that the ways and means are continually renewed thanks to a systematic process of innovation – technological as well as organizational and social.

These reforms and programs are structured around two major changes. First, a refocusing on the specific competencies of the governmental and competitive sectors. For the former: design PSGS and manage their production and distribution through incentive or performance contracts with providers in the competitive sector. For the latter: produce and distribute PSGS at the best possible cost, under incentive contracts with the governmental sector. Second, a systematic recourse to open and transparent competitive processes in the attribution of contracts for the production, distribution, and delivery of PSGS.

To ensure that these changes bear the desired fruit, programs and policies need to be designed to promote the development of appropriate open and transparent competitive mechanisms and the emergence of competitive-sector businesses capable of positioning themselves as credible competitors in markets for those contracts.

These reforms and programs will generate heated debate regarding their implementation and the transition from the current under-performing and wealth-destroying mechanisms and policies to more efficient, wealth-creating, and welfare-increasing ones. Resistance to the required changes will be strong – understandable, but strong. Even though the CSD model is fully consistent with the social values specific to the social democratic view of life, society, and well-being, the far-reaching reforms it requires will elicit aggressive resistance from many individuals and organizations. These opponents will vigorously declare their allegiance to the social democratic ideal while fiercely defending their vested interest in the current system, no matter how inefficient it is.

It is a legitimate concern that private or competitive-sector firms and organizations systematically try to make supra-competitive profits. But few succeed. A very large majority of businesses make no excess profit at the public's expense. On average, half of them lose money (make profit below their normal level) and half make money. It follows a random walk over time. It does happen surely that illicit profits are made. That is why competition authorities and offices of fair trading exist in different countries. Even if some customers are robbers, not all customers are. The competitive private sector is liable to corruption and gaming just the same as a public organization. But overall, maintaining competitive conditions is the objective of such authorities. Maintaining monopoly is the objective of public bureaucracy.

Implementing the required reforms will, as a consequence, require a strong, committed, well-informed, and persuasive political voice to overcome political inertia and thwart the efforts of interest groups invested in and benefiting from the current dysfunctional system.

Developing a broad consensus on these reforms will take time and a great deal of persuasion. In this battle to educate populations and reform institutions, the inherent reasonableness and analytical underpinning of the CSD model are its greatest selling points. It doesn't mean that the CSD model is immune to fraud, corruption, or excess profit taking, but the role that a more intense competitive environment can play in raising this immunity protection cannot be understated. Maintaining a proper intensity of competition in the PSGS sectors is the best policy in that regard.

The CSD model is, first and foremost, a vision of human beings as social animals, a vision in which the pursuit of improvements to the well-being of individuals, the central tenet, involves an explicit recognition of three fundamental principles: the capacity of individuals to make rational choices; the social partnership that defines and shapes the individual; and, finally, the crucial need for explicit and effective coordination and motivation mechanisms allowing the optimal use of available resources.

This characterization allows for a direct contrast between traditional versus competition-based social democracy models. While both proceed from the same point of departure, the former has not only lost its true purpose along the way, but has increasingly sunk into the quagmire of magical thinking. Under magical thinking, the mere affirmation of an objective is deemed sufficient for achieving it, without having to worry about putting in place appropriate and realistic mechanisms for evaluation, coordination, and motivation.

THE RELATED NECESSARY REFORM OF CAPITALISM

There is a vocal demand for an in-depth reform of capitalism in the wake of the developments of the last four decades. These include an increase in income and wealth inequalities, the climate emergency, the perceived increase in environmental and industrial disasters, the expansion of global trade, the internationalization of cultures, the financial crisis of 2007–10, and the transformation of Marshall McLuhan's "global village" into a local/global whole.

We need to begin by understanding how these phenomena came about and what they really mean before we can even begin to imagine solutions. We already know the two principal causes of the 2007–10 financial crisis: the economic policy of easy credit and congressional pressures on the US government–sponsored Fannie Mae (officially the Federal National Mortgage Association) and Freddie Mac (the Federal Home Loan Mortgage Corporation) home mortgage companies to issue high-risk "subprime" mortgages that led these companies not so much to underestimate as to completely ignore these risks.

Even if we concede that reforms are needed to the functioning of capitalism, we must take heed not to throw the baby out with the bathwater – a threat that is no less real for being metaphorical. There is a danger that governments, under pressure from a variety of poorly informed interest groups, will be tempted to play the role of Goethe's sorcerer's apprentice,[1] with the result of losing control of the intended reform of the powerful engine of growth that capitalism represents.

The market economy, entrepreneurial freedom, responsible capitalism, and the freedom to challenge the established economic order remain the best guarantors of development and a rising standard of living. A rising standard of living should bring about the expansion of representative diversity, the eradication of poverty, and a decline in inequality in consumption and opportunities. Casual observations show that more developed countries are more respectful of representative diversity than are poor ones. It is simply because they can afford to be. Not all citizens are respectful of such diversity, but more end up accepting it.

All businesses are competing for limited resources to produce goods and services for their customers. The fact that both the NCC model, described in chapter 3, and the CSD model, described in chapter 2, are competition-based makes them intimately related. A properly functioning NCC model is as important for economic growth and social welfare and well-being as a properly functioning CSD model.

I

Basic Socio-economic Concepts Revisited

In this chapter, I look at some basic economic concepts that may not be well known to all readers. Some of these concepts are present in a confusing way in the public discourse. Clarifications on these topics are important to understand what CSD and NCC models are really about and why they are necessary to help us reach a new level of economic development. Some readers may want to skip this chapter, although a quick reading may be fruitful.

The concepts I discuss are the following: organizational challenges; value, profit, and trust; businesses, entrepreneurs, and competition; creative destruction and job creation; the origin and power of the status quo; and the tragedies of the commons and the anticommons.

THE ORGANIZATIONAL CHALLENGES OF ECONOMIC ACTIVITY

Organizational efficiency is central to the CSD and NCC reforms. Our understanding of what makes a firm capable of successfully facing the challenges of survival and profitability has evolved significantly in recent decades. Communications and technological innovations have altered the competitive environment in which firms operate. New interaction and decision-making organizations have emerged, such as Amazon, Walmart, and Alphabet, each with their own complex value chains and networks.

In conjunction with developments in the international socio-economic environment (more free trade alliances, international energy infrastructures, large monetary unions), communications and technological innovations, such as telephony, the Internet, and artificial intelligence–based value chains and networks, have important repercussions for all institutions – businesses as well as organizations run and sponsored by the government. At their core is the increasingly widespread realization that efficient coordination and incentive mechanisms, such as competitive markets, prices as coordination mechanisms between buyers and sellers, and incentive mechanisms inducing people to engage in productive activities to generate products and services that have true value for intended customers and fellow citizens, are central to the organization of human and social activities, and of economic activities in particular.

This new economic understanding of organizations is articulated around the following three observations. The first is that information that is vital to the organization's performance is often only known to certain members of the organization, who in turn may wish to conceal or manipulate this information. For example, a department head may have an incentive to report biased data on the profitability of a program of activities to his or her superiors when that bias cannot be directly identified or detected. A second observation is that it is often the case that certain actions undertaken by a member of the organization, and having a significant impact on its performance, are not directly or easily observable by other members of the organization, especially those in management. For example, the manager of a department may have an interest in providing a sub-optimal level of effort in performing his or her task when that effort is not observable by other managers. The third observation is that maximizing the performance of the organization often requires that some members invest efforts in acquiring skills or competencies that are specific to the organization. For example, a company may be reluctant to make an investment if the profitability of that investment depends on future co-operation from a supplier or customer, who may be unable or unwilling to make a credible commitment – thus jeopardizing the future value of the skills investment for the company.

Coordination and incentive mechanisms implemented within organizations can be seen as institutional responses to these three issues. Competitive markets and prices are particular mechanisms for coordinating the decisions of consumers/buyers and producers/sellers and for motivating both sides to make good decisions. Companies and organizations exist because they can sometimes prove more efficient than markets alone in coordinating decisions and motivating agents.

Inasmuch as accelerating technological advances and more competition lead to further decentralization, it follows that they should encourage more incentivizing structures. An incentivizing mechanism essentially refers to a situation in which the compensation received by agents, which may be businesses or individuals, depends at least in part on their performance or the performance of their organization. By linking the compensation, understood in a broad sense, received by individuals or groups to the organization's performance, it becomes possible to ensure that it is in everyone's interest to contribute to this performance, even in contexts that are susceptible to manipulation. Even a partial understanding of incentive problems and constraints can significantly improve the performance of an organization.[1]

VALUE, PROFITS, AND TRUST

Assigning a *value* to a good, a service, an investment, an hour of work, a public good or asset, or a durable creation such as a sculpture or a sound recording is one of the most important issues not only in economics, but also in sociology, philosophy, psychology, and other fields of the human and social sciences. On more than one count, economists are the scientists of *value*. Their fundamental proposition is that a fair and equitable price is a competitive price, a price that respects the interests of suppliers/producers and those of buyers/users in a setting in which both suppliers and buyers are free to participate.

The best guarantee that suppliers will be fairly compensated for their goods and services lies in the competition between the demanders of those goods and services, including labour services. And the best guarantee that demanders will pay an appropriate compensation lies in the competition between suppliers of those goods and services. Thus, a competitive price is fundamentally equivalent to a fair and equitable price, because it respects the freely expressed interests of both suppliers and demanders. However, a fair and equitable price is not necessarily above cost; it may well be below cost if the good or service in question has no or little value to customers. It would not be fair and equitable to ask that my fellow citizens (customers) pay a price above my cost if my product has value below my cost or even no value at all to them.

If for some reason markets are not competitive, this guarantee does not hold. If a firm or group of firms have market power on a given product market, the non-competitive equilibrium price will settle at a level higher than the competitive price (in what's called the monopolistic or oligopolistic equilibrium). As a customer, I would end up paying more than I should, although I remain free to buy or not. Firms would like to sell more at that price, but they refrain from doing so to avoid having to reduce their prices. They are constrained by the demand for their goods or services. As firms with market power, they are facing a downward sloping demand curve, while a competitive firm with no market power faces a horizontal demand curve.

Similarly, if a firm or group of firms have market power on a given labour market (or any input market), the non-competitive equilibrium wage will settle at a level lower than the competitive wage (assuming what's called a monopsonistic or oligopsonistic equilibrium). At that non-competitive equilibrium wage, firms would like to hire more workers (they will express a shortage of workers, possibly through unfilled job openings or vacancies), but refrain from doing so to avoid having to increase wages. They are constrained by the supply of labour. Again, as firms with market power, they are facing an upward sloping labour supply curve, while a competitive firm with no market power faces a horizontal supply curve. Being starved for labour is a characteristic of monopsonistic and oligopsonistic firms.

Competition and competitive prices are subtle concepts that may be put to improper uses. The intensity of competition is neither a local nor a timeless concept. Competition may take some time to materialize. Once seated in a restaurant, one may decide to leave after seeing the prices of the different meals. But leaving is costly. The consumer's decision will often be to stay and choose a reasonably priced meal while never coming back to that restaurant. Eventually, the restaurant will lose its clientele and be forced to shut down. Similarly, the decision to leave a job to take a new one at a higher wage takes some time to bear fruit. The new job must be searched for, possibly in a different industry or city. Searching and moving are costly activities. But eventually, the low-wage employer will lose its workforce. Hiring and training new workers as well as adjusting wages are costly activities for the firm. The exercise of market power is tricky and may be profitable in the short term but costly in the long term. Market power in static versus dynamic environments are very different realities.[2] Moreover, there is more to compensation than the wage as working conditions and fringe benefits, including lifestyle, may be the determinant factors.

Competitive markets, or alternative institutions or mechanisms such as administrative tribunals or commissions (for example, copyright boards – under different names in different countries, such as copyright tribunal or office, or intellectual property office – make decisions on copyright rates by estimating the competitive value of copyright), whose mission is to emulate them, are essential to eliciting the socially fair (just) and equitable value of things, whether factors and products, goods and services, in the private or public sphere. When goods and services are not fully paid for by the customers, as in education or health-care services, they must be evaluated from the customers' willingness to pay for them in competitive or competition-emulating contexts. Clearly public and elected officials, in deciding on the allocation of budgets to different PSGS, do implicitly if not explicitly evaluate the benefits and costs or net value for citizens of each PSGS (including the true cost and value of a child's education!). Whatever the service considered, there are always trustworthy people demanding very honestly that more money be allocated and spent to improve it. Needs are infinite, resources are limited. Economics is the dismal science – sorry!

There is widespread confusion in public policy circles, among other contexts, about the concept of profit. It is useful to repeat here the error briefly discussed above regarding this notion. It is often argued that private firms must earn profits in addition to covering their costs, and therefore that the prices of their goods and services will necessarily be higher than the prices that a government-owned enterprise would charge in the absence of this profit constraint or objective. This statement is erroneous.

The error here lies in the confusion between accounting profit and economic profit. Accounting profit is the difference between revenues and costs, including interest charges on debt but excluding equity capital costs. Economic profit, sometimes referred to as economic rent, is the difference between revenues and all costs, including interest charges on debt *and* the costs of equity capital. These two notions of profit coincide when a company is financed entirely by debt – which is generally the case in the governmental sector, provided that the public firm is subject to the same tax regime as private companies, which is seldom the case.

Providers of capital, whether in the form of debt or equity, will normally receive a competitive level of compensation based on the non-diversifiable (or systematic) risk level of those funds, which is generally lower for debt than for equity (except where the business is 100 per cent debt financed). Competitive pressures, in particular free entry and exit in the sector, will almost certainly ensure that no excess profits will be earned on a sustainable basis.

If the company belongs to the governmental sector and is, accordingly, financed by taxes and/or government-backed debt (and therefore by taxpayers), it must be able to pay fair, equitable, and competitive compensation to all its factors of production: labour, resources, capital, and others. Thus, the claim that profit-seeking firms would produce at higher prices than government enterprises because of the profit constraint is wrong – persistent, but wrong.

Governmental-sector firms and organizations should typically operate with a goal of zero economic profit, allowing them to compensate all factors of production used, including public capital, at a level equal to the opportunity cost or value of foregone activities – that is, the best possible activities displaced by the activities effectively pursued. However, the presence of profit-seeking firms in a competitive market will actually lead to lower prices because of their incentive to pursue and attain high levels of efficiency, compared to firms in the governmental sector.

As to *trust* between members of a society, and between strangers in particular, it is both valuable as a private asset and as a public one, as trust allows a significant reduction in transaction and interaction costs. The governmental sector has a crucial role to play in developing and maintaining trust. This role is central to the CSD and NCC models.

At the World Economic Forum in Davos in January 2003, one of the main topics of discussion was how to restore and foster trust, both within the business community and in society at large. The reason for this interest at that time was twofold: First, a wave of large-scale bankruptcies and financial scandals had shaken confidence within and toward the business world, and second, "trust" is the most important form of social capital because it can significantly reduce transaction costs of all kinds within a society.[3] The 2007–10 financial crisis, which was fundamentally a crisis of confidence *within* the banking sector in general, brought the issue of trust to the forefront.

Trust is a form of both private and social capital, and as such, developing and maintaining it poses difficult problems of organization and therefore coordination and incentives. It is a form of private capital because a company will benefit from the confidence of its partners. But the trust thus privately created has a positive impact on trust across all firms. This social effect is sufficiently important for public authorities to have a particular responsibility to ensure that trust capital is fostered and sustained.[4]

Trust is a form of capital that is built up with difficulty over the medium and long term and easily destroyed in the short term – in the private, public, and social spheres. The manipulation and falsification of information transmitted by public and private organizations, particularly with regard to risk measurement, is a first pernicious factor in the destruction of social capital. A second comes from the complacency of watchdogs responsible for regulated companies – the cases of Fannie Mae and Freddie Mac come to mind as particularly egregious examples. A third comes from flaws in performance incentive mechanisms, which too often neglect to correct for reckless risk taking.[5] A fourth one revolves around formulaic application of market-based accounting rules, such as market-based evaluation,[6] in a setting in which evaporating confidence makes the relevant markets disappear. This exacerbates the contagion of non-confidence.[7]

Trust is an especially important type of social capital. Consequently, the *loss of confidence* within the financial system in 2007–10, and particularly in interbank financial relations, helped precipitate the financial crisis and then the economic recession. After an interim period of quasi-stability in financial markets, we may be heading back toward chaos in the financial markets with a resurgent risk of *loss of confidence* in sovereign debt of important countries and its impact on bank liquidity and solvability, a sign of this being the increasing role of central banks as lenders of last resort for governments. Private lenders (banks), who are always searching for good opportunities, consider the yield on government bonds too low given the risk and wish to avoid the bad publicity if they were to call in this government debt.

Rules that could make the regulation of the financial system more efficient and allow for semi-automatic adjustments and reorganizations, for a better control of systemic risks, could and should be designed.[8] For instance, Luigi Zingales, professor of economics, entrepreneurship, and finance at the University of Chicago, recently suggested a two-part plan to facilitate the adjustment of mortgage conditions to major variations in housing prices.[9] The government should favour the inclusion in mortgage contracts of clauses giving the owners of dwellings the option of renegotiating their mortgages downward when the value of houses in their neighbourhood or region (based on postal codes, for instance) has fallen more than 20 per cent. In return, the mortgage lender would receive a portion of the eventual selling price – for example, 50 per cent of the difference between the selling price and the renegotiated mortgage. This is a win-win solution compared to traditional foreclosures.

Next, to help banking institutions in difficulty, the government would make available to them a quick partial bankruptcy process under which debt (commercial paper and bonds) would be converted to equity capital and the current shareholders would see their equity liquidated while getting the option, to be exercised within seven days, of buying back the debt at nominal value.

Similar types of options could be included in other contracts to allow for continuous adjustments to economic conditions in case of recession or financial crisis, avoiding sudden cascading adjustments that only aggravate poor economic conditions needlessly. These options obviously will be incorporated into contracts at a certain cost to the parties. But, to the extent that enough of these adjustment clauses are effectively included in contracts, they will help reduce the undesirable collateral effects of recessions.

Such rules could provide the means to address the four causes identified above – the two causes related to incentives: ensuring the independence of regulators and making greater use of private regulatory bodies under performance incentive contracts given clearly expressed objectives, and fostering a better understanding of the effective structure of performance incentive mechanisms; and the two causes related to information: tightening up the disclosure of information on risks (easier said than done!), and relaxing the mark-to-market accounting obligation in light of the economic rule of net present value.

Risk mitigation and management considerations are part of the public policy discourse, but there is room to bring risk issues even more to the forefront of public debate. It would be a socially responsible policy to promote the development of tools to help individuals and companies better manage the various risks they face: financial, technological, environmental, legal, health, and organizational. The development of those tools themselves is an example of PSGS. Change, even if desirable, is inherently difficult and risky.

This objective requires analysis at different levels. The concepts and techniques of risk measurement and management can be applied and extended to a broader social context than their current applications in corporate finance.[10] The ultimate goal is to contribute to better social policy through a greater understanding of how individuals respond to uncertainty in various contexts and circumstances, a development that must draw on psychology, political science, sociology, and economics.[11]

Examples are numerous. Employment insurance can and does actually provide protection for individuals against labour market downturns. A progressive tax system can be considered a hedge against future social unrest. Some public policies deal with the problems of youth at risk,[12] in education and security contexts in particular. Other examples include end-of-life (long-term care) insurance policies,[13] flood insurance,[14] insurance against the effects of pandemics, disruptions of cultural or sporting events,[15] semi-automatic adjustments in mortgages in case of a significant drop in housing prices, as discussed above (i.e., the second part of Luigi Zingales's two-part plan), as well as risks to "human capital" in education and lifelong training.

BUSINESSES, ENTREPRENEURS, AND COMPETITION

The discussion of notions of value, profit, and trust leads directly to the discussion of the role of businesses, entrepreneurs, and competition. It is important to properly understand the different types of business organizations that together constitute the competitive sector. The real and potential presence of these different organizations underlie the power of competition, a central element of the CSD and NCC models.

A firm can be understood as an institution that harnesses different factors of production for the generation of goods and services useful to customers, so that the total (social) value of its products is not less than the total (social) cost of all the factors used. When this is the case, the firm is a true wellspring of net value and wealth.

The difference between the total value of products (revenues) and the total value of all factors used (costs) will vary over time, sometimes positive and sometimes negative. How is the balance between revenues and costs realized? By defining priority factors, those inputs paid first, and a residual value, equal to total revenues minus total costs of priority factors, which become the compensation, sometimes positive and sometimes negative, of the last paid factor or stakeholder.

To enhance our understanding of the role of businesses, entrepreneurs, and competition, let us consider four types of firm: the capitalist enterprise (with private or public capital); the co-operative enterprise; the workers' enterprise; and the IP (intellectual property) enterprise. A socialist enterprise will typically be of the second or third type. The four types discussed here are abstract and generic; in the real world, businesses can of course combine different types.

Residual decision-making power accrues to, or is vested in, the stakeholder who is paid last. This stakeholder is compensated from the residual value generated by the operations of the firm, unless specified otherwise by contract. The residual value may be in part accumulated over time to assure some predictability of compensation to the residual stakeholder. The identity of this stakeholder is determined by the nature of the firm: equity capital (capitalist enterprise, whether private or public), co-operators or members of the co-operative (co-operative enterprise), labour or human capital (workers' enterprise), and intellectual capital (IP enterprise). The amount paid for each factor (labour, resources, IP, capital) to their owning stakeholder as well as the value of best alternative uses must and will account for the risk incurred in the compensation scheme. For a given factor of production, a more secure compensation will be lower than a riskier one on average.

The capitalist enterprise compensates in priority all factors other than equity capital, whether private or public, which is compensated last from the residual value. This residual value may be positive or negative and can vary over time, but it must on average be equivalent to the expected value of this equity capital in its best possible alternative use (the opportunity cost of the equity capital, whether private or public). Indeed, in the case of a state-owned enterprise, the compensation of the public equity capital may be virtual only but must nevertheless be estimated from its best possible alternative use (the opportunity cost of the public equity capital, whether public or private).

The co-operative enterprise compensates all factors of production, including borrowed capital, before co-operators (whose contributions may be in capital, labour, or some other resource), which are compensated last from the residual value, through a form of co-operators' dividend. In a financial co-operative (credit union), for instance, the dividend (the *ristourne*) paid to a member is usually a function of interest paid by the member on his mortgage and other loans and of interest paid to the member on different forms of deposits and savings through the co-operative. The yearly dividend paid depends on the financial performance of the co-operative. Hence the compensation of co-operators will be uncertain (risky) and variable over time. However, for the co-operative to be a true wellspring of net value and wealth, this co-operators' compensation must, on average, correspond to the expected value of co-operators' invested resources in their best alternative uses.

The workers' enterprise pays in priority all factors other than labour. Labour is compensated from the residual value, once all suppliers as well as borrowed capital (the workers' enterprise is, by assumption, 100 per cent financed by borrowing at market conditions) have been paid. More typically, labour will be paid in part through a lower fixed wage and in part through a share of "profit" or residual value generated by the firm. Again, this residual value is generally unknown, may be positive or negative, and can vary over time, but must on average be equivalent to the expected value of labour in its best possible alternative use for the workers' enterprise to be a true wellspring of net value and wealth.

Employee ownership may take different forms. In Canada, EllisDon is an example of a major employee-owned construction services company.[16] Founded in 1951, the company announced on 28 February 2020 that a final agreement with private owners (owning 50 per cent of the company) was executed under which 100 per cent of the company's equity will be transferred to the company's employees.[17] It is the second-largest (as per 2021 revenues) construction company in Canada. Among an extensive list of projects, EllisDon was awarded the construction management contract for the Metro Toronto Convention Centre project (1982), and built the SkyDome (1989; now the Rogers Center), which, when completed, was the world's first retractable-rooftop stadium. EllisDon participated in the public-private partnership (PPP) William Osler Health Centre in Brampton, Ontario (2004). The company completed construction and installation work on the Dubai Waterfront, the largest waterfront development of its kind in the world (2008). It built the terminal building at the Winnipeg International Airport (2010), the first building of its kind in Canada to receive the LEED (Leadership in Energy and Environmental Design) certification. In 2018, EllisDon acquired the interests of joint venture partner Carillion (in liquidation in the United Kingdom) in four Ontario hospital projects, becoming the sole service provider at Royal Ottawa Hospital, Oakville-Trafalgar Memorial Hospital, Brampton Civic Hospital, and Sault Area Hospital.

The IP enterprise pays in priority all factors other than intellectual property. Paid last, this intellectual property is compensated from the residual value, hence once all suppliers and borrowed capital (the IP enterprise is, by definition, 100 per cent financed by borrowing at market conditions) have been paid. In the IP enterprise, the IP owner is paid from the residual value generated by the firm. This residual value is generally unknown, may be positive or negative, and can vary over time, but must on average be equivalent to the expected value of the idea or the intellectual property (or the efforts that went into creating the intellectual property) in its best possible alternative use for the IP enterprise to be a true wellspring of net value and wealth.

Thus, it is important to realize that the forms and structures of competitive enterprises may vary. All can compete for contracts with the public sector for the production and distribution of PSGS. This competition will benefit citizens, whether individuals or enterprises, both suppliers and customers or consumers of PSGS. In each case, the prime stakeholder, owner, and key entrepreneur is that stakeholder who is paid last, once all the so-called priority factors are paid at their competitive value, that is, at their opportunity cost or value (the expected value of the factors in their best possible alternative use, which is to say in the best foregone activities and projects displaced by the activity being undertaken).

The intensity of performance incentives in the production and distribution of PSGS falls primarily to the prime stakeholder, who, being compensated last, is given the decision-making power authority within the firm. This prime stakeholder is the one who in the end is responsible for meeting the objectives set by the governmental sector in the contract. In the tender process, the prime stakeholder will be able to demand the budget level deemed necessary to reach those goals. Competition between different firms of different types and structures, all under incentive contracts, will ensure that the governmental sector, as representative of the citizens, gets the best possible deal.

If IP owners in a capitalist firm consider that their contribution is not properly evaluated and recognized, they can create their own IP enterprise, provided that they own the IP itself,[18] and compete on the market for contracts. Similarly, if a subgroup of workers or a labour union in a capitalist or co-operative firm consider that their contribution is not properly evaluated and recognized, they can create their own enterprise and compete on the market for contracts. An important CSD and NCC policy is that such movements be considered positive and normal.

In each case, the entrepreneurs are supposed to be innovators par excellence, maestro conductors, master chefs who mix up ingredients to concoct finished products and services that will increase social well-being: the total value of those products and services must be larger than the total cost or value of all factors used in their production. In the modern firm, this entrepreneur is personified by the CEO (or equivalent), the officer ultimately responsible for the success and growth of the business, whatever its type. The roles and responsibilities of the CEO vary from one company to the next, partly depending on its organizational structure and size.

Of course, reality checks are around every corner. It is entirely possible for an entrepreneur to make mistakes, to behave irrationally, or to be incompetent.[19] The examples of this are legion. It is important to realize that in the real world, best practices do not always hold true or are not always properly implemented. Whatever the quality of the arguments, there will always be exceptions/mistakes/wrongdoing, etc.

Nevertheless, competition encourages and incentivizes all firms, active and potential, to solve organizational issues regarding production management, labour management, investment choices, and intellectual property development and management, in order to produce goods and services whose value exceeds the opportunity costs of all factors, inputs, and resources used. Otherwise, the current firms should and will be replaced by others. The development of best practices is a trial-and-error process encouraged by competition, that is, by competitive markets and the prices of products and factors.

It impossible for a firm in a competitive situation and surrounded by competitive markets and institutions to continuously and systematically exploit its workers, gouge its suppliers, or cheat its customers. Competition, including the threat of entry, is a powerful force that will or should prevent firms from generating excess or supra-competitive profits over a sustained period of time. However, in industries or markets with a small number of firms (oligopolies, due possibly to economies of scale or a small market size), the market power of firms may push prices above their purely competitive levels. That said, those higher-than-competitive prices may still be lower than counterfactual prices that would be observed if we were to break down the firms into a larger number of units, thereby losing the benefits of economies of scale, meaning higher costs for all, and hence higher prices.[20]

THE COMPLEXITY OF JOB CREATION AND CREATIVE DESTRUCTION

The process underlying the constant turnover of job losses and job creation – the latter typically in more promising sectors or more productive firms[21] – is one of the most important mechanisms for growth and wealth creation. Economists refer to this process as creative destruction: new jobs (created) replace old ones (destroyed).

To the extent that the stimulus packages launched by various governments are primarily aimed at preserving existing jobs, they can seriously harm social welfare by preventing the adjustments brought about by creative destruction in the commercial and industrial fabric of economies. Jobs are lost or destroyed to make room for jobs newly created. The process by which destroying jobs give rise to jobs created is a complex one. It is also a subtle issue in public policy analysis. It is important to understand why and how to manage those subtleties through a better understanding of creative destruction itself.

The process of creative destruction manifests itself through four different channels: the number of jobs, the number of establishments, the distribution of establishment size, and the increase or decrease in employment in all sizes of businesses. We will here focus on the number of jobs.

Data on employment dynamics in the United States (shown in table 1.1) show that over the 119 quarters from the third quarter of 1992 (1992.3) to the first of 2022 (2022.1), private-sector establishments created an average of 7.67 million jobs per quarter, of which approximately 80 per cent were in existing establishments and 20 per cent in new ones. During the same period, those establishments lost an average of 7.36 million jobs per quarter, with about 80 per cent in existing establishments and 20 per cent in closing ones.[22]

If we restrict the analysis to those quarters (98) where the *net* number of jobs created is positive, private-sector establishments created on average 7.77 million jobs and lost 7.11 million jobs per quarter. Hence, over those 98 quarters, a single net job is the result of 11.6 jobs created and 10.6 jobs lost. During the quarters (21) where the net number of jobs created is negative, private-sector establishments created on average 7.18 million jobs and lost 8.54 million jobs per quarter. Hence, over those 21 quarters, a single net job lost is the result of 5.3 jobs created and 6.3 jobs lost. Thus, during those 21 quarters with

Table 1.1
Gross job gains and losses

A(B)	C	D	E: C–D	F: C/E	G: D/E
Period (no. of quarters)	Average gross job gains per quarter ('000)	Average gross job losses per quarter ('000)	Average net job change per quarter ('000)	Average gross job gains and losses/ average net jobs change	
1992.3–2000.4 (34)	8,095	7,440	655	12.4	11.4
2001.1–2003.2 (10)	7,808	8,192	–384	–20.3	–21.3
2003.3–2007.4 (18)	7,719	7,310	409	18.9	17.9
2008.1–2010.1 (9)	6,668	7,696	–1,028	–6.5	–7.5
2010.2–2019.4 (39)	7,297	6,755	542	13.5	12.5
2020.1–2020.2 (2)	6,377	14,089	–7,712	–0.8	–1.8
2020.3–2022.1 (7)	9,013	6,912	2,101	4.3	3.3
All quarters with positive net change (98)	7,774	7,106	668	11.6	10.6
All quarters with negative net change (21)	7,183	8,541	–1,358G	–5.3	–6.3
All quarters 1992.3–2022.1 (119)	7,670	7,359			

Italics refer to periods of quarters with negative net change.
Source: US Bureau of Labor Statistics, "Business Employment Dynamics" (as of 26 October 2022), https://data.bls.gov/cgi-bin/surveymost?bd, and "Table 1: Private Sector Gross Job Gains and Job Losses, Seasonally Adjusted," https://www.bls.gov/web/cewbd/table1_18_ind3.txt.

net job losses, the gross number of jobs created by US private-sector establishments is nevertheless quite large.

The process of job gains and losses is complex and involves large movements of jobs throughout businesses and the economy. This is creative destruction at work. Job creation is intimately related to job losses. It is worth questioning just how disruptive government interventions might be to this process, in particular when the often expressed desire is to protect jobs. As a rule of thumb, these policies are poorly adapted to the complexity of job gains and losses.

THE POWER OF THE STATUS QUO

Social development and economic growth may be impaired by the power of the status quo. It is important to understand why and how. It is also important to understand how competition can help fight the status quo when necessary or useful.

Societies and individuals develop habits that, once they have been dynamically accepted and entrenched, become very difficult to change. At the individual level we speak of habit formation. At the social level we call it the status quo. In both cases, change is difficult, if not impossible, even if there seems to be no compelling reason to stick to acquired habits or to fight to preserve the status quo. What is normal in one region or country appears unacceptable in another. Simply observing that people in country A accept as normal certain social traits may not convince people in country B that they should accept them as normal too. Moreover, change is inherently difficult and risky. The power of the status quo may therefore prevent the emergence and acceptance of *best* practices if such practices come into conflict with *accepted* practices (the status quo).

To further illustrate the entrenched quality of the status quo, consider two regions that are socio-economically and politically similar, Quebec and France, and two important areas of social interaction, education and health care. It can be said with reasonable confidence that both regions share a certain cultural heritage: similar national language, similar social democratic spectrum of public services, similar economic orientation based on free markets, similar levels of development. The health-care and education sectors in both regions are dominated by public providers under strong government control. But the regions differ significantly in their conceptions of interactions with private for-profit companies in their respective education and health-care sectors.

In Quebec, the public health insurance board will typically refuse to reimburse the costs of treatment in private clinics, even if similar treatment is fully covered in public clinics. It is also illegal for private insurance companies to offer insurance plans for health-care treatments covered by the state-controlled health insurance plan. In fact, private for-profit health-care providers are in Quebec seen as the devil incarnate!

In France, private for-profit health-care providers operate under an agreement with the public social security system and represent an important part of the public health-care system. The social security health authority will reimburse expenses incurred by a citizen who has chosen to be treated in a private for-profit clinic on the same basis as if the care had been received in a public hospital.

Private for-profit establishments play an essential role in the French hospital landscape: they account for around 37 per cent of all health-care establishments with hospital capacity and represent more than 20 per cent of acute-care beds; this is twice as high as in the United States, where private for-profit establishments account for about 15 per cent of all hospitals and 12 per cent of beds.[23] French private for-profit health-care institutions specialize mainly in surgery and acute care. They are responsible for 60 per cent of all surgeries, 50 per cent of digestive system surgeries, 40 per cent of cardiac surgeries, 75 per cent of cataract surgeries, and 30 per cent of childbirths. With regard to the treatment of serious cases, the activity of private hospitals is comparable to that of the public sector (aside from university hospitals). Since 2000, a form of universal medical coverage (*couverture maladie universelle*, or CMU) has been available for low-income earners (bottom decile) with no user fees. It turns out that 50 per cent of those covered by CMU choose to be treated in the private for-profit sector.

Let us now turn our attention to university education systems and their relationship with the private sector, private companies, and other private entities. In Quebec, all universities court private donors to fund not only chairs and research centres but also infrastructure (buildings, laboratories, etc.). It is common for universities to name major buildings and classrooms after large corporate or individual donors. The boards of governors of public universities usually include senior executives from private companies, and are sometimes even chaired by them. As a result, the ties between public universities and the private corporate sector are very strong in Quebec.

In France, there are virtually no such links at any level within universities. In fact, private money and senior executives of private companies are viewed with considerable suspicion. This is less the case today than it was a few years ago, but it is still the predominant perception.

How can two otherwise similar societies end up with such entrenched and contrasting views of the private sector? What is beyond the pale in one society – private for-profit hospitals in Quebec, and private funding of universities in France – is ubiquitous and perfectly normal in the other. Moreover, the extent to which these positions are entrenched in each region make this a linchpin of the status quo, rendering it very difficult to initiate or even suggest that the position or characteristics of the other region should be adopted.

There's nothing a priori natural about either position. As for tastes and habits at the individual level,[24] the characteristics of the status quo at the social or political level slowly crystallize over time in an ongoing process of becoming the immutable and unalterable rule of the land. The problem this status quo raises is that it creates a quasi-religious attachment to the local system and prevents the introduction of ideas for improving the education or health-care systems. The message here is that the search for best practices is seriously impaired by the power of the status quo. Such restrictions and constraints on the search for best practices are value destroying if they result from an entrenched status quo. And we must be careful not to let status quo phenomena gain an undue importance – namely, by allowing concurrent ideas to thrive. Price control is a nice example: once in place for a few years, it becomes impossible to roll back.

Among the most efficient tools to fight the status quo is open and transparent competition between groups and companies interested in taking an active place in the provision of PSGs. Open and transparent competition means new ideas and new players, more innovations, and better services to the population. To achieve the goal of building a more innovative society based on competition, modularity, flexibility, experimentation, and change, it is imperative that proper signals be sent to stakeholders in order to guide their search for more efficient ways of producing and distributing PSGs. To this end, competitive prices and mechanisms must be encouraged at all levels and in all sectors. Price controls must be abandoned in favour of competitive prices determined by markets.

THE TRAGEDIES OF THE COMMONS AND THE ANTICOMMONS

The "tragedy of the commons" relates to the over-exploitation and depletion of a common resource due to individuals who, acting independently and rationally according to their own self-interest, behave contrary to the whole group's long-term best interests. Hardin, who coined the expression, writes,

> The tragedy of the commons develops in this way. Picture a pasture open to all. It is to be expected that each herdsman will try to keep as many cattle as possible on the commons. Such an arrangement may work reasonably satisfactorily for centuries because tribal wars, poaching, and disease keep the numbers of both man and beast well below the carrying capacity of the land. Finally, however, comes the day of reckoning, that is, the day when the long-desired goal of social stability becomes a reality. At this point, the inherent logic of the commons remorselessly generates tragedy ... Each man is locked into a system that compels him to increase his herd without limit – in a world that is limited. Ruin is the destination toward which all men rush, each pursuing his own best interest in a society that believes in the freedom of the commons. Freedom in a commons brings ruin to all.[25]

The "tragedy of the anticommons" refers to the under-exploitation of a common resource due to numerous rights holders who can prevent others from using it, frustrating what would be a socially desirable outcome. Heller, who coined the expression, writes, "A tragedy of the anticommons can occur when too many individuals have rights of exclusion in a scarce resource. The tragedy is that rational individuals, acting separately, may collectively waste the resource by under-consuming it compared with a social optimum."[26]

The over-exploitation of shared property (tragedy of the commons) as well as its under-exploitation (tragedy of the anticommons) are fundamentally due to a failure of concerned parties to coordinate one way or another in setting proper institutions to govern the shared property – that is, to define rules favourable to its socially responsible exploitation. Why and when is that so? Elinor Ostrom, laureate of the 2009 Nobel Memorial Prize in Economic Sciences, offers a more optimistic analysis of real world situations in which people have been able to co-operate and avoid the tragedies depicted by Hardin and Heller. She argues for a more realistic modelling (game theory) of "common-pool resources" challenges participants are facing. She insists in particular on the dynamics of participants' repeated interactions, internal and external constraints, and dependence on policies (and so-called policy analysts) improperly designed on the basis of faulty representations of common property situations:

> empirical cases of successfully governed common-pool resources provide theoretical and empirical alternatives to the assertion that those involved cannot extricate themselves from the problems ... Some individuals have broken out of the trap inherent in the commons dilemma, whereas others continue remorsefully trapped into destroying their own resources ... The differences may have to do with factors *internal* to a given group. The participants may simply have no capacity to communicate with one another, no way to develop trust, and no sense that they must share a common future ... The differences may have to do with factors *outside* the domain of those affected. Some participants do not have the autonomy ... and are prevented from making constructive changes by external authorities who are indifferent to the perversities of the commons dilemma, and may even stand to gain from it.[27]

Internal and external constraints form a complex system surrounding and exacerbating the commons problems. Standard solutions often advocated in such commons-related conflicts – namely, privatization (through the definition of property rights on the commons), nationalization (through the imposition of state-determined, top-down regulations of the use of the commons), or decentralized self-governance of the commons by the participants themselves – may each be appropriate in some but not in all cases.

Ostrom argues that "getting the institutions right is a difficult, time-consuming, conflict-involving process ... that requires reliable information about time and place variables as well as a broad repertoire of culturally acceptable rules ... Institutions are rarely either private or public – 'the market' or 'the state.' Many successful common-pool resource institutions are rich mixtures of 'private-like' and 'public-like' institutions defying classification in a sterile dichotomy."[28] Besides the traditional pasture-for-all example discussed by

Hardin, more modern and acute (sometimes catastrophic) cases will be discussed in this book.

One is the 1959–61 agricultural crisis in mainland China, analyzed in chapter 3. Following the success of community-based agricultural collectivization during the period 1952–58, the state decided to "nationalize" the experience by changing the institutions, modifying the rules, and nullifying the incentives set at the community level. Properly managed community commons (with competence and rationality) gave place to centrally managed commons (with incompetence and ideology). The changes ended up causing a major drop in productivity and a famine resulting in some thirty million deaths.

Another is the competition-based social democracy reforms of the school and health-care systems discussed in the conclusion. Education and health-care systems, under free access and population growth and aging, may become the commons of tomorrow, if they aren't already today. As mentioned above (and argued in more detail below), the competition-based social democracy model is structured around two major changes. First, the newly defined specific competencies of the governmental sector (to design PSGS and manage their production and distribution through incentive or performance contracts with providers in the competitive sector) and the competitive sector (to produce, distribute, and deliver PSGS at the best possible cost, under incentive contracts with the governmental sector). Second, the systematic recourse to open and transparent competitive processes in the attribution of contracts for the production, distribution, and delivery of PSGS.

These reforms will often call for local community involvement in overseeing schools and health-care facilities, with proper incentives, accountability, and monitoring being key factors in facing the potential commons problems raised by the education and health-care systems.

2

Competition-Based Social Democracy

The competition-based social democracy, or CSD, perspective on politics and economics is simultaneously a continuation (mainly with regard to fundamental principles) and a significant departure (mainly in terms of the ways and means) from the many reforms of social democracy that have sprung up and been developed over the past two centuries.

Most of these "reforms" have striven for a balance between market economics and social democratic ideals. Their failures and qualified successes are most probably due to a confusion between objectives and means, and to an inability to plan the needed transformation from a heavily bureaucratic command and control system to a decentralized competitive (market) system for the supply of PSGs.

The traditional social democratic model – the one that dominates the landscape today – has become obsolete, and an impediment to growth. The reason is that it relies on non-competitive ways and means for producing and delivering PSGs and emphasizes the protection of incumbents' rights, privileges, vested interests, and of sacred cows and institutional icons.

The tandem of technocratic central planning and bureaucratic management has come to weigh heavily on the shoulders of citizens. The various reforms enacted over the past thirty or forty years in different countries or regions were often designed to reduce or contain the greatest failures of this decaying system. These facelifts have largely made it possible to avoid tackling head-on the true underlying causes of the system's inefficiency. Significant resources have also been devoted to challenging or denying the existence of systemic failures and to claiming that reforms would only generate more problems and worse outcomes.

The CSD model I envision emphasizes the need for flexibility and modularity, and insists that competencies must be the source of power and authority. In so doing, it come down squarely on the side of efficiency and accountability in the supply of PSGS. The CSD model purports to be a truly powerful engine of growth, fuelled by open, competitive processes and a spirit of freedom that invites citizens to become engaged. It is based on redefined boundaries between the responsibilities and activities of different stakeholders and sectors.

In the CSD model, the "public versus private" dichotomy gives way to the "governmental versus competitive" one. The governmental sector consists of officials chosen through the electoral process as well as their close collaborators, while the competitive sector is comprised of various forms of organizations (coalitions of citizens), such as NGOs, co-operatives, civil society organizations, social economy organizations, commercial enterprises, and other entities. The distinction is not simply a matter of semantics but is instead intended to alter and clarify the boundaries of each sector's sphere of intervention and responsibility in a more transparent and useful way.

In a CSD, goods and services that are currently produced by the private sector will naturally be produced and supplied by the competitive sector. As for goods and services that are presently produced by the public sector, they may remain "public" in the sense that the government remains the primary funder and monitor of their production and distribution. However, they would now be produced and distributed by the competitive sector in partnership with (more precisely under contract with) the governmental sector. I maintain the expression "public and social goods and services," or PSGS, but it must be understood that this terminology never means goods and services produced and distributed by the governmental sector.

As mentioned above, the generic policies and programs of the CSD model will elicit opposition and criticism and be resisted and contested by many interest groups. Hence, the importance for social democratic institutions (including citizens and their leaders) to clearly demonstrate the intelligence and courage of their ambitions: the intelligence to design the ways and means whereby the reforms necessary to systematically achieve social democratic objectives are to be implemented, and the courage to deliver and persevere with these reforms.

In all likelihood, there is no single best way to achieve the objectives of a competition-based social democratic society. Moreover, things can and probably will go wrong at times and in some cases. Occasional misfires and deviations will occur. People will cheat, people will "game" the system – but they already do anyway. Open and transparent competition between different types of firms as providers of PSGS under incentive contracts with the governmental sector is an effective guarantee that a rigorous awareness of these possibilities is maintained and a strong will brought to bear so as to engineer them out of the system. But perseverance will be crucially required. One thing is certain: If current suppliers of PSGS cannot be competitively challenged in a reasonable and recurring fashion, and if the supply of PSGS can be captured and monopolized in one way or another by individuals, groups, or private or public organizations, then the quality and reliability of PSGS will eventually and inexorably deteriorate to an unacceptable level.

Unfortunately, many social democratic societies are already on this trajectory. Facing strong resistance to change, they are perched on a social and economic time bomb and are thus, with each tick of the clock, nearer to a dramatic collapse. Numerous symptoms can be observed: a reduced rigour in managing public funds (increasing deficits), rising taxes, falling public-sector standards (education, health, infrastructure), increasingly dysfunctional multi-layer bureaucracy. The remedy most often mentioned and called for is "more money." But just throwing more money around squeaky wheels won't solve the problem. Indeed, this has given rise to a fundamental dilemma: As society has grown richer and more productive, PSGS have become more expensive (opportunity cost), creating substantial pressures to reduce their level and coverage. Why not instead reduce their cost by improving productivity, organizational efficiency, and fostering innovation through competition?

We need something new – a revitalized social-political-economic philosophy – together with an efficient set of policies designed to supply an appropriate array of PSGS: a model in which objectives are clearly defined; means are chosen for their efficiency; political and economic rights and freedoms (including the right to challenge and replace existing suppliers of PSGS) are reaffirmed; and transparent competitive processes (the ultimate embodiment of equality of opportunity, innovation, and motivation) are encouraged.

This new model is the competition-based social democracy. It has an ambitious goal, one that may even seem a little utopian. It is not!

The CSD model is based on a logically consistent framework with concrete political implications and applications. The necessary tools and instruments are already in place. However, a thorough revamping of governments' activities and priorities is necessary.

THE CSD MODEL: FOUNDATIONS AND PRINCIPLES

The CSD model is a "new" social democratic philosophy that emphasizes the importance of a strict separation between the goals (optimizing the well-being of all citizens through social cohesion, maximum growth, and economic freedom) and the ways and means (production and distribution processes, economic contestation). The model relies on the explicit design and implementation of behaviourally realistic policies to attain overall efficiency. It fosters the refocusing of existing, and eventually new, competitive institutions to enhance collective well-being by capitalizing on the diversity of citizens' knowledge, innovative capacities, and skills. The CSD model that I propose here is structured around these pillars, but it is also anchored in a deep underlying belief in a new form of social liberalism. CSD is not, however, an ideology in the sense of a world view or philosophy of life. Therefore, many of the aforementioned macroeconomic and sociological issues will not be resolved, at least not directly, in this manifesto.

I will attempt to convince skeptics that these principles are valid, realistic, and pragmatic. I will show how these principles relate to competitive processes and will propose a new dichotomy between the governmental and competitive sectors. The CSD is a social democracy that seeks not only to ensure that the quantity and quality of PSGS are optimal now and over time, but also that they are supplied in the most efficient manner possible. When so produced, these goods and services favour a stable and unifying social cohesion.

The foundations of this new approach are in line with recent developments in the social democrat vision of the world, but they go further. In so doing, the CSD model raises social democracy's chances of success. The foundations remain those enunciated in the 1999 Blair-Schröder manifesto: liberty, equal opportunity, solidarity, responsibility to others, and, finally, fairness and social justice (democratic rationality).[1]

Liberty and equal opportunity are articulated around individual autonomy, pluralism, and meritocracy. Each member of the social or political community should enjoy the basic resources and capabilities required to survive and flourish in an advanced market economy. The emphasis here is on standards of social protection, health care, and training (qualifications, competencies, employability). Furthermore, this equality of opportunity must persist from start to finish, as outlined in anti-discrimination plans and procedures and in checks on asymmetric power relationships.

Solidarity and responsibility to others entail accepting moral responsibility and practising social virtues. This paints a picture of the market as a sphere of harmonious and productive expression of individuality and sociability. Participating in a market involves much more than merely engaging in occasional exchanges; it also includes compliance with local laws and conventions (with contracting parties), decency and honesty in transactions, participating in co-operative ventures as the collective interest dictates, and demonstrating social initiative on the basis of one's ability to pay. Solidarity and responsibility to others translate into reciprocity. The notion that there can be "no right without responsibility" means that those who wish to reap economic benefits from social co-operation, in the broadest sense, have an obligation to contribute to the best of their ability to the well-being of the community in exchange for those benefits.[2] Governments are obliged to adopt policies that foster autonomy, or, more precisely, that encourage citizens to take their own lives into their own hands.

Fairness and social justice promote the compatibility of the pursuit of social democratic objectives not only with democratic legitimacy, but also with competition and competition-prone institutions. Any arbitrage between conflicting political objectives must be dealt with through public deliberation based on civil dialogue and democratic process for all groups and organizations. These foundations enable us to identify some characteristics shared by all incarnations of social democratic governance. A partial list of those characteristics would include the following, although not always at the same level or with the same commitment. Nonetheless, they constitute the currently dominant conception of social democracy.

Social democracy should welcome globalization as a primary source of economic growth in a regime of economic freedom and pluralism. Growth policy has two dimensions. On the one hand, growth originates from new technologies (computing, Internet, biotechnology) and from new business and distributive services. On the other hand, growth should be qualitative and cause the least possible environmental damage, particularly by means of the invention and adoption (innovation) of better methods of production and management. The process of growth must strike a balance between private and public goods, toil and leisure, old and new risks, as well as competition and the ties that bind local communities. The first and most important purpose of economic growth is to expand and extend human freedom, both individual and social.

Social democracy should create a level playing field for basic opportunities while maintaining the ability to accept differentiated outcomes in terms of income, wealth, lifestyle, and status. This "celebration of creativity, diversity, and excellence" is, however, constrained in two senses. Social democrats seek to abolish or limit extreme differences in unearned income and inherited wealth. Poverty should be fought with a policy mix of safety nets, the fiscal and moral promotion of job acceptance at the proper level of skills, schooling, childcare facilities, sanctions (workfare), urban renewal (against segregation, ghettoization, organized crime, and no-go areas), family values, as well as access to social services (no poverty trap). Moreover, tax-evasion strategies (transfer pricing and exporting profits to tax havens) and double-dipping (PSGS consumed at home but earnings declared and taxes paid abroad) should be discouraged and combated.

Social democracy should reinforce its commitment to an open society and various humanitarian missions via a wide range of measures. These include, among other things, participation in peacekeeping operations and regional stability pacts, welcoming political refugees with a long-term objective of helping them reintegrate their societies, and helping migrant communities (language courses, special programs for migrant employment and migrant entrepreneurship) to contribute to national and international value chains.

Social democracy should also promote open and fair global trade based on competitive processes and the rejection of political interventions, export-promotion subsidies, and trade-distorting grants in favour of national champions. Social democracy should design development aid to foster good governance.

Finally, social democracy should promote inclusive citizenship and strong democracy. This reform entails, among other things, social pacts, regional autonomy, interactive policy-making, legal protection of ethnic minorities and women, adequate financing of political parties and NGOs, institutions and practices of representative and direct democracy (fiscal responsibility, powers of parliament, referenda), and personal freedoms and responsibilities.

THE ULTIMATE GOAL OF CSD: MAXIMIZING THE WELL-BEING OF ALL CITIZENS

Ultimately, the rationale for the CSD initiative is the optimized improvement of social well-being, which embraces civil liberties, environmental quality, and subjective welfare. However, social well-being is more than the sum of the well-being of all individuals. It also needs to reflect society's preferences and values with regard to equality of opportunity, civil liberties, the distribution of resources, and opportunities for further learning.

"Well-being" is a complex concept. Rather than engaging in a quasi-philosophical debate on this, let us focus on a relatively short list of clearly definable metrics that can be measured by citizens.

Social Cohesion

There are two major threats to social cohesion: The first is *exclusion*, which is considered involuntary; and the second is *defection*, which, in contrast to exclusion, is voluntary. When pursuing the goal of increasing social cohesion both of these phenomena must be resisted in order to promote what is generally called *social inclusion*, which Amartya Sen (the 1998 Nobel laureate in economics) characterizes as a shared social experience, an active participation, an equality of opportunities, and a basic level of well-being for all citizens.[3]

The concept of social exclusion is relatively new, having appeared in the seventies with the rise of new forms of social marginalization. Social defection is a phenomenon of alienation and withdrawing from mainstream society. Preventing someone from participating in social relationships and contributing to society is referred to as exclusion. Exclusion, for its part, should not be confused with poverty: Poor societies are not necessarily marked by high levels of exclusion. Poor societies usually maintain strong links between individuals. A low income is only one aspect of exclusion. Albert Hirschman examines the concept of defection, which he defines as behaviour consisting of disengaging from society's rules, dropping out, and refusing to participate. This represents a clear loss of social capital.[4]

What role should the government play in fighting exclusion and poverty? Is it better to give a fish to a starving man, to teach him how to fish, or even to create opportunities for him to learn how to fish? Should voluntary defection also be resisted?

Maximum Sustainable Growth

Simon Kuznets, the 1971 economics Nobel laureate, writes, "Distinctions must be kept in mind between quantity and quality of growth, between costs and returns, and between the short and long run. Goals for more growth should specify more growth of what and for what."[5] The reply given by CSD to this first question (more growth of what?) is relatively forthright: Growth is defined as the increase over a long period of time of a volume-based indicator of production, such as gross domestic product (GDP), or real per-capita GDP. Regardless of the volume indicator chosen, the goal would be to maximize this indicator while taking care to not undermine attainment of the other objectives, namely, social cohesion and freedom. Consequently, an analysis of the connection between growth and social cohesion is of fundamental importance.

As to the second question (more growth for what?), the CSD model rests on the causal relationship between growth and well-being. The position of the CSD model is completely consistent with the broad definition, suggested by Sen, of well-being being determined as much by what we do as by what we have. Growth is thus not an end in and of itself, but rather a means for expanding the palette of choices.

Freedom and Economic Contestation

As stated at the top of this chapter, the policy initiative proposed here is concrete and practical. We seek to integrate the concept of the "right to economic contestation," which represents a significant and distinctive element of the CSD model.

Economic rights are conferred by economic freedom: entrepreneurial freedom, freedom to hire, and adaptability, which together ensure the realization of economic rights. Beware, however, not to confuse adaptability with precariousness. Rather, this economic freedom must be accompanied by measures that buttress and fortify social cohesion. The right to economic contestation allows individuals to challenge the current structure or organization of the supply of PSGS. Indeed, the supply of PSGS, currently ensured by the government (provided outside of markets and thus shielded from competition), will typically represent a significant share of GDP. This supply is often characterized by inefficiency, undermining citizens' economic rights.

The CSD model is based on four principles that most people would accept as reasonable and even indisputable: individual rationality, the power of incentives, the efficiency of competitive processes, and the value of modularity and experimentation.

Individual Rationality

What does the concept of rationality entail? Opinions differ as to the proper definition and use of this concept in economics. I use the following definition: behaviour is rational if it is characterized by the pursuit of a coherent set of objectives and the use of appropriate means to attain them. Rationality is a morally agnostic concept, in that saints as well as sinners, not to mention ordinary citizens, may be considered rational: rationality can be applied both to bettering or enslaving society. However, properly understood, rationality is a powerful tool that allows human behaviour, and, specifically, changes to human behaviour, to be predicted.

The concept of rationality is central to the construction of economic models, and the assumption of rationality has deep roots in economic thought. However, there is not an economist alive who would assert that every individual or agent is rational in all circumstances and at all times in the sense described above. The notion of rationality must be understood broadly to include constrained and bounded rationality.

Some traditionalists propose a sharp divide separating economic decisions from the social and historical contexts in which they are taken. They believe that the economic principle of rationality means that individuals make the best use of the resources at their disposal given the constraints they face, but they also point out that rational individuals are fundamentally selfish: taking only their own interest into account and ignoring established social practices acquired consciously or unconsciously. I do not share this view of rationality.

Instead, I position myself more within the framework of what is generally referred to as systemic rationality. This concept, suggested by James March,[6] can be summarized as follows: The individual makes decisions in an "open" environment, permeable to the influence of the other agents' behaviour, and relying in part on "computational" rationality. Current decisions depend on past decisions (adaptive rationality) and concurrent decisions (contextual rationality), and preferences evolve within a given community (social rationality). Thus, systemic rationality is conceived simultaneously as a social, endogenous, and evolving phenomenon.

In adopting this conception of systemic rationality,[7] I clearly take issue with the narrowly defined "selfish" version. To be fair to the traditionalist view, we must bear in mind that the assumed selfishness of the individual also accounts for the interests and opinions of others. The individual is much more than the caricatural *homo economicus*, the isolated and self-contained cold calculator who is without passion, even if a good part of individual behaviour can be understood, and therefore predicted, with this simple representation in mind.

Behaviour is conditioned by preferences and incentives. It is difficult to change preferences, but incentives can be used to guide individuals to contribute not only to their own well-being, but also to the general good: a demanding but at the same time rather exhilarating agenda.

The Power of Incentives

Individual rationality leads quite naturally to the second principle: incentives are a powerful instrument for efficiently pursuing the objectives of the CSD model. I begin my presentation of the importance of incentive mechanisms with a factual illustration, which brings up the fundamental situation economists refer to as moral hazard and adverse selection. In a nutshell, moral hazard relates to a change of behaviour after an agreement is reached. For instance, once I get my automobile insurance contract, I start to drive in a less prudent way; once the government or my employer announces a relatively generous unemployment coverage, I choose to reduce my effort at work, raising the probability of losing my job. Adverse selection relates to taking advantage of proprietary (asymmetric) information. For instance, I know that my probability of sickness is high but my insurer believes it is low and therefore offers me a health insurance contract on better terms than I deserve; I know that my project is unprofitable but my employer doesn't, so I can take advantage of him by not reporting the information or by falsifying it so that I can get bonuses for a few years. There are different ways to control these contractual problems, such as partial insurance (deductible and co-insurance), tests and verification of past performance, or incentive pay based on the success of the project. But it is a challenging task.[8]

A particularly stark illustration of the consequences that can ensue from failing to recognize or ignoring the impacts that reforms to individuals' economic environments can have on their incentives is the agricultural crisis in mainland China that took place between 1959 and 1961. Agricultural collectivization was a resounding success when it was first introduced around 1952. This success was due to several incentive factors, one of which was that all members of a co-operative had the option of withdrawing, along with their capital (family labour and farming equipment) if they were dissatisfied with the output or their share of the profits. This possibility was eliminated with the reform that took place in 1958–59 – catastrophically undermining productivity. Intentions may have been good, but replacing competence and rationality with incompetence and ideology ended up causing thirty million deaths!

Not every misunderstanding of the incentive impacts of reforms leads to such a disastrous outcome. However, expanding the use of efficient incentive mechanisms, in particular to sectors where they have never been tried, such as the production and distribution of PSGS, will enable us to find more appropriate solutions to counter many harms that afflict our society, such as free riding, moral hazard, and adverse selection. In this way we can benefit from significant efficiency and productivity gains that will improve quality and reduce the cost of those goods and services.

Moral hazard exists when individuals' behaviour cannot be observed directly. Individuals may then provide a sub-optimal level of effort – reducing the probability of success of a project. Adverse selection exists whenever an agent takes advantage of inside information, reducing the efficiency of contracts because some information about the salient characteristics of the tasks to be performed are distributed asymmetrically among the parties.[9] Other, similar problems associated with asymmetric information can give rise to opportunism by one or both parties to a contract, including free riding and holdup.[10]

The Efficiency of Competitive Processes

The third basic principle of the CSD model is that competition leads to efficiency and growth and to increases in well-being. Given the central role played by competition, and financial and insurance markets, in the creation and development of a true social democracy, we must first address some misunderstandings regarding competition.

All too often this proposition that competition can produce efficiency, growth, and, as a consequence, well-being is the target of ill-conceived and biased attacks. A typical criticism might be summarized as follows: Competition is not the way to build a strong community. If you are your neighbour's rival, there will be a winner and a loser. We don't want any losers.

The CSD model is premised on the fact that the absence of competition produces mainly losers, aside from the enlightened central planners who think they know better than the citizens themselves what's good for them; or the monopolists/monopsonists who enrich themselves unduly on the backs of their clients and suppliers. In all countries, antitrust authorities within competition bureaus aim to counter illegal attempts to stifle competition. Appropriate competition policies must enforce a level playing field, in particular antitrust, anti-cartel, and anti-monopoly rules, as part of an explicit policy in favour of competition upstream (between suppliers and between trade unions, among others) and downstream (between retailers and between assemblers of products and services, among others).

A properly regulated competition that is open and transparent floats all boats and creates a win-win society in which markets and solidarity are reconciled for the benefit of all. The last few centuries of history leaves little doubt as to the truth of these claims. Detractors need only look at the record of central planning and the absence of competition in recent times[11] – reduced productivity, increased corruption, and an equality of shared penury under the tutelage of visionary despots. The lessons of history are corroborated by many statistical studies that examine the connection between competition, efficiency, wealth creation, growth, and well-being, not to mention technological and organizational innovation.

Only open and transparent competitive mechanisms (that make optimal use of information and communication technologies) can guarantee the emergence of a society in which the interests of citizens prevail. This requires that decisions pertaining to public and private production, consumption, and investment are made efficiently on the basis of the best available information, the strongest competencies, and the most promising development prospects.

The economists William Baumol, John Panzar, and Robert Willig define a competitive market as a contestable market (one with free entry and exit).[12] It is on the basis of this definition that the CSD model assigns a pre-eminent place to the right to economic contestation – that is, the right to challenge and potentially replace incumbent suppliers, producers, and distributors of PSGS.

The Value of Modularity and Experimentation

As a concept, modularity is relatively old. Modular production organizations can be found in the vast industrial standardization movements that occurred in the automotive and railway industries over a century ago. From Wikipedia:

> Broadly speaking, modularity is the degree to which a system's components may be separated and recombined, often with the benefit of flexibility and variety in use ... The following are contextual examples of modularity across several fields of science, technology, industry, and culture: in biology, modularity recognizes that organisms or metabolic pathways are composed of modules; in ecology, modularity is considered a key factor – along with diversity and feedback – in supporting resilience; in nature, modularity may refer to the construction of a cellular organism by joining together standardized units to form larger compositions, as, for example, the hexagonal cells in a honeycomb; in cognitive science, the idea of modularity of mind holds that the mind is composed of independent, closed, domain-specific processing modules; in the study of complex networks, modularity is a benefit function that measures the quality of a division of a network into groups or communities.[13]

More specifically, modularity in the wide field of PSGS is the recognition that complex systems (in health, education, infrastructure) may be seen as composed of modules (links in production chains) that can be produced separately and recombined. In education, for instance, science students may be bussed to lab facilities shared by many schools; an on-site math and science module, composed of teachers, technicians, and equipment, may be shared by many schools. Similarly in health care, autonomous diagnosis facilities may be shared by many hospitals.

A modular product often gives rise to a modular organization. The relationships between the components of the finished products are mediated by their interfaces. An architecture is said to be perfectly modular when the interfaces are perfectly decoupled (i.e., a modification to one of the modules connected by the interface does not necessitate a modification to the other elements connected by this interface) and perfectly standardized (i.e., accepting connection with a wide variety of components). At the opposite end of the spectrum are integrated finished products. In terms of cost and efficiency, a perfectly modular architecture is ideal.

Organizational modularity means that each team can work independently on the parameters and characteristics of a subsystem of the finished product. In the CSD model, the concept of organizational modularity permeates the production and distribution of PSGS.

What role should modularity play in the production of PSGS? What degree of modularity do we want or need to target in order to optimize the production and distribution of these goods and services? Is there a connection between modularity and the right to economic contestation as an expression of economic freedom? These questions will be addressed below.

The Dichotomy of Governmental versus Competitive Sectors

Two love-hate relationships of human behaviour are particularly important in economics: those with risk and those with competition. Many people enjoy controlled-risk activities in sports, love, culture, and business, but at the same time buy all kinds of insurance and financial options to avoid the potential consequences of risky activities or events. Similarly, many enjoy strategic competition games in sports and movies and games of chance (casinos, lotteries), but at the same time typically engage whenever possible in cartels and agreements (e.g., marriage) to avoid competition. The fear of uncertainty, insecurity, and risk, along with the fear of competition, generate efforts to cut them off at the root: to socialize and transfer risks and to reduce or eliminate competition by whatever means possible. The proliferation of financial and insurance instruments, markets, and institutions has gone a long way toward helping individuals and businesses deal with risk. As for competition, many consider it an overall source of efficiency, wealth, and well-being, but most would agree that it is good that others compete with each other, but not with oneself. Many governments in particular are pro-competition except for their own activities or fields of intervention. Numerous social democratic governments are at the forefront of daily battles to suppress their competitors: a great many governments control, if not suppress, the development of non-public schools, non-public hospitals, and non-public health insurance. In that sense, public figures lead the way in attacking and attempting to subvert the development of competition and in undermining the efficient management, sharing, and transfer of risk, especially as this relates to policies governing the production and distribution of PSGS.

Competition is the foundation on which more efficient means of producing PSGS will, or should, be built in the future. This is in everyone's interest. In the absence of competitive production and distribution systems, mounting economic pressures will lead to a reduction, contraction, or even abandonment of government programs one way or another. This abandonment may not be officially sanctioned, but it will certainly result in practice through lower-quality PSGS characterized by less choice, greater uncertainty, and a loss of reliability. This won't be because we cannot afford them, but rather because these PSGS are being produced less efficiently in the absence of competition.

Confusion between the objectives and the means of attaining them has led to the proliferation of gargantuan bureaucracies that are not only shielded from competition, but also subject to capture by a parallel web of organizational, trade union, political, and bureaucratic power brokers. This works to the detriment of citizens as ultimate beneficiaries and funders of the system. The dichotomy between the governmental and competitive sectors, both having clearly delineated responsibilities, becomes vital to ensure that the well-being of citizens is optimized. This new dichotomy lies at the very heart of true social democracy.

Competitive-sector organizations will be called upon by the governmental sector to respond to open and transparent calls for tenders for the right and obligation to supply, for a defined and generally renewable span of time, clearly identified PSGS. The contracts thus concluded will specify the rights, responsibilities, commitments, and compensation of stakeholders.

Contracts between governmental-sector authorities and competitive-sector organizations should be designed in such a way that the retained supplier is incentivized to achieve its objectives and honour its commitments. The contract duration must be calibrated to the useful lifespan of the equipment and/or the estimated duration of the governance strategies, so that the government – or the evaluator – can determine the performance of the provider with regards to objectives stipulated in the contract, and the provider can internalize the effects of its strategies on its performance. The governmental sector thereby ensures that the selected competitive-sector entity will properly manage its operations and the inherent risks. The tendering process itself should be repeated at regular and sufficiently frequent intervals, ranging from several months to several years, depending on the good or service in question.

Competition between the suppliers, producers, and distributors that are under contract with the governmental sector is favourable to multi-source, diversified procurement that is conducive to objective evaluation, benchmarking, innovation, as well as performance incentives. Competition means multi-source procurement – as in, "don't put all your eggs in one basket – and watch them closely."

This characterization of the roles of the governmental and competitive sectors makes it possible to avoid the conflicts of interest that undermine the efficiency of the traditional social democratic model, in which the design, financing, provision, and evaluation of suppliers typically all fall under the purview of a single organization: the government.

These conflicts of interest are endemic to the traditional social democratic model, where they tend to create a climate conducive to scheming, lack of transparency, kickbacks, and the granting of undue perks at the expense of citizens, consumers, and taxpayers. Examples are numerous. The following are based on my own experience. If the minister of environment comes up with a report that water is "unfit" for consumption in some localities, the minister of municipal affairs may advocate for postponing the publication of the report as funds for reinvesting in filtration and purification plants are not available. If a researcher files a report that recommends an action that the deputy minister does not like, the deputy minister may lobby to change the recommendation, and, if necessary, may even refuse to pay for the report. Similar problems are present, too, in the private sector. The difference is that in the latter case, the firm and its officers will eventually suffer the consequences.

Separating the roles and responsibilities of the governmental and competitive sectors should allow for the deployment of credible accountability and performance incentive mechanisms. Too often, these are at best unclear and subject to manipulation, and at worst non-existent in the traditional delivery of PSGS.

THE TEN GENERIC CSD POLICIES AND PROGRAMS

The CSD model builds on ten major and ambitious generic policies and programs.

1. Clearly define the core competencies of the governmental and competitive sectors.

As the name indicates, the governmental sector answers directly to the government. The main responsibilities of this sector are (1) to identify citizens' needs for PSGS, including regulations of different kinds, both in terms of quantity and quality; (2) to determine the characteristics of PSGS; (3) to arbitrate, as required, between different baskets of PSGS and between different coalitions of citizens according to available resources; and (4) to manage contracts and partnerships for the production, distribution, and delivery of the chosen basket of PSGS. These functions of identification, design, arbitrage, and choice in terms of the baskets of PSGS are closely linked and are brought about through the process of democratic elections.

The competitive sector is broadly defined to include the private business sector, the co-operative sector, the NGO sector, non-profit enterprises, as well as other organizations such as civil society and social economy organizations. The role of the competitive sector is to produce, distribute, and supply PSGS – as well as private goods and services, of course – in the most efficient way possible, using the best available technologies, human resources, and organizational structures. This role of the competitive sector is framed by well-defined incentive-compatible contracts with the governmental sector.

The new responsibilities of the governmental sector represent a major change, as new competencies must be developed and acquired. New people, with those management competencies, must be hired. In the end, a significant reduction of the public bureaucracy must be envisioned. Most public servants presently working in the public sector will move into the workforce in competitive-sector production and distribution entities, now under incentive contract with the governmental sector.

2. Promote open and transparent competitive mechanisms in the attribution of contracts for the production, distribution, and delivery of PSGS.

For competitive mechanisms to be universally embraced, a significant effort must be made to communicate and foster a better understanding of economic laws and rules. The emergence and pervasiveness of competitive prices and processes throughout the economy, in the PSGS sectors in particular, are key to avoiding waste and for generating innovative solutions to problems and challenges. This is why they are considered central to the CSD model. If we are to succeed in this endeavour, contracts must be attributed through open and transparent processes with no favouritism or predatory behaviour. Competitive-sector organizations must face a level playing field; if some participating organizations are to benefit from any advantage, this must be made known and quantified clearly at the outset.

3. Support the creation and development of competitive-sector organizations with the ability to effectively bid on contracts for the provision of PSGS, by making use of best practices and public and private counselling services. In so doing, creative destruction (and innovation) is promoted with better services being implemented on a continuous basis.

The emergence of competitive markets for the production, distribution, and delivery of contracts regarding PSGS requires that a sufficient number of organizations participate in the tendering process. It is a fundamental responsibility of the governmental sector to make sure that contract-awarding processes be immune to significant expression of market power by competitive-sector organizations. The latter organizations must be capable of submitting credible bids for governmental contracts in a setting purged of all favouritism. The governmental sector has a responsibility under this generic policy to make sure that best practices are promoted through well-understood creative destruction and innovation. Nothing would prevent the governmental sector from promoting information gathering and dissemination (possibly through counselling activities) on such best practices at all levels.

In order to achieve the highest possible level of efficiency, it is preferable for the government to explicitly favour the emergence of competitive-sector organizations without directly interfering in the allocation of contracts. In the long run, this type of policy would be much more profitable than trying to tilt the playing field to benefit a preferred organization.

4. Promote the emergence of competitive prices and mechanisms (market creation) in all sectors of the economy, including the PSGS sector.

Competitive mechanisms are best for allowing citizens and organizations to make choices based on appropriate information. By sending distorted signals and indicators of relative costs and scarcity of goods and services, price manipulations have become a major source of social and economic waste in our societies. These manipulations result in poor consumption and investment decisions. They also lead firms and organizations in all sectors – including PSGS sectors, such as health care and education, for instance – to make production, investment, and R&D choices that are more in line with the interests, wishes, and private objectives of political authorities and well-organized interest groups than with the needs of their customers and clients.

Faced with the right signals (competitive prices and processes), individuals as well as firms and organizations can adapt their consumption and production activities – including their investments in human capital (portfolio of competencies) and in R&D and innovation – to the relative social value of those activities. In some cases, well-informed decision making will require the creation and establishment of competitive markets in lieu of traditional bureaucratic decision making, whose interests nearly always end up trumping those of the people. This is inexorably and most perniciously the case even when well-intentioned political leaders take it upon themselves to impose their own tutelary preferences.

This is not to say that it is never appropriate for political or social leaders to seek to shape the behaviour of the people, but rather that it is always better to proceed through competitive institutions and mechanisms, respecting citizens' freedom and encouraging a sense of responsibility.

5. Promote modularity, flexibility, experimentation, and change through multi-source or diversified procurement.

Innovation, both technological and organizational, must rely on an explicit process by which experimentation and change become normal, which not to say frequent or continuous. In order to reduce the costs of developing, selecting, and deploying innovations, and, by extension, promoting the emergence of an innovative society, the governmental sector must explicitly develop a multi-source procurement policy when awarding contracts. The conditions surrounding the awarding of contracts aimed to implement multi-source procurement can be designed in such a way that no single competitive-sector organization can monopolize or dominate a significant part of the production, distribution, and/or delivery of a given PSGS.

In order to advance competition among providers and to identify those capable of performing better in the production, distribution, and delivery of PSGS, there must always be some level of modularity and experimentation, with proper safeguards, allowing the evaluation of new ways and means – so as to implement known best practices as consistently as possible. By explicitly favouring multi-sourcing, the governmental sector strives to encourage a proper level of modularity and experimentation in the provision of PSGS, and in so doing, encourages the search for and the discovery of best practices.

6. Favour the development of mechanisms and institutions to help individuals as well as firms and organizations better adapt to changes caused by creative destruction.

A significant source of opposition to socio-economic change, even when this change appears desirable, is the absence of mechanisms or institutions to help individuals and businesses cover the direct costs they incur in adapting to such changes. The following three factors are equally important for social well-being: flexibility in adapting to altered conditions and the willingness to take on new challenges created by exogenous and endogenous changes in a volatile socio-economic environment; the education sector's capacity to meet the needs of industry and society in terms of skills and competencies; and the scale and effectiveness of R&D investments in generating new ideas and useful products and services.

Hence, adaptability in a volatile environment must be a characteristic of all sectors producing and distributing private as well as public and social goods and services. Flexibility counters inertia, which can be triggered by the fear of change. Unless people understand the reasons for change and are given tools to manage it, they will resist any change in the economic and political arenas. Therefore, the level of social receptiveness to change will depend on the existence of institutions (tools, organizations, and markets) that allow individuals, companies, and the various levels of government to manage the risks and opportunities caused by volatility in the socio-economic environment. A proper set of institutions for managing the risk associated with change is a prerequisite for a flexible society – that is, for a society in which innovation, both technological and organizational, thrives.

7. Promote direct and transparent income- and wealth-support policies while resisting the development of a culture of dependence among individuals and businesses/organizations.

It is normal that a certain number of individuals will end up making decisions that prove, *ex post*, to have disastrous and socially undesirable outcomes. Entrepreneurs and innovators take risks when developing a new technology, a new product, or a new process. Risk means that, sometimes, the project ends up in failure. Similarly, undertaking a job-training program does not guarantee the individual a job at a high salary. But taking risks is an important source of productivity gains, and of social well-being. Hence, a governmental income- and wealth-support program (a PSGS) may not only be unavoidable, it may also be essential to growth and overall social well-being. However, this type of government program must be properly designed and implemented. In lieu of the paternalistic control and manipulation of prices that have often been the preferred policy, the CSD model advocates implementing direct and transparent policies of income and wealth support with strong incentives for the beneficiaries to exit them. It is desirable that such programs be administered by a single government authority and provided by competitive-sector partnering organizations in order to increase overall accountability.[14]

A CSD policy for the needy, the unlucky, and the poor must be as compassionate as possible, but for the well-being of the beneficiaries themselves it must be designed to prevent long-term dependence. It is necessary that beneficiaries, be they individuals, companies, or industries, be properly incentivized to leave government income- and wealth-support programs as quickly and successfully as possible, thereby allowing better and more generous programs to be designed and implemented in their place.

8. Foster systematic, transparent, and credible evaluations of government programs and policies, including subsidies and supports for businesses.

Every government program should contain a sunset clause to force a periodic re-evaluation of its purpose. Independent and credible organizations and bodies, well versed in the use of state-of-the-art and transparent methodologies and open to scrutiny and criticism from the public, should be tasked with performing these evaluations. In most cases, current socio-economic evaluations of government programs make use of incorrect, controversial, and biased self-gratifying methodologies. Programs designed to boost (regional) job creation or increase targeted investments, as well as endeavours to reintegrate the chronically unemployed, are all examples of government initiatives costing vast sums of money with practically no significant tangible results.

The problem may not be with the objectives of these programs as much as their implementation. Current evaluation procedures applied to these programs are not only of dubious value, but most often amount to little more than a means to justify (*ex post*) a bad, politically motivated decision.[15] The CSD model rejects these feeble evaluation procedures and methodologies in favour of systematic, transparent, independent, and credible evaluations. By stressing the need for more rigorous and regular evaluation procedures, in addition to requiring that the programs be subject to competitive processes leading to incentive-compatible assistance programs, the CSD model will favour programs whose design and implementation are better.

9. Reform the tax system to make it simpler, more consistent and inclusive, and more informative. This will promote social cohesion and incentivize individual and business contributions to social well-being.

The changes proposed in the CSD model favour a redesigned tax system that could raise its capacity to attain two objectives. First, ensuring balanced funding of PSGs, and second, providing individuals and organizations with the appropriate incentives to contribute to the well-being of their fellow citizens. This contribution relates to the labour-market-participation decisions (how, at what level of effort) and the business decisions needed to develop and bring to market high-quality goods and services.

To accomplish this, the following elements must be put in place. The CSD supports taxes on consumption (such as sales taxes and value-added taxes, which should be included in posted prices so as to promote transparency in pricing) rather than on income, where they create greater potential distortions in taxpayers' decisions, in particular in labour-market-participation decisions. If it is necessary to maintain a certain level of income taxation (during the transition to generalized consumption taxes), the CSD would reduce the implicit marginal tax rates on the unemployed or welfare recipients when they manage to find full- or part-time jobs. Similarly, it would reduce the marginal tax rates applicable to significant year-over-year increases in earnings, reduce income tax rates and their complexity (number of tiers) while including all income in the tax base, and impose a minimum rate on overall income to promote social inclusion.

In order to impart a sense of responsibility and reduce resistance to paying income taxes, the CSD model would allow every citizen to directly allocate a certain percentage (3 per cent?) of his or her tax bill to an educational or health-care foundation or institution, or perhaps more generally a charitable foundation or institution, of his or her choice.

Economists have long known and advocated that efficiency in resource allocation must be based on taxing consumption rather than labour (income). Hence the need to move toward reducing, and eventually abolishing, personal income taxes in favour of consumption taxes (sales taxes or value-added taxes) so that taxation causes as little distortion as possible. In their consumption decisions, consumers will typically consider the relative value of goods and services and their relative prices: a fundamental result of economic analysis is that if relative prices (costs) between two goods are in a ratio of 2:1, consumers will aim at consuming quantities of both goods such that the relative values for them are in a ratio of 2:1. Similarly, in their production decisions, firms will typically consider the relative costs of goods and services and their relative prices: if relative prices are in a ratio of 2:1, a producer will aim at producing quantities such that the relative costs are in a ratio of 2:1. With the same relative prices, the interests of buyers (consumers) and suppliers (firms) are met in a consistent way: the rate at which consumers will consider substituting product A for product B is the same as the rate at which the producer will consider substituting product A for product B.[16] To reach this tax neutrality, a unique percentage should be applied to all goods and services so that relative prices are not distorted.

Consumption must be defined in a broad sense. For instance, an amount distributed as a gift to friends, family, and charities must be considered as consumed by the donor as it generates "love and recognition." Efficiency requires that all goods and services, including tomatoes, "love and recognition," and vacation trips, be taxed at the same rate. Consumption taxes should thus be collected at the time of purchase, or at death, on the principle that individuals are considered to have consumed all their accumulated wealth at the time of death.

10. Promote free trade alliances with developing countries in order to contribute to their development and to obtain strategic advantages in competing with developed countries.

The CSD model stresses the search for social and economic efficiency within a given country or region in order to provide the best possible opportunities for improving productivity, stimulating growth, and enhancing social well-being. Amid these opportunities, free trade policies cutting across various sectors and levels of the commercial and industrial landscape occupy a special place.

The CSD model stresses the importance of identifying and acting on different strategies for forming alliances with producers and suppliers from countries of the Global South in order to acquire, maintain, and consolidate competitive advantages among countries of the Global North and, in so doing, favour the development of countries of the Global South. With this type of strategy, developing countries could become key allies as providers of much-needed inputs (not only intermediary products but also, in due time, new technologies, products, and services) in the rivalries between developed countries.

A foreign aid policy based on free trade with developing countries and their inclusion into value chains and networks would be much more efficient that simply offering financial grants and giving subsidies to businesses and organizations in developing countries, notwithstanding the necessity of such grants and subsidies in emergency situations. Free trade and foreign outsourcing and offshoring of proper links in value chains could be much more efficient and respectful than economic immigration policies, whose objective is to attract valuable workers (with proper competencies) from developing countries, hence robbing those countries of their most valuable resource.[17]

3

The New Competition-Based Capitalism

Numerous economists and economic bodies have proposed reforms of capitalism, but eight of them are of particular interest in the present context due to their content and/or grounding in economic theory.[1] In this chapter, then, we will look at the arguments put forward by Luigi Zingales, Jean Tirole, a team from *The Economist* magazine, Joseph Stiglitz, Philippe Aghion (with Céline Antonin and Simon Bunel), Mariana Mazzucato, Thomas Piketty, and the World Business Council for Sustainable Development (WBCSD).

The first six of them reaffirm the efficiency of competitive markets and their ability to generate growth and well-being, while acknowledging the shortcomings of a system of prices and markets dominated by big business with market and political power. In particular, they show the materialization since 1980 of significant income and wealth disparities. They recognize that correcting these "flaws" will require truth in market pricing and more emphasis on promoting open competition, which is as challenging as it is beneficial. The seventh reform initiative (Piketty) is more along the lines of participatory socialism. The eighth (WBCSD) stresses the notion of "real value," asserting that capitalism needs to be reoriented toward the pursuit of true value, preserving and enhancing natural, social, and financial capital, rather than simply the pursuit of financial profits and economic efficiency.

Before proceeding with brief descriptions of the eight reform proposals, we need to define capitalism and give a succinct overview of its currently most popular manifestations. Recall the discussion of the different types of firms in chapter 1, in particular the capitalist one. A capitalist (private or public) firm is a firm where the suppliers of capital, equity holders not lenders, are compensated last, from the residual revenues, if any, once all other (priority) factors of production are paid. Branko Milanovic will serve as our guide here.[2] In his view, capitalism has not only become the dominant economic paradigm, especially after the spectacular collapse of communism at the beginning of the 1990s, but it is, in fact, essentially the only one still present on the international scene.

The capitalist nature of this (sole) system lies in the fact that the production of goods and services is primarily motivated by profit, equal to the residual revenues, if any, once all other (priority) factors of production are paid, bringing together labour, resources, and privately owned (it could also be publicly owned) capital, while the production process is coordinated by a decentralized system of prices. Capitalism comes in two flavours: liberal meritocratic capitalism, principally exemplified by the United States and the European Union, and state capitalism, of which the best example is China.

Under liberal meritocratic capitalism, investments are essentially determined by private firms and independent entrepreneurs in a setting characterized by equal opportunity based on merit (or talent), entrepreneurial freedom, and social and economic mobility driven by performance in wealth creation. According to Milanovic, over time this brand of capitalism leads to a high level of income and wealth inequality and the emergence of an upper class, the renewal of which is less and less ensured by merit-based equality of opportunity. Through a process of entrenchment, this upper class manages to form an elite and resist challenges from new talents and skills and from new entrepreneurs seeking upward mobility. The biggest challenge in liberal meritocratic capitalism is to find a way to prevent this oligarchy from using the various tools at its disposal to become immune to competition, thereby undermining equality of opportunity based on merit.

State capitalism also has as its primary motivation profit, and it is also organized around firms that bring together labour, resources, and private capital and choose their output and prices in a decentralized fashion. According to Milanovic, Chinese government control of production, which was nearly 100 per cent prior to 1978 and still over 50 per cent in 1998, represented only about 20 per cent of GDP as of 2022. As for the share of private investment, it has attained 65 per cent, and private employment 85 per cent. In a recent working paper for the Peterson Institute for International Economics, Tianlei Huang and Nicolas Véron state, based on Fortune 2022 Global 500 rankings, that the aggregate revenue of the private-sector companies reached 19 per cent of the aggregate revenue of Chinese companies in 2021, and that the private sector's share of market value in the top one hundred listed Chinese companies crossed the 50 per cent threshold in 2020.[3]

The main feature of this state capitalism is the existence of a powerful bureaucracy whose role is to implement policies designed to promote the pursuit and attainment of robust economic growth. Its second key characteristic is the absence of rule of law and checks and balances on government interventions. Arbitrating conflicts between these two characteristics and resisting systemic, endemic, and inequality-generating corruption, which is inevitable in the absence of rule of law, are the two main challenges to state capitalism.

PROJECTS FOR REFORMING CAPITALISM

Luigi Zingales's Reform of Capitalism

Luigi Zingales sets himself the dual goal of sounding the alarm over the cancer of collusive and crony capitalism and of defining a program for eradicating this cancer before it metastasizes.[4] This program is spearheaded by a reaffirmation of the power of competition. Zingales claims that the absence of competition and major distortions caused by all sorts of government subsidies underlie all of today's economic ills (he published his book in 2012), including declining real incomes of the middle class. His goal is thus to harness the power of competition and to define the conditions conducive to it playing a positive role, in particular the affirmation of a simplified and transparent regulation of property rights, the right to compete, and the information sharing required for balanced transactions between economic agents.

For Zingales, competition curbs the ability of firms to earn supra-competitive profits, makes the benefits of innovation available to consumers, and promotes efficiency and thus meritocracy. Under this system, responsibilities fall on the shoulders of those most able to bear them and for whom equitable compensation is ensured. Consequently, economists should be more concerned with assessing the actual state of competition rather than simply assuming that it exists and deriving all sort of conclusions therefrom. For the potential benefits to materialize, markets have to be open and transparent and welcoming to new entrants. Robust competition is the best protection against monopolization and the proliferation of crony capitalism.

Zingales also warns against PPPs in which the government and business are partners. It is necessary to be vigilant regarding the promises of these PPPs, so that the vision of the efficiency of the private sector and the social goals of the public sector are not somehow reversed. The example of Fannie Mae and Freddie Mac in the United States is the most eloquent illustration of a PPP gone bad. According to Zingales, the greatest advantage of such government-sponsored enterprises (GSEs) within PPPs was that GSEs benefit from government backing of their debt. It is estimated that the value of the government-backed debt in the Fannie Mae and Freddie Mac case amounted to some $10.9 billion in 2000 and $19.8 billion in 2003.[5] Only two-thirds of this was recuperated by the intended beneficiaries (housing market borrowers), while one-third was misappropriated by private shareholders and managers at the expense of taxpayers.[6]

The program championed by Zingales is designed to strengthen competition and the economy of competitive markets by several means, including a more aggressive stance against the development of crony capitalism,[7] and a more vigorous defence of freedom, democracy, and social mobility.

The battle against income and wealth disparities, which are attributable to inequality of opportunity (education) and barriers to entry, is waged by intensifying competition at all levels, yielding better measures of performance, developing an incentive social safety net focused on the benefits of insurance[8] and conducive to productivity gains, and driving a reinvention of competition policy that makes it more focused on protecting competition.

It is not always straightforward to distinguish between good and bad approaches for protecting competition. It is here that economic ethics, social capital, social norms, limits to lobbying, efficient taxation, responsible finance, and the creation of markets for common resources (the environment, for instance) come into play, which are addressed directly or indirectly by Zingales. This list could include the creation of markets and institutions, including community-based institutions, to counteract the misfortune of the over-exploitation of shared property (tragedy of the commons) and the misfortune of socially desirable exploitation being blocked (tragedy of the anticommons) by too many veto rights of different kinds.

In conclusion, Zingales reiterates that a pro-market policy is not a pro-business policy, and that the true genius of capitalism is not in private property or the pursuit of profit, but rather in competition. In the final analysis, the reason for the phenomenal success of the market economy lies in competition, properly framed and promoted by appropriate rules of social and financial responsibility, accountability, freedom, democracy, and ethical and responsible governance.

Jean Tirole's Reform of Capitalism

Jean Tirole broaches the reform of capitalism from the angle of relationships between an imperfect system of competitive markets and an imperfect government with essential responsibilities.[9] The choice isn't between markets or government, but rather between more or less efficient markets, and a government that is more or less clear-sighted, including about its own limitations. Reforms are needed for both markets and government.

Tirole recalls how the presentation by Jean-Jacques Laffont of his 1999 report *Étapes vers un État moderne – Une analyse économique*[10] to the French Council of Economic Analysis unleashed a wave of indignation among the policy-makers, academics, and top bureaucrats in attendance (the report was denounced as heresy). However, Laffont was only presenting an economic perspective in which the government reacts to incentives, can be captured by various interest groups, and may wish to pursue objectives other than the well-being of the population: economics – the ultimate dismal science.

Tirole issues a reminder of the power of the efficiency and integrity harnessed by markets, undergirded by freedom of entrepreneurship and commerce, and by dynamic competition between companies. He also speaks to the failures of markets insofar as, left to themselves, market exchanges can affect third parties without their consent, reflect the temporary irrationality of the participants, lead to over-indebtedness of consumers who are poorly equipped to resist the lure of easy credit, succumb to the sway of non-competitive markets, and ultimately generate significant inequalities if only because of the absence of useful "markets," such as various insurance markets and social safety nets, among others.

Similarly, the government, when left to its own devices and without effective checks and balances, is in danger of being captured by lobbyists, sinking into collusive and crony capitalism, lying to ill-informed voters (populism), and profiting from policies whose costs are barely noticed and whose benefits are concentrated. This list is by no means exhaustive.

If capitalism is to be at the service of the common good, it must receive ongoing tune-ups, both situational and routine, to improve the functioning of markets and businesses. For the latter, this refers to their social responsibilities, the prevalence of truth in pricing, and improvements to government interventions, which are sometimes necessary correctives, and sometimes ill-advised meddling.

Hence, Tirole advocates for a relatively traditional but continuously fine-tuned capitalism. He advocates also for a similar refocusing of the role of government, whose actions and interventions often suffer from incomplete information and potentially perverse incentives.

The Economist's *Reform of Capitalism*

In September and November of 2018, *The Economist* magazine published two special reports on the future of capitalism. The first states that liberals have become a complacent and inward-looking elite who need to rediscover their fire.[11] The second contains a series of articles on the common theme of a pro-competition liberation movement to bring companies earning excessive profits to heel and to ensure that innovation continues to blossom.[12]

According to *The Economist*, since 1977, indices of concentration have increased in three out of four industries, such that dominant businesses are increasingly difficult to de-throne. Although globalization has allowed excess profits to be curbed, returns have increased greatly in protected industries while the quality of the goods and services they supply has deteriorated. *The Economist* proposes a three-prong plan of attack, asserting that the true spirit of liberalism is not self-perpetuation, but rather radicalism and disruption.

First, intellectual property should serve to foster innovation rather than protect established firms. Two measures would be particularly effective here: require platforms to grant access to challengers under competitive terms, as was done in the case of networks (like telecoms, for example), and tighten controls on patents to make them harder to obtain, shorter in duration, and easier to contest in court. Maintaining vigorous competition should have precedence over protecting intellectual property.

Next, antitrust authorities should aggressively dismantle barriers to entry and pursue pro-competition policies with greater emphasis on stronger measures to encourage the arrival of new players on the market. To do this, governments must prohibit abusive non-compete clauses and non-essential professional certification requirements and simplify the complex regulations too often written by industry lobbyists.

Finally, antitrust authorities must pay more attention to the overall level of competition in the economy and to excess profits in various industries.

Joseph Stiglitz's Reform of Capitalism

Joseph Stiglitz starts from the premise that the United States has the highest level of inequality among advanced economies, and one of the lowest levels of social and economic opportunity and mobility.[13] He asserts that there is an alternative, which he calls progressive capitalism. This is not an oxymoron: it is based on the idea that the power of competitive markets can be harnessed to the service of society in general, owing to their role as engines of growth and well-being.

According to Stiglitz, standards of living have been rising for over two centuries because of scientific innovation and the evolution of social organization, as reflected in institutions such as the rule of law and democracies endowed with checks and balances. The true source of a nation's wealth is its citizens' capacity for creativity and innovation.

To increase their wealth, individuals can either add to the nation's "economic pie" (wealth creation), or they can seize a bigger piece of the pie by either exploiting others or by abusing market power or insider information. Just as government policy in the United States was increasingly relying on unleashing its market system and reducing social protections, information economics (which deals with ubiquitous situations in which information is imperfect and incomplete),[14] behavioural economics, and game theory were clearly demonstrating that markets left to themselves can be inefficient.

The result is a US economy that is characterized by more exploitation and less wealth creation. The gutting of antitrust laws and lax application of what regulations remained, combined with the inability of regulators to adapt to innovations in the accumulation and abuse of market power, have had the effect of rendering markets more concentrated and less competitive. In order to play their role, markets must be structured around rules and regulations, and these rules and regulations must be vigorously enforced.

Stiglitz proposes that the way out of this morass begins with recognizing the vital role played by the government in placing markets at the service of society, in ensuring that market regulation guarantees robust competition without abuses, and in aligning the interests of businesses with those of their workers, suppliers, and clients.

At the level of government policy, Stiglitz identifies many other areas in which government intervention is required: protection against unemployment and disability, pensions with low administrative costs, protection against inflation, the development of adequate infrastructure, provision of high-quality universal education, and adequate support for fundamental research.

According to Stiglitz, progressive capitalism amounts to a new social contract, with a basket of public policies centred on the production and distribution of PSGS that are typically the responsibility of the government, and a policy of safeguarding, overseeing, and promoting competitive markets and effective pro-competition institutions.

While several characteristics of Stiglitz's progressive capitalism are compatible with the CSD model, especially with their shared emphasis on the development of the basket of PSGS and an effective, even aggressive, competition policy, the two models have several important differences.

Philippe Aghion and Colleagues' Reform of Capitalism

Philippe Aghion and his collaborators Céline Antonin and Simon Bunel see capitalism through the lens of Schumpeter's creative destruction, more or less tempered by the presence of a social safety net.[15] According to Aghion, we must accompany this process of creative destruction without impeding it, mainly by means of appropriate regulation.

The power of creative destruction lies in its formidable ability to generate growth. Because of this phenomenon, the market economy is intrinsically disruptive. Historically, creative destruction has proven to be a remarkable engine of prosperity, raising our societies to levels of development unimaginable two hundred years ago. Thus, the issue is to better understand the driving forces behind this power in order to channel it into directions that we want as a society – namely, the quest for a prosperity that is more sustainable and equally shared.

In developed economies, capitalism has become more caring and inclusive over time, largely due to the struggles of civil society (unions, progressive parties, media). Interventions from visionaries seeking to change the posture of government to make it more responsive to pressure from civil society has also played a key role.

Aghion strongly advocates for a marriage of convenience, or merger, between a more cutthroat and aggressive capitalism and a softer and more inclusive one for at least two reasons. First, reforms to provide more protection and inclusion in the United States have been delivered without hampering innovation; likewise, reforms to facilitate innovation and creative destruction in Germany and Scandinavia have not led to a fundamental rethinking of welfare systems and public services. Second, the stakes involved between innovation and inclusion (or between innovation and protection) do not amount to a zero-sum game – in fact, quite the opposite.

Facilitating the entry of innovative new companies and triggering the potential of researchers promotes innovation and growth as well as inclusivity. A well-designed and incentivizing flexicurity on the labour market can protect individuals against the negative consequences of job loss, while at the same time providing an incentive to acquire training in order to ensure they are better prepared for a new job. This provides greater protection for individuals without hampering the process of creative destruction.

Mariana Mazzucato's Reform of Capitalism

According to Mariana Mazzucato, capitalism has no answers to a host of problems, including disease, inequality, the digital divide, and, perhaps most blatantly, the environmental crisis.[16] She looks at the grand challenge facing us: reshaping the capacities and role of government within the economy and society, and recovering a sense of public purpose.

She claims that modern economies reward activities that extract value rather than create it, a situation that must change if we are to ensure a type of capitalism that works for the general population. She scrutinizes the way in which economic value is determined and how the difference between value creation and value extraction has become increasingly blurry. Mazzucato argues that this blurriness allowed certain actors in the economy to portray themselves as value creators, while in reality they were just moving existing value around, or, even worse, destroying it. It is not clear if she is referring to politicians or business persons in such a statement.

Mazzucato raises questions of significant importance: If value is created collectively, including by direct investments of state-led institutions, how can it also be shared collectively? Regarding the key role of the state in driving innovation-led growth as an investor of first resort, what are the ways to ensure the state gets a fair return for its investment? How can innovation be governed in the public interest?

Mazzucato debunks the so-called myth of a lumbering, bureaucratic state versus a dynamic, innovative private sector. She claims that the opposite is true: the private sector only finds the courage to invest after an entrepreneurial state has made high-risk investments. Hence, Western capitalism is in crisis: investment has been falling, living standards have stagnated or declined, and inequality has risen dramatically. She claims that, while traditional economic theory sees policy as a means to fixing markets, inclusive and sustainable growth require active market creation and "shaping not only fixing."

For Mazzucato, global companies have become increasingly driven by short-term returns and maximization of shareholder value. How, she asks, can "purpose" become central to how business interacts with other economic actors, fostering a more symbiotic and mutualistic ecosystem?

Thomas Piketty's Reform of Capitalism/Socialism

The last chapter of Thomas Piketty's monumental book *Capital and Ideology* is entitled "Elements for a Participatory Socialism for the Twenty-First Century." So it is, in fact, less an initiative to reform capitalism than to reform socialism. Be that as it may, Piketty's project is strongly focused on mechanisms allowing the reduction of "hyper-inequality" in favour of a "just inequality."

Piketty proposes some reasons or explanations for the so-called hyper-inegalitarian narrative we have observed over the last forty years of so: a product of history, a consequence of the communist debacle, of the failure to disseminate knowledge, of too-rigid disciplinary barriers, and most importantly of the insufficient appropriation of economic and financial issues by citizens. Important elements of his project are temporary ownership and just inequalities:

The notion of permanent private ownership will need to be replaced by temporary private ownership, which will require steeply progressive taxes on large concentrations of property. The proceeds of the wealth tax will then be parceled out to every citizen in the form of a universal capital endowment, thus ensuring permanent circulation of property and wealth ... A just society in no way requires absolute uniformity or equality. To the extent that income and wealth inequalities are the result of different aspirations and distinct life choices or permit improvement of the standard of living and expansion of the opportunities available to the disadvantaged, they may be considered just.[17]

According to Piketty, proprietarism (defined as a defence of the primacy of private property) and capitalism (defined as the extension of proprietarism to industry) are grounded in a concentration of economic power that allows the owners of capital to sovereignly decide whom to hire and at what wages.

This is clearly a particularly reductionist view of capitalism, in particular when it is exposed to competition. In characterizations of enterprises, be they capitalist, socialist, or co-operative, workers' or IP' enterprises (see chapter 1 above) residual decision-making power always lies with the group that is paid last: financial capital (capitalist enterprise, whether private or state-owned), human capital (co-operative or workers' enterprise), or intellectual capital (IP enterprise). The compensation paid to the various resources used in the production of goods and services that are useful to a buying clientele have to respect two constraints. First, the total compensation paid out cannot systematically exceed the total revenue that citizens agree to pay to the company in exchange for the goods and services produced. Second, the compensation of all the factors and the value of their best alternative uses must reflect, or be calculated on, a risk-adjusted basis. Value-creation mechanisms are well-known and, unfortunately, not magical.

For Piketty, the progressive property tax appears to be an indispensable tool to ensure the greater circulation and wider dissemination of property. Piketty recognizes that the progressive tax has never made it possible to distribute property to the poorest 50 per cent, which can only limit their participation in economic life, and in particular in the creation of companies and their governance. To get there, we have to go further. According to Piketty, the most logical way to do this would be to put in place a system of capital endowment paid to every young adult (for example, at the age of twenty-five) and financed by a progressive tax on private property. By design, such a system makes it possible to diffuse ownership at the base while limiting its concentration at the top.

Before looking at a few questions raised by this particular reform initiative, let us recap Piketty's view in his own words: "The model of participatory socialism proposed here rests on two key pillars: first, social ownership and shared voting rights in firms, and second, temporary ownership and circulation of capital. These are the essential tools for transcending the current system of private ownership. By combining them, we can achieve a system of ownership that has little in common with today's private capitalism; indeed, it amounts to a genuine transcendence of capitalism."[18]

Two comments come to mind when considering these purported excesses of capitalism. First, accounting is not economics. And second, you can't increase the size of the cake by cutting it differently: pooling property will not by itself prevent the tragedy of the commons from occurring. Indeed, when a shared or common property good or asset is not adequately managed one way or another (for instance, through community-based rules and regulations, or through prices, or both), economic agents tend to over-exploit it and threaten its survival. Pooling property is not synonymous with adequate management.

An example of a tragedy of the commons is China's agricultural crisis of 1959–61,[19] briefly mentioned above. Agricultural collectivization in China began around 1952 and initially was a stunning success, with farm output skyrocketing between 1952 and 1958. Production co-operatives can be extremely profitable when certain organizational characteristics are present, such as those that allow for the coordination of effort. It appears that the organizational structure of the first Chinese agricultural co-operatives satisfied these requirements.

However, in 1959 grain production fell by 15 per cent, and in 1960 and 1961, they remained at more than 30 per cent below 1958 levels. Justin Yifu Lin, an economist at Peking University, attributes most of the fall in production to a modification in the organization of the co-operatives, which significantly reduced the scope for effective coordination and eliminated incentives, resulting in an estimated thirty million deaths.[20]

In 1957, there were 735,000 co-operatives with 119,000,000 member households, or an average of 160 households per co-operative. Following the success of these first ventures, the Chinese government decided in 1958–59 to extend the collectivization project to all of China. The co-operatives were amalgamated into 22,000 communes that covered almost the totality of the Chinese territory and comprised an average of 5,000 households.

Prior to 1958–59, co-operative members had the option of withdrawing their families' labour and/or physical capital such as tractors in order to possibly join another co-operative if they believed that productivity, or their share of the proceeds, were inadequate in the co-operative they belonged to.

Various organizational changes were instituted in 1958–59. Among them, the right of withdrawal was abolished to simplify the administration of the system. The compensation method was also changed from a redistribution of the benefits based on merit points to a system primarily based on members' needs, independent of productivity. Furthermore, the monitoring of each member's effort, which was possible when there were 160 households in the co-operative, as members could keep an eye on each other, became impossible with 5,000 households. Removing the member's right to leave the co-operative and join another voided the threat that made all members more productive in their best interest.

Although there is no consensus on the specific effect of each of these organizational changes, it is clear that their overall impact on effort and productivity levels could only be disastrous. Intentions were most likely sound, but replacing competence and rationality with incompetence and ideology ended up causing thirty million deaths. Ultimately, it's not intentions that matter, but results. China had to wait for the de-collectivization of the 1980s to recoup the productivity levels posted before 1959.

WBCSD's *Reform of Capitalism*

The World Business Council for Sustainable Development, an organization bringing together more than two hundred large companies from all regions of the world, is dedicated to developing governance focused on the pursuit of "true value" rather than exclusively on financial returns. Pursuing true value means promoting value creation that takes into account long-term environmental impacts and both individual and social well-being. True value is also based on prices that integrate all externalities. It is also a matter of (re)orienting capitalism to strive for true value based on the protection and enhancement of natural, social, and financial capital rather than striving solely for financial profit and economic efficiency.

The language used by WBCSD distinguishes between the extraction of value, as supposedly practised by contemporary capitalism, and the creation of true value by a renewed capitalism.[21] Renewed capitalism is oriented toward stakeholders rather than the single-minded maximization of shareholder value. It also has a long-term vision[22] focused on regeneration rather than degeneration, and accepts responsibility rather than sloughing it off.

WBCSD recognizes that capitalism – more specifically, the ensemble of profit-maximizing companies with competitive markets – has made an essential contribution to living standards, innovation, and value creation. But this capitalism, which has historically been the main engine of increases in prosperity and progress, has become the greatest threat to the continuation of this development. The future lies in the promise of harnessing the power of the convergence of for-profit businesses with the creation of value that internalizes environmental and social costs and benefits. These costs and benefits must be reflected in the relative prices of products, goods, and services, in the profitability of companies, in the costs of capital, and in market valuations.

Few economists would dispute WBCSD's proposed reforms, which are very similar to the goals championed by Business Roundtable, an organization gathering the CEOs of leading US companies.[23] The difficult trick is to identify the means to be used to achieve this better governance. The language of both WBCSD and Business Roundtable are suspiciously lofty. All too often, a virtuous discourse on the governance of public and private companies and organizations provides a foil for deflecting responsibility, aided by the impossibility of measuring performance in the way that was originally intended. As we all know, if you take on too much you may crash and burn. This is the case for WBCSD and Business Roundtable programs; they are "fine and good," but they chase the wrong target.

THE CENTRAL ROLE OF COMPETITION AND REGULATION

The model of competitive markets may derail if it is poorly framed and left to run itself. Competition is beneficial and generates efficiency, growth, and well-being when it corresponds to the principles elaborated by the authors of the different reform projects examined above. This is the competition that underlies competition-based social democracy, which will be in more detail discussed below.

This effective competition will be resisted by all who benefit from its deficiencies or abuses, whether that be fly-by-night crony capitalists, the ill-informed would-be defenders of the public good who long for command and control, or the consumers happy to take advantage of a bargain at the wrong price (free, for example) even if this bargain will ultimately harm their well-being and that of their fellow citizens.

The true source of wealth and well-being for all is not low prices but right prices – that is, prices that send the right signals of scarcity to consumers and producers. These prices are competitive, and so they are bounded or set by competition or by mechanisms that emulate competition. One could also argue that antitrust authorities should place more emphasis on, and have more resources at hand for, maintaining competition in the medium and long term by limiting the scope of legal justifications for mergers and acquisitions on the basis of potential or assumed economies of scale.

Two examples, chosen among many, will suffice to illustrate this policy. To concretely recognize the presumption of the benefits of developing and fostering competition, there should be a reasoned prohibition of requirements for professional licensing and certification by professional bodies when professionals are not in direct contact with the generally poorly informed public. Likewise, antitrust authorities should defend and apply relevant total-cost sharing rules, rather than avoidable-cost sharing rules, in cases relating to predatory pricing practices in order to focus on maintaining competition in the medium and long term rather than capturing short-term gains.

The reform of capitalism proposed here, the new competition-based capitalism, or NCC, is designed around this type of model of effective competition.

THE NCC MODEL IN TEN POINTS

For a capitalism-reform program to be credible to economists, it must stress the role of for-profit businesses, entrepreneurs, competitive markets, and externality "taxes" – all within a sound regulatory framework that is both incentivizing and constraining.

The right signals are thus sent to companies, allowing them to pursue their quest for profit first by producing goods and services that are useful to customers; second, by providing their employees with compensation that is competitively aligned with the value of their best alternative use; and third, by compensating their suppliers of intermediary goods and services as well as financial resources at a level that is competitively aligned with the value of the best alternative use of those goods, services, and capital.

The term "suppliers" is used in a broad sense here, to include providers of the environmental and social goods (ESG) and services as well as the financial capital (in the form of loans or equity) needed by businesses to produce the goods and services they offer customers. A sufficiently intensive competitive environment will drive economic profits (but not accounting profits) – defined as the expected difference between revenues and all costs, including the appropriately measured costs of borrowing and equity – to zero.

1. Encourage companies to express in their mission statements their reluctance to do business with "heavily" subsidized firms, whether suppliers or customers.

Effective competition, competition-emulating institutions, and competitive prices (including carbon levies and their equivalents in other areas) are important for providing incentives, generating innovation, inducing productivity gains, and raising social welfare. Hence, an ESG-like requirement for companies in the NCC is that they refrain as much as possible from actively transacting with companies that profit from direct or indirect government subsidies. This is because the prices of products, goods, and services bought and sold by heavily subsidized companies do not represent a credible signal of their value or scarcity. The total amount of these government subsidies is difficult to determine, but it is likely astronomical.

One of the ambitions of the NCC should be procurement and investment policies that penalize price manipulations. In this vein, it would be of some interest to develop a price-manipulation index by industry, sector, region, and even country. Price manipulations, whether originating from the private sector (cartels) or the governmental sector, are irreconcilable with NCC. The true economic ethic is first and foremost an ethic of efficiency based on competitive prices. The quintessential example of this pattern is the environment, the price of which can be set at an inefficiently low level (such as zero).

> 2. *Impose strict limitations on the power of business and labour unions to intervene directly in politics and the power of politicians to intervene directly in business in order to decouple business from politics and separate capitalism from the electoral process in democracy.*

This separation of business from politics, which we see in not only in Zingales's account but also in the arguments advanced by Raghuram Ramaswamy,[24] is an essential component of the NCC model. As mentioned in the introduction, robust competition will ensure the emergence of value-generating companies and the disappearance of value-destroying ones. Competitive markets for factors of production and for end products (goods and services) foster an accurate representation of value, ensuring that businesses pay their factors of production at the rate of their best alternative usage and bring goods and services of value to final consumers.

When all factors of production are compensated at their competitive value and all final products are sold at competitive prices, competing firms, including innovative new entrants, will be forced to either use the optimal mix of correctly compensated factors to produce an appropriate set of final products generating net social value and creating wealth, or go bankrupt. Companies have no business being involved in politics, especially if they are seeking anti-competitive advantages. The role of CEOs is to lead businesses, not society or government. And the role of social or political leaders does not include running businesses.

> 3. *Promote environmental protection (e.g., against greenhouse gas, or GHG, emissions) by creating markets, property rights, carbon levies (high enough to make a difference over time), and incentive regulations. The objectives must be to promote collective well-being by averting the tragedy of the commons, the tragedy of the anticommons, as well as the misguided blanket rejection of petrochemical resources and their derivatives.*

In January 2019, a group of economists stated that the best instrument for reducing carbon emissions to the desired level is a carbon levy (often misrepresented as a carbon tax).[25] Regulations that emulate carbon levies could also be a viable alternative. Carbon levies should increase every year to favour inter-temporal efficiency. The same principle applies to water pollution and other instances of market failure. A key consideration for these levies is their social acceptability, which could be increased by redistributing the generated revenues equally among citizens.

When calibrating these environmental levies for the use (pollution) of common resources such as air and water, there are two pitfalls to avoid. The tragedies of the commons and anticommons are directly related to inadequate coordination, pricing, and/or regulation. User fees and/or regulations regarding rights and responsibilities that emulate a competitive equilibrium, including community-based and possibly informal agreements or codes of conduct, are the preferred, if not the only, processes for avoiding the two tragedies.

It should also be noted that petrochemicals and their derivatives are responsible for significant improvements to overall welfare, which we would be hard-pressed to go without. Promoting the beneficial uses of petrochemical resources while curbing their emissions may require, in addition to an appropriate carbon levy, regulations that support beneficial uses within an overall reduction.[26] But in general, the best policy is to fix a proper price or levy on carbon emissions and let the industry develop under this proper price.

To this end, it's worth considering the words of Michael Smith:

> Look around you: chances are that every object within your field of vision contains refined petroleum. The varnish on your desk, the paint on your walls, the finish on your floors. Unless the chair you are sitting on is made of untreated wood, then your butt is resting on synthetic materials derived from petrochemicals. Plastic is petroleum based: the components of your phone and computer, your printer and audio speakers. Take a sip of coffee and think about it. The glaze on our mugs comes from oil. Oil was once thought to have mystical properties.[27]

Smith mentions that oil has also been a major factor in the development of medicine: in fact, gel caps, balms, salves, and gelatin pills contain petroleum. He mentions that nearly 99 per cent of pharmaceutical feedstocks and reagents are derived from petrochemicals. This suggests to him that in a sense "medicine is oil." He concludes by saying that "we must begin to treat petroleum with the respect it deserves. We must value it, like our very lives, as a precious, almost magical, but certainly finite resource. Then we can begin to do the meaningful work that nurtures our planet, nurtures our friendships, and creates lives of joy."[28]

This requires proper pricing of the resource to induce people to use it with care and respect, not only for environmental protection reasons, but also for reasons of civilizational development, so that our children and grandchildren can keep on using it beneficially for centuries to come.

> *4. Implement extended liability rules for industrial accidents and environmental disasters. The financial and technological partners of the responsible company, as well as their management consultants, must be made jointly and severally liable[29] in order to protect active and retired workers, ensure the rapid cleanup of contaminated sites, and provide strong incentives for companies to better manage these risks.*

Rules that limit liability and govern bankruptcy impede the proper compensation of damages. A proper alignment of incentives between borrowers and lenders for environmental protection requires lenders (with deep pockets) to be jointly and severally liable for damages. In this way, creditors will price the risk they face, and debtors will have a strong incentive to improve their treatment of hazardous waste. In addition, creditors will find it in their best interest to monitor their clients' hazardous waste treatment systems and policies and insist on compliance as a condition for financial support. The same arguments apply in the case of technological suppliers and, ultimately, management consultants. Ensuring that (all) costs and benefits of business activities, including the risk of bankruptcy, are properly accounted for is a central tenet of the NCC.

Incentive-compensation schemes could be developed and implemented as a complementary tool to motivate companies, especially senior management and board members, to manage risks properly. The full discussion of such a concept exceeds the scope of this book, however.[30]

> *5. Abolish corporate income (profit) taxes to help companies focus on their core missions of wealth creation, the promotion of R&D investments, and productivity gains, which are important drivers of growth and social welfare.*

If generalized, the elimination of corporate income taxes would render obsolete inter-country tax competition aimed at attracting businesses. Acrimonious arguments about how tax competition between countries allows companies to avoid paying their fair share of taxes through tax-evasion schemes would become moot. This would help entrepreneurial resources focus more sharply on the company's mission rather than on finding sophisticated tax loopholes.

To illustrate with a well-known example, it is often said that the so-called Big Tech GAFAM+ companies (Alphabet-Google, Amazon, Facebook, Apple, Microsoft, Netflix, etc.) avoid paying their fair share of taxes. To some extent, this is a question of perspective. Based on their estimated total payroll, income and consumption taxes paid by their employees amounted to some US$65.3 billion in 2021–22.

These income and consumption taxes are moreover distributed among countries where those employees reside. If we were to include the taxes paid by shareholders on dividends, capital gains, and any other additional activities generated, we might discover that the net impact on government revenues of abolishing corporate income tax would be barely perceptible.[31] This finding applies to all businesses.

Moreover, whether corporations pay their fair share of taxes is in part a matter of perspective. Suppose that a corporation tells its employees that it will pay directly or will reimburse their income and consumption taxes. Hence, their salary or total compensation paid is net of those taxes. Then the corporation pays the governments involved the taxes due, which would appear in its accounting books for the year. That's how the six Big Tech corporations shown in table 3.1 could claim to have paid a tax bill on the order of US$65.3 billion for 2021–22.

Tax systems have reached an unsettling level of complexity, spawning a plethora of exemptions and loopholes and setting the stage for crony capitalism. This has become a major obstacle to the proper allocation of resources and investments, including management efforts, as well as R&D and innovation efforts.

6. Foster the expansion of inter-regional and international free trade while acknowledging differentiated levels of economic development.

Political leaders are frequently heard trumpeting the principles and benefits of international trade and lamenting the harm caused by tariffs, quotas, and other barriers to trade. These generate unnecessary

Table 3.1
Taxes generated by Big Tech

Reported to the SEC (2022)				*Estimated taxes paid by employees*		
Company	Median salary A	Number of employees B	Estimated total payroll C=A*B	Income taxes D=%*C	Other taxes @20% on 90% of income net of taxes E	Total taxes F=D+E
Alphabet-Google	$295,884	156,500	$46.3B	@30%, $13.9B	$5.8B	$19.7B
Amazon	$32,855	1,608,000	$52.8B	@10%, $5.3B	$8.6B	$13.8B
Meta (Facebook)	$292,785	71,970	$21.1B	@30%, $6.3B	$2.7B	$9.0B
Apple	$68,254	164,000	$11.2B	@20%, $2.2B	$1.6B	$3.9B
Microsoft	$190,302	221,000	$42.1B	@30%, $12.6B	$5.3B	$17.9B
Netflix	$201,743	11,300	$2.3B	@30%, $683.9M	$287.2M	$971.2M
					GRAND TOTAL	$65.3B

Source: US Securities and Exchange Commission. Calculations of the author.

and unjustified costs to the detriment of the country's workers, citizens, and national security. However, these leaders often follow up with assurances that they are committed to protecting the interests of workers in industries likely to be affected by a loosening of trade restrictions. In so doing, they are prone to echo nearly word for word the statements made by the opponents of free trade.

From another perspective, some might want to use free trade and its expected benefits as leverage to persuade or incentivize potential trading partners to change their economic, social, or environmental policies. Thus, they might oppose free trade with a potential partner because of the latter's policies, or lack of policies, on matters such as working conditions, worker safety, child labour, pollution, deforestation, property laws, intellectual property regulation, antitrust legislation, etc. This use of free trade agreements, while not wholly unreasonable and unjustified, too often conceals the goal of protecting vested interests, be they economic, social, cultural, or environmental.

Too often, the specific characteristics of certain trade partners are ignored under the cover of lofty posturing. However, economic development takes time, and we cannot reasonably expect that a poorer and less developed partner will immediately adopt the policies and lifestyle adjustments that richer partners have worked out and implemented over a period of fifty years or more. An operational free trade agreement may well be the best way to nudge a poorer country toward benefiting from its comparative advantages while allowing the developed country to benefit from its own comparative advantages.

We are also likely to hear political and economic leaders call for preferential treatment for products "made locally" over those "made abroad." They often follow with generous actions toward certain chosen businesses and industries that they deem to be national treasures or essential.[32] This is basically a populist crony capitalism approach. Rather than focusing on the true determinants of economic and social well-being and contributing to a better understanding of how the economy works, they prefer to play the role of big spender – dispensing other people's money – and banking on the ignorance of a non-negligible subgroup of the population and its elites. This approach is incompatible with the NCC model.

The expansion of free trade is a pillar of this model because it increases the intensity of competition, the value of innovation, and the well-being of all stakeholders.

> 7. Strengthen legal constraints (competition law) on anti-competitive practices (refusal to deal, predatory pricing, price fixing, tie-in sales, abuse of market power, etc.) so as to foster the development and protection of competition, shield competitors and new entrants from potential anti-competitive practices by incumbent businesses, and allow creative destruction to play its role.

Philippe Aghion and his collaborators make a convincing case that creative destruction is a fundamental factor of innovation, growth, and social well-being. In this respect, quarterly data from the US Bureau of Labor Statistics reveal to what extent net job creation is the result of a complicated interaction of gross job creation and destruction.[33]

We observed in table 1.1 (which uses US data) that between 1992 and 2022, a net job created during the 98 positive job growth quarters during that period was the result of 11.6 jobs created and 10.6 jobs lost in private-sector establishments, while a net job lost during the 21 negative job growth quarters during the same period was the result 5.3 jobs created and 6.3 jobs lost. This creative destruction can be largely undermined by two policies: first, the use of avoidable cost criteria by antitrust authorities to determine whether a firm has engaged in abusive or illegal predatory pricing, and second, public direct and indirect subsidies to businesses to either improve their competitiveness or shield them from competitors. Both policies reduce the intensity of competition by preventing competitors from challenging incumbent firms.

Regarding the first undermining policy, the NCC approach would replace the avoidable cost criteria,[34] whose measure is a perennial source of conflicts,[35] with a formula for sharing the total cost among products. Each product of a company, along with each good or service or node in a network (air travel, for example), would be assigned a share of the total cost, yielding a total of 100 per cent when they are summed. If a firm prices a product below its assigned cost, antitrust authorities could accuse it of predatory pricing. This change would, admittedly, reduce the efficiency of resource allocation in the short term in favour of a more robust competition in the long run.[36]

With regard to the second policy, the NCC approach would be to auction off individual government assistance programs. The objective is to transfer the responsibility for providing the subsidy, loan, loan guarantee, or equity injection to a private local or international financial consortium. In exchange for a premium paid by the government to the winning consortium, the latter would assume responsibility for the disbursements while benefiting from repayments as stipulated by the terms of the government assistance contract.[37] The premium paid is the best estimate of the fiscal cost of the program for citizens.

The main reason for auctioning off these government assistance programs is to reduce the ubiquitous risk of crony capitalism or collusion. Regardless of how lofty the intentions voiced by the government and the various stakeholders, this risk of crony capitalism will eventually materialize at the expense of not only the intensity of competition itself, but also of citizens, taxpayers, and businesses. This is transparency at the service of competition.

8. When analyzing proposed mergers and acquisitions, opt for a weight greater than 1 for the impact of reduced competition and efficiency gains; for example, a ratio of 2:1 or even 3:1.

In our contribution to the fiftieth-anniversary edition of the *Canadian Journal of Economics*, my colleagues Thomas Ross, Ralph Winter, and I claimed the following:

> Provisions to protect Canadians from anticompetitive mergers have been part of Canadian competition law since the passage of the first Combines Investigation Act in 1910. Canadian merger law enforcement, however, was quiet until the passage of the Competition Act in 1986 ... Perhaps the most notable of all merger cases under the new law was the Superior Propane (2003) case. In defending this merger, the efficiency exemption was invoked by the merging parties and the Tribunal had to address directly the welfare standard to be applied. Despite new arguments from the Commissioner that the appropriate standard is not the total welfare standard, the Tribunal initially took the view that the total welfare standard was exactly the right basis on which to trade off harms to competition and efficiencies.[38]

Balancing the potential harm caused to consumers or to competition itself by a merger or acquisition against potential efficiency gains from economies of scale, scope, network, and the like is certainly a very difficult task. Among the hardest challenges to be dealt with is the fact that the analysis is of "potential," which is to say not yet realized, impacts. Another challenge is determining what criteria to use for "balancing" the impacts, requiring the weighting of impact measures of varying quality.

In taking an unequivocal position in support of competition in the medium and long term, the NCC approach prescribes relative weights of 2:1 or even 3:1 for the reduction of competition versus efficiency gains, by whatever means the impacts are measured.

9. Impose regulatory provisions to ensure access to networks, digital platforms, essential licences, and patents at prices and terms that are fair, reasonable, and non-discriminatory (FRAND) on the basis of a complete sharing of costs, including the value of real options exercised.

There are two broad approaches to funding network infrastructure. The first derives from sharing network costs, in particular investment costs, between the main partners and users of the network. In its purest and most rigorous form, this approach is primarily based on the theory of co-operative games.[39] The second involves charging regulated access fees whereby the network is assumed to have been developed by a specific company. Various potential network users, including those who are competitors, may wish to use the network, or at least some of its critical, or essential, parts, rather than develop an alternative network.

With the advent of electronic networks and platforms for the transmission of information, communications, commerce, etc., the danger of new forms of market power is very real. For managing and mitigating these risks, the regulation of access to networks and platforms under reasonable competitive prices and conditions plays a central role. It is important to remember that "it is more the end product that counts: connectivity, flexibility, safety, dependability, accessibility, capacity (high speed and broadband) and user-friendliness. In that sense, the demand expressed by consumers for different telecommunications devices (wireline, wireless, cellular mobile, satellite-based mobile, Internet Protocol … telephony, and so on) is a derived demand rather than a direct demand."[40]

Electronic communications, commerce, and information networks and platforms are like highways travelled by communication, commercial, and informational goods and services. Rather than free, the use of these highways is, or can be, subject to certain tolls. In some cases, duplicating highways is not an option. Thus, a certain degree of regulation must govern open access to these highways.

The characterization of these access rules, prices, and terms is a difficult and information-intense task. One potential approach that emulates competition is particularly promising: the global price cap suggested by Jean-Jacques Laffont and Jean Tirole.[41] The cap is defined by both the prices of final products and services and access prices. The two main benefits of this formula are, first, that it derives from sound economic theory, and second, that it has more modest information requirements than other approaches. Once the global price index ceiling is determined, firms can set their prices, including access fees, to be compatible with the pressures of competition and consistent with the global price index ceiling.[42]

Whatever the case may be, the new regulatory framework should be based on the principles of promoting competition and global economic efficiency, even if in some cases efficiency is reduced in the short run (see policy 7 above). The first principle demands appropriate incentives to ensure dynamically competitive prices and access conditions and efficient investment programs in network maintenance and development. The second one requires the design of nonpredatory pricing rules through the full sharing of total costs, including the value of real options exercised in network development.

> *10. Reiterate that capitalism is synonymous with radicalism and disruption (recall the proposals from* The Economist *discussed above) and not with managed or defanged competition. To this end, "abusive" professional certification (in particular for businesses and individuals who do not interact directly with the poorly informed public) and "abusive" non-compete clauses, as well as business and trade union lobbying, designed to limit and curtail competition, must be fought and eliminated.*

In his 2022 presidential address to the American Economic Association, Nobel economics laureate David Card describes a lawsuit that

> concerned "no poaching" and "no solicitation" agreements affecting software and animation engineers in Silicon Valley ... To avoid bidding wars over employees, Lucasfilm and Pixar agreed (1) not to "cold call" each other's employees; (2) to notify the other company should they receive an application for employment; and (3) that all offers to employees at the other company would be "final," with no further bidding. Ultimately this agree-

ment was extended to other high-tech firms (e.g., Google, Microsoft, and Oracle) and lasted over 20 years, until 2008. The size of the settlement to affected engineers ($585 million in two suits), and other wage adjustments made after the agreement was made public (e.g., a 10% across-the-board increase offered by Google to all its employees in November 2010) suggest that the suppression of between-firm competition was successful – a validation of the idea that at least some labor markets are vulnerable to wage fixing ... While one might be tempted to think that "no hire" and "no poaching" agreements affect only highly skilled workers, Ashenfelter and Krueger found that no poaching clauses were widespread in U.S. franchise agreements ... These agreements typically prohibit a franchisee from hiring another franchisee's employees for some pre-specified period of time after an employee's departure ... Another strand of recent research has focused on the prevalence of non-compete agreements, which prohibit employees from moving to jobs at "competitor" firms for a specified period ... Again, a surprising fact is the prevalence of these agreements even for relatively low-wage workers ... The popularity of no-poaching and non-compete agreements seems to confirm [that] ... limits on poaching or firm-to-firm mobility will reduce quits and increase monopsonistic power.[43]

Clearly, abusive non-compete or no-poaching clauses have been around longer than is generally recognized.

Rather than proceeding with a long list of measures to dismiss as being inimical to healthy competition in labour markets, let us examine the particular and informative case of the construction industry. Regulations in Quebec limit the mobility of construction workers across administrative regions and organize in silos the different trades and competencies. The regulations were born in a specific historical situation, but today these are an anachronism from an earlier time. The regulations persist because they shield certain companies, trade unions, and regulatory bodies from competition: a form of crony competition management, to the detriment of citizens.

While this regulation may have had its benefits at the time of the major conflicts between trade unions, which the industry experienced, today it serves to undermine the resilience and growth of the economy. Regional development, including development of construction in the regions, would be better served by an opening to competition and mobility, which should be promoted rather than restricted. An opening like this would likely lead to a better allocation of resources, labour, capital, a better matching of supply and demand in the construction labour market, faster penetration of best practices, better development of skills, higher productivity gains, and more effective cost control, all of which translate into gains in individual and collective well-being. The NCC leaves no room for this type of counterproductive regulation.

Regarding the different forms of skill certification and professional corporatism, they may still be useful as a credible "proof" of competence and experience, even when the customer does not belong to the so-called uninformed or poorly informed public. If this is the case, then market-based, or "branded," certification systems should be the method of choice for accomplishing it. Some businesses may decide to use certified workers (of a certain "brand") while others may develop their own internal process for verifying competencies. In the final analysis, the important thing is to avoid reducing or constraining competition through arbitrary certification measures.[44]

4

The "Fab Four" Factors of Growth

Trade and specialization, encouraged by mechanisms of increasingly efficient coordination and incentives, are foundational factors in human history and civilization.[1]

The main purpose of the CSD model is to improve the well-being of all citizens by fostering social cohesion, promoting growth, and safeguarding economic freedom – including the right to economic contestation (challenging the current providers of PSGS). This chapter discusses the four main growth factors that contribute to social and economic development. The model is associated with an assortment of policies designed to promote general economic expansion and growth that need to be implemented in many sectors: health care, transportation, education, energy, the environment, etc. These will be presented and elaborated below.

There is a broad consensus among economists that the most critical factors explaining differences in the performance of countries and regions in terms of economic growth, social well-being, and improved living standards are the following: the per capita quantity and quality of human capital, the ability to invent and innovate, the quality and strength of performance incentives, and the quality of private and public resource-allocation mechanisms, the latter two defining the general concept of good governance of organizations and institutions.

The centrality of these "fab four" factors to growth, and, by extension, to social well-being and welfare, permeates all sectors of society, all networks of stakeholders, all mechanisms of conflict resolution, and all fields of human activity – hence the importance of presenting them here. Equally important is the fact that these four factors are strongly complementary. More of any given one increases the incremental value of the others, and more of the others increases the incremental value of that one.

Consequently, while it is useful to present and explain these four factors individually, their impacts on growth and hence social well-being and welfare are quite interdependent and intertwined. For instance, a core tenet of the CSD model is that intelligence and creativity are uniformly distributed across time periods, societies, and regions or countries. At any point in time, those societies' relative performance in terms of innovation and commercialization might vary considerably, not because of differences in endowments in creative abilities, but rather because of differences in the portfolios of incentive frameworks and resource-allocation and coordination mechanisms (governance) faced by their members, individual or organizational.

Growth, along with productivity and welfare gains, primarily depend on the quality of governance rules in organizations and institutions, including the efficiency of incentivization and resource-allocation mechanisms. Indeed, skills, human capital, inventions, innovations, and natural resources all significantly contribute to growth and well-being, but good governance in private business and government affairs is probably the most important factor. This is true because good governance shapes the development and adaptation of human capital, the choice of investments, and, by extension, the portfolio of advanced technologies. Good governance also determines the way natural resources are exploited for the good of all. Under these conditions, the factor "good governance" is given a position of preeminence among the various policies characterizing competition-based social democracy.

THE FIRST GROWTH FACTOR: HUMAN CAPITAL

Education, or more generally the training of workers, is defined as the individual and social portfolio of distributed knowledge and high-level competencies together with cognitive capability, dexterity, and (basic, soft, and specialized) skills. It is a major determinant of growth.

Countries and regions must efficiently develop their stock of human capital in order to fully benefit from accelerated growth opportunities offered by the globalization of markets, new information and communications technologies, and the internationalization of cultures. The efficient development of human capital allows a country to ensure that all individuals can hone their skills regardless of their initial endowment, such as their early access to human capital development tools and programs. To achieve this objective, the supply of training programs must be diversified to reflect a context of lifelong periods of education/training and work.

Levels of competitiveness and productivity, as well as innovation and commercialization of inventions and, by extension, improvements to living standards in a society, depend on the following building blocks: (1) the ability of its broadly defined education sector to respond to industrial and social needs in terms of required skills and competencies of different types in both quantity and quality; (2) the level and efficiency of its R&D investments and the capacity to transform them into successful innovations and bring them to market, or, in other words, to transform new ideas into useful processes, products, and services; and (3) the flexibility with which it can adapt to changes in its social, economic, and business environment, in addition to the determination it shows in confronting the significant challenges posed by exogenous and endogenous changes.

Reaping the full benefits of these investments in human capital formation is not an easy matter. In order to do so, a country or region must successfully address the "skills challenge" – the benefits secured will be greater, most likely by a significant margin, when the acquired skills are properly integrated with the needs expressed by society on labour markets for the near and distant future. Hence the importance of reviewing national and sectorial levels of investment in human capital training and the allocation of those efforts across the different skills and competencies being developed in quantity as well as quality.

According to the Organisation for Economic Co-operation and Development (OECD), human capital is the knowledge, skills, competencies, and other attributes relevant to economic activity embodied in individuals. In short, human capital is associated with the economic behaviour of individuals, which can be defined as the sum of the knowledge and aptitudes that allow individuals to increase their productivity and their incomes, thus contributing to an increase in the productivity and wealth of the firms and organizations in which they operate. Human capital and economic growth reinforce each other, though the former often precedes the latter. A 2004 study suggests that differences in average skill levels among OECD countries explains 55 per cent of differences in economic growth since 1960.[2]

The same study claims that "the long run effects of human capital investment in literacy are much more important – around three times – than investment in physical capital."[3]

Human capital underlies growth, but it can also support the creation and maintenance of social capital. Education and training can encourage practices, aptitudes, and values conducive to co-operation and social participation.

THE SECOND GROWTH FACTOR: INVENTIONS AND INNOVATIONS

The second main factor is the promotion of inventions and innovations that contribute to improvements in the manner by which social, public, or private goods and services are produced and delivered. As mentioned in the introduction, economists consider the ability and desire to identify, adopt, and implement inventions and innovations, whether technological, social, or organizational, to be an important source of economic growth. This ability is rooted in individual attitudes toward change as well as in the stances taken by political institutions with regard to flexibility.

Inventions are scientific discoveries and, more generally, new knowledge resulting from fundamental research, appearing quite often as ideas without concrete applications. Innovations sometimes follow inventions. They represent successful application and/or commercialization of inventions.

Inventions and innovations contribute to increased productivity. These benefits can assume various forms concurrently: a fall in prices and a corresponding increase in the purchasing power of households, reduced hours of work, an increase in profits and a corresponding increase in real incomes and/or investments to yield still more increases in productivity, or an increase in wages insofar as pressures develop on labour markets, among other benefits.

Designing a truly efficient invention and innovation policy framework requires strong support for both elements, but particular attention is needed for innovation because while inventions are common, innovations are less so. An effective policy begins with redefining the roles played by various stakeholders in the commercialization of inventions/innovations, including individuals, universities, grant-giving bodies, and the government.

Given the complementary and highly modular relationship between the four main growth factors, it will appear as no surprise that the creation and successful implementation of inventions and innovations (whether technological, social, or organizational) is strongly correlated with the level of human capital, the quality of incentives directly geared toward inventions and innovations, and the appropriate governance of intellectual property laws and provisions. Not everyone needs to, or can, be involved in researching, discovering, or implementing sophisticated technologies or discoveries, but those who are active in invention- and innovation-generating sectors, or in sectors relying on the growth and adoption of such inventions/innovations, must be well trained. Thus, by supporting the accumulation of human capital, the government of a social democratic society supports inventions and innovations as well as growth.

However, to promote this dynamic, the policies of social democracies must encourage the emergence of teams composed of researchers and entrepreneurs, all while ensuring the presence of well-enforced patents and copyrights to provide safeguards against the plundering of discoveries. According to Hernando De Soto,[4] underdevelopment is in large part attributable to the absence of legal and social safeguards for the value of physical and intellectual capital.

THE THIRD GROWTH FACTOR: INCENTIVES (INFORMATION, CONGRUENCE, COMPATIBILITY)

Whenever organizations and individuals make decisions, they have an impact on the use of social resources, and therefore on the value of those resources. If decisions are made efficiently, they create wealth directly or indirectly, either by increasing the level of resources available or by increasing their value. It is therefore important to understand what motivates organizations and individuals to make the decisions they make regarding the allocation of the resources over which they exert some form of control.

Two broad sets of factors can be brought forward to explain the decision-making process of economic and social agents: "preferences" and "incentives." Preferences are deeply ingrained factors emerging from the lifelong process of socialization through which every human being acquires social values and learns proper behaviour from parents, families, teachers, and peers. It is very difficult to change preferences in the short and medium term. As a result, factors and policies influencing growth are better understood as dealing with the second explanatory factor for the decision-making process of economic and social agents: incentives. Incentives are flexible and powerful tools for shaping the contribution of organizations and individuals to social wealth and well-being. In that sense, growth, productivity, and welfare gains depend directly on the quality and intensity of incentives that organizations and individuals face.

Sufficiently strong incentive mechanisms require that individuals' compensation and firms' profitability reflect their performance. Too many compensation schemes in social democratic societies, whether at the level of individuals, groups, businesses, or organizations, are either too weak or misaligned with social objectives. Consequently, these societies can suffer from free riding, the destruction of wealth, and situations that hobble economic growth. It would therefore be useful to identify the relative importance of low- versus high-intensity incentivization mechanisms for determining compensation in different sectors of a given social democratic society and relate them to the relative innovative capacity or commercialization performance of the different sectors.

Incentive pay is for higher-skilled workers, which is to say workers whose productivity characteristics are difficult to evaluate initially. For example, in an academic (university) setting, it is difficult to know who is going to be successful in research and teaching. Another example is when it is difficult to observe work effort – that is, when the job is less standardized, and hence more individual initiative is desirable and welcomed. And lastly, productivity can be difficult to evaluate in situations where individual or team performance is crucial for the success of the organization in attaining goals or fulfilling its mission.

As we will see, while there are major issues related to observation and information, that is no reason to abandon incentive pay. Incentive pay should be understood as a compensation mechanism that creates an environment in which the individual's pursuit of personal interests is aligned with the objectives of the organization for which they work.

In this context, the dangers of not using incentive pay are numerous. In any organization, the compensation formula is a fundamental tool used by management to direct the efforts of the different divisions and individuals toward their most productive uses (measured in terms of the overall objectives and mission of the organization). Failure to appreciate the importance of this tool can jeopardize an organization's ability to fulfil its mission. Incentive pay is the most efficient way to make key members of the organization responsible for their own contribution to the success or failure of this mission. Moreover, it forces the organization to explicitly articulate its mission and objectives.

THE FOURTH GROWTH FACTOR: RESOURCE-ALLOCATION AND COORDINATION MECHANISMS

As mentioned above, competencies and human capital, state-of-the-art technologies, and natural resources are significant determinants of growth and well-being, but good governance in private business and government affairs is probably the most important factor. It is important to stress again that, in the CSD model, good rules of governance are seen as having a profound impact on the development, evolution, and adaptation of competencies and human capital, the choice of investments in social, technological, and organizational inventions and innovations, and, by extension, the portfolio of advanced technologies, as well as the way natural resource endowments are developed for the benefit of all. Good governance covers both appropriate performance-related incentive mechanisms discussed above, and the efficient resource-allocation and coordination mechanisms explained below.

The analysis of governance made its appearance in 1937 in the article "The Nature of the Firm" by Ronald Coase, which examines explanatory factors for the existence of the markets-prices duo. The duo was said to guide the decisions made by buyers and sellers, and by firms within which the role played by markets and prices is secondary, or even absent, aside from the entrepreneur's leadership.[5] Prices/markets and entrepreneurs are part substitutes and part complements in the organization of social activities, and, consequently, in the allocation of scarce resources.

Initially applied to the boundaries of management in private corporations, governance has grown as a domain in itself, such that today it includes the governmental and political spheres. Although this concept is encumbered by a myriad of definitions and covers many sub-topics, it can be understood in a relatively comprehensive way. Good governance, understood in its form specifically tailored to a CSD approach to the production, distribution, and delivery of PSGS, corresponds to a radically different form of government action and intervention.

In this concept of governance, different competitive-sector organizations, both currently active ones and those that could potentially emerge, and individual citizens themselves, participate in an incentive-compatible framework for the formulation and implementation of policies designed to meet the single most important objective of social well-being. To elicit this explicit and organized participation requires an extensive use of competitive mechanisms: modularity, transparency, and individual and institutional accountability. Hence, CSD "good governance" calls for a major reform of the government: its place, its role, and its scope, as well as its operations.

CSD good governance must be designed to underlie, create, and support efficient resource-allocation and coordination mechanisms not only for the production, distribution, and delivery of PSGS, but also for the economy as a whole. Efficient resource-allocation mechanisms require that proper signals be sent to individuals and firms regarding the relative scarcity of goods and services. In most real-world situations, mechanisms with the greatest efficiency are those compatible with the competitive market/open auction mechanisms.

To the extent that, in social democratic societies, too many prices are at levels that differ from their competitive values, the ability of the economy to efficiently generate value and wealth for citizens is significantly compromised. These manipulated prices cause distortions in the overall level of innovative effort and in its allocation across businesses and activities. When prices are set too low, there is either an overproduction (if demand must be satisfied, social welfare is reduced because the last units of the good or service produced are worth less to consumers than the cost incurred to produce them) or an underproduction (if the freedom of supply is enforced, social welfare is reduced because some units are not produced whose value for the consumers would be larger than the cost to be incurred to produce them). The same applies, *mutatis mutandis*, if prices are set too high above competitive levels. Whenever such price controls are used, some resource misallocation occurs. Social cost will vary as a function of the extent of the control or with the distance between the administered price and the competitive equilibrium price.

In general, these price controls are used to directly "benefit" consumers or producers, to "induce" consumers to consume more of some product or service than they would otherwise choose to consume, or to "protect" consumers or customers against the exercise of market power by suppliers. Regardless of the rationale or intent of these price controls, there is always a better way to achieve the desired objective without unduly distorting the allocation of resources.

In some situations, such as for network architecture, system design, public goods, or surplus sharing between a monopsonistic buyer and a monopolistic seller, it is necessary to consider more advanced coordination mechanisms. Among those, one finds patent and copyright pools,[6] standard essential patents licensing regulations (with FRAND pricing),[7] and Lindahl pricing.[8] Those alternative mechanisms follow from the efficiency principles of competitive price equilibrium.

A society's prosperity and growth, as well as its competitiveness and capacity to adapt to change, mainly depend on its ability to innovate and accumulate human capital. However, the quality of institutions and organizations within said society has a considerable influence on those growth factors. Thus, the basic growth policies proposed as part of the CSD model fall under the umbrella of good governance – that is, appropriate incentive schemes and frameworks and the right resource-allocation and coordination mechanisms.

5

Ethics, Equity, and Socially Responsible Behaviour

Environmentalist Joan Roughgarden writes, "Economists are not about to cede the moral high ground to ecologists just because humanity is contained in a giant ecosystem. In principle, economics deals with 'ethical efficiency' – trying to achieve the most good for the most people given a 'budget constraint' of either time or money. Of course, matters may not work out so ideally, but it's important to realize that the ethical starting points for both ecologists and economists are equally noble."[1]

Two broad topics illustrate the complexity of the relationship between competition, ethics, and equity: the ESG movement (which seeks corporate social responsibility) and the fair value of the environment, especially water.

THE ESG COMPACT AND CORPORATE SOCIAL RESPONSIBILITY

According to the latest report from the Forum for Sustainable and Responsible Investment, ESG funds totalled some $12.0 trillion in assets at the beginning of 2018 and $17.1 trillion at the start of 2020, a 42 per cent increase, representing 33 per cent of total assets under private management.[2] Jon Hale, of the American financial services firm Morningstar, estimates that assets invested in ESG funds in the United States increased by 400 per cent in 2019.[3] Leading asset managers have made significant commitments to ESG principles. Black-Rock, the world's largest asset manager, has announced that ESG criteria will be its "new standard," and it has urged corporate CEOs to recognize that "climate change has become a defining factor" in the long-term prospects of their companies. State Street Global Advisors, the world's third-largest asset manager, contacted boards of directors to inform them that the ESG approach is no longer just an option for a long-term strategy, announcing that the firm would use its proxy voting power to ensure that companies identify and incorporate ESG principles or criteria into their long-term strategies. Goldman Sachs said it intends to put $750 billion into ESG investments over the current decade. More and more investors are realizing that global warming is an impending crisis accompanied by significant societal and financial risks, and that a long-term focus on creating value for all stakeholders will increase the value created for shareholders and society in the long term. The situation is similar in Europe.[4] Clearly, the socially responsible investment movement has given rise to a large and growing industry.

Business Roundtable's 2019 about-face is symptomatic of the changes that are occurring. Since 1978, Business Roundtable has periodically published principles of corporate governance, and these have always reaffirmed the primacy of shareholders. In August 2019 it changed course.[5] It now affirms that the economy must enable everyone to thrive through work and creativity and to lead a life of meaning and dignity, and that the free market system remains the best way to achieve this – that is, to create good jobs in a strong and sustainable economy, to foster innovation, and to create a healthy environment and economic opportunities for all. These CEOs now proclaim that they share a fundamental commitment to all stakeholders in their respective companies.

Some Caveats

In October 2020, the US Department of Labor published a new regulation that could limit the use of ESG criteria in the choice of investments in pension plans. According to the US secretary of labor,

> Protecting retirement savings is a core mission of the U.S. Department of Labor and a chief public policy goal for our nation ... This rule will ensure that retirement plan fiduciaries are focused on the financial interests of plan participants and beneficiaries, rather than on other, non-pecuniary goals or policy objectives ... Our goal is to ensure that retirement security remains the top priority of those who manage the retirement assets that millions of

Americans have worked so hard to earn. Plan fiduciaries should never sacrifice participants' interests in their benefits to promote other non-financial goals.[6]

The Department stated that so-called ESG investment analysis raises important and far-reaching concerns in terms of both rigour and the demonstrated prudence and reliability of the exercise. The regulation stipulates that pension plan managers are to opt for investment strategies that mostly, even exclusively, focus on financial performance.

In a recent *Wall Street Journal* editorial, the CEO of Roviant Sciences, Vivek Ramaswamy, asserted that expecting businesses to take a stand and advance environmental and social programs (the ESG approach) gives them entirely too much power. It was his opinion that this type of authority should be reserved for the government:

> My main problem with stakeholder capitalism is that it strengthens the link between democracy and capitalism at a time when we should instead disentangle one from the other ... Speaking as a CEO and a citizen, I don't want American capitalists to play a larger role in defining and implementing the country's political and social values. I think the answers to these questions should be determined by the citizen – publicly through debate and privately at the ballot box ... I believe the reason many corporate executives are speaking up in favor of stakeholder capitalism is that they think they will gain popularity at a time when it is unpopular to be perceived as a pure capitalist. The crux of the populist concern about capitalism is not that companies serve only their shareholders, but rather that capitalism has begun to infect our democracy through the influence of dollars in buying political outcomes. The answer is not to force capitalism into an arranged marriage with democracy. What we really need is a clean divorce.[7]

ESG and the "Fab Four"

Recall the "fab four" factors of quality growth discussed above (chapter 4), which are, by extension, the fab four of an ESG policy. These four growth factors are highly complementary: an increase in one factor raises the incremental value of the others. This allows us to group societies into two large sets: those in which all these factors are well-developed and pervasive, and those in which they are lacking in quantity and quality. Differences in the relative performance of societies are less attributable to variations in their endowments in human and material resources and in creative capacities than to variations in the incentive structures and mechanisms for allocating resources and coordinating the decisions under which the members – whether individuals or organizations – of the society operate.[8]

Efficient resource allocation requires that good signals be sent to individuals and businesses about the relative scarcity of goods and services. Usually, the most effective mechanisms are those consistent with competitive markets. To the extent that too many prices are administered, manipulated, and controlled at levels that deviate from their competitive values, the ability of the economy to efficiently generate value and wealth for citizens is significantly compromised.

These manipulated prices cause distortions and losses due to over- or under-production of goods and services. In general, these price manipulations are intended to support consumers or producers or to give consumers an incentive to consume more of certain goods and services. Regardless of the rationale or intent of these price controls, there is always a better way to achieve the desired objective without unduly distorting the allocation of resources.

Consequently, the emergence of competitive prices and markets, including the creation of markets and improvements to their functioning, should be promoted in all sectors of the economy, including PSGS sectors.

In the case of energy, for example, the artificial downward (or upward) manipulation of prices always leads to misguided resource-use policies that ultimately benefit only the users (or producers) specifically targeted, while the benefits that could ensue from socially optimal resource exploitation are forgone. These policies necessarily and inevitably lead to collective impoverishment. The policy of tampering with prices, up or down, always results in higher levels of taxation and public indebtedness, which may in turn lead to a deterioration of social services and infrastructure, thus undermining future economic development. This is not only an inefficient subsidy to energy-intensive consumers, but also a regressive transfer from low-income households to those that are better off.

The case of agricultural prices is similar. The channels through which political assistance is provided differ from one region to the next: direct financial aid, supply management, price floors, import restrictions (tariffs and quotas), etc. If farmers and ranchers need to be subsidized, it is best to do so through direct transfers, which should be offered through competitive incentive mechanisms without opaque price manipulations. In this way, the social cost of such support is minimized while any potential social benefits are maintained.

Similar analyses could be applied to education and health care – sectors in which prices are manipulated to benefit certain interest groups, creating costly distortions in the allocation of resources and undermining social well-being.

It is not low prices that generate growth and welfare, it is the right prices. This leads to my first proposition with regard to ESG: one objective of ESG should be investment policies that oppose price manipulations on principle. For example, one ESG criterion should be avoiding direct or indirect investments in companies and sectors that demand, promote, or benefit from price manipulations, including large and ongoing direct or indirect subsidies.

It would be interesting to develop an ESG price-manipulation index by industry, sector, region, or even country. Price manipulations, whether from the private sector (from cartels) or the public sector (in the form of price controls), should be anathema to the "socially responsible public and private management" movement.

The true economic ethic underlying the CSD and NCC models is first and foremost an ethic of efficiency based on competitive prices.

ESG Is First and Foremost a Governmental Issue

To the extent that ESG is concerned about the environment, it is significantly hampered by the absence of markets. Creating and developing markets, with the associated institutions and regulations to ensure their emergence and efficiency, is a vital and central job of the governmental sector.

Implementation of the right level of environmental protection can be achieved through competitive pricing of environmental services. If firms and individuals have to pay to use environmental services, such as clean air and water (the quantity used should vary according to the different pollutants released), they will rationally equate the marginal value, specifically the value of the marginal product, to the price.

Sound use of the environment is socially efficient if it results from trades in a well-designed competitive market system. Similarly, it is socially responsible for the firm to maximize its value rather than its profit, which is a short-term or periodic measure. Moreover, sound use of the environment implies a certain level of degradation or destruction, and sometimes improvement or protection, which are basically different facets of the same prism.

When Milton Friedman wrote that "the social responsibility of business is to increase profits,"[9] he fully if implicitly understood that the link between ESG principles and profit maximization is based on the existence of competitive markets and prices and sound regulations that reflect the value of a firm's products and services to consumers and the opportunity costs of the human, material, social, environmental, and financial resources it uses. It is by reacting to those prices that it maximizes its profits, and hence its contribution to society.

The modern capitalist firm is a formidable wealth creator, transforming valued human, natural, material, and technological resources into products and services of greater value. However, this transformation must be based on reliable and appropriate indicators of relative values, such as competitive input and output prices, which would generally be set by competitive markets but sometimes by administrative mechanisms and regulations emulating competitive markets.

ESG is first and foremost a public-sector issue. It is in response to a failure of the governmental sector to create the conditions for the emergence of competitive markets, prices, and processes that ESG has become a business- or private-sector issue. What should have been a clear-cut case of "business as usual" has become an issue that instigates division among, and detracts from the shared missions of, both businesses and individuals.

Nobel economics laureate Oliver Hart and Luigi Zingales recently argued for replacing the currently dominant shareholder value maximization paradigm with one based on shareholder welfare maximization, where firms could engage in social and environmental issues if they have a comparative advantage over individual shareholders in addressing ESG-type issues. Their discussion builds on the economics of externalities and of firm boundaries in a context in which governments fail to properly manage externalities. In some cases – namely, those in which competitive prices and markets are not available or feasible – profit maximization may require firms to internalize the externalities, positive or negative, they impose on or generate for others. Hart and Zingales write, "In a more populous and interdependent world, the importance of externalities has also greatly increased, and many feel that governments are not dealing with them ... We think that the paradigm needs to change. This is true even if one accepts, as we do, the idea of shareholder primacy, that is, that companies should act on behalf of shareholders. When externalities are important and at least some investors are prosocial, we argue that shareholders will want companies to pursue *shareholder welfare maximization*."[10]

Another recent discussion of ESG criteria from a mainstream economics viewpoint is provided by London Business School economist Alex Edmans. He builds on the existing mainstream literature on corporate finance to show that ESG concerns are neither new nor different from the evaluation of investments that create long-term financial and social value. Among the relevant literature, Edmans mentions the following: the asset pricing literature, which explores how the stock market prices risks; the welfare economics literature, which investigates externalities; the private benefits literature, which analyzes manager and investor preferences beyond shareholder value; the optimal contracting literature, which considers how to achieve multiple objectives; and the agency theory literature, which examines how to ensure that managers pursue shareholder preferences, including non-financial preferences. He identifies how the conventional ESG thinking on ten key issues is overturned when applying the insights of mainstream economics. Among those issues, one finds the following:

1. Shareholder Value Is Short-Termist *(No, shareholder value is a long-term concept).*
2. Shareholder Primacy Leads to an Exclusive Focus on Shareholder Value *(No, shareholders have objectives other than shareholder value).*
3. Sustainability Risks Increase the Cost of Capital *(No, sustainability risks lower expected cash flows).*
4. Sustainable Stocks Earn Higher Returns *(No, sustainability may be priced in; tastes for sustainable stocks lead to lower returns).*
5. Climate Risk is Investment Risk *(No, climate risk is an unpriced externality).*
6. A Company's ESG Metrics Capture Its Impact on Society *(No, partial equilibrium differs from general equilibrium).*
7. More ESG Is Always Better *(No, ESG exhibits diminishing returns and trade-offs exist).*
8. More Investor Engagement Is Always Better *(No, investors may be uninformed or undermine managerial initiative).*

9. You Improve ESG Performance by Paying for ESG Performance *(No, paying for some ESG dimensions will cause firms to underweight others).*
10. Market Failures Justify Regulatory Intervention *(No, regulatory intervention is only justified when market failure exceeds regulatory failure).*[11]

Human Rights and Child Labour

My third proposition addresses human rights, another key concern of ESG. I am thinking in particular of child labour in poorer economies.

On the basis of 105 national household surveys, in collaboration with several national and international statistical agencies, the International Labour Organization estimates that in 2016 some 152 million children aged 5–17 (58 per cent boys) were victims of child labour, nearly 50 per cent of them in Africa and 40 per cent in the Asia-Pacific region.[12] Of these 152 million children, almost 50 per cent were aged 5–11, 28 per cent 12–14, and 24 per cent 15–17. Some 73 million of these children were engaged in hazardous work (62 per cent boys and 25 per cent under the age of 12). Child labour was found mainly in agriculture (71 per cent), but also in services (17 per cent) and industry (12 per cent), including mining. Nearly 69 per cent of child labour occurs in family-owned farms and businesses, while contract work and self-employment accounts for 27 and 4 per cent of these jobs, respectively.

The same report notes that 32 per cent of child labourers are not in school, and that 68 per cent of children attend part-time but are educationally penalized because their work interferes with their ability to fully benefit from their presence in the classroom. Their dropout rate is high and academic achievement falls short of expectations.

How can we define an ESG policy on child labour? In a 1998 special report on human rights entitled "The Power of Publicity," *The Economist* wrote, "In many circumstances too much pressure can be counterproductive, especially when it comes to labour standards. If western firms are persuaded by a torrent of criticism to reduce their investment or withdraw from low-wage countries, then local workers are the ones who suffer."[13]

Sam Vaknin reminds us that the issue of child labour "gave rise to a veritable not-so-cottage industry of activists, commentators, legal eagles, scholars, and opportunistically sympathetic politicians. Ask the denizens of Thailand, sub-Saharan Africa, Brazil, or Morocco and they will tell you how they regard this altruistic hyperactivity – with suspicion and resentment."[14] It is difficult to refute those denizens when they say, and sincerely believe, that behind the arguments for preventing or outlawing child labour, which appear convincing in the abstract, lies a program of trade protectionism.

The inclusion in international treaties of articles that impose strict working conditions and environmental protection indiscriminately is a form of protectionism – a trade policy designed to eliminate imports of products that intensify the competition some well-established domestic industries and their political allies are facing from countries that appropriately rely on cheap labour. These interventions are not only anti-ESG – they also ignore the benefits from international trade accruing to both partners.

Vaknin asserts that there are important nuances to be considered in the matter of child labour. There is a consensus that children should not be exposed to dangerous conditions and long working hours, be used as a means of payment, be physically punished, or be used as sex slaves. But in many poor communities, the work performed by children is a way to prevent the breakdown of the family unit. Depriving children of the opportunity to work, and, in so doing, preventing them from helping their families avoid disease and famine, is the height of immoral hypocrisy. It should be remembered that child labour was common in the United States in the nineteenth century, and even until the middle of the twentieth century. Miriam Wasserman writes,

> At the beginning of the twentieth century, pressure for [US] federal legislation covering child labor was growing nationally, but especially in the North. It was greeted with resentment in many segments of southern society. They saw it as interference from a richer North which – after having benefited from child labor in its own industrial development – was trying to limit the South's development ... The plight of working children in the developing world today is not very different, and in some cases even less harsh, than that prevalent in countries such as the United States and England during the nineteenth and early twentieth centuries.[15]

Likewise, Catherine Paul argues that

> In the late 1700s and early 1800s, power-driven machines began to replace hand labor for the making of most manufactured items. Factories sprung everywhere, first in England and then in the United States. The owners of these factories found a new source of labor to run their machines – children. Factory owners preferred hiring children because they were cheaper, less likely to strike, and more manageable than adults. However, factory work was grueling; a child working in a factory worked 12 to 18 hours a day, six days a week, for only one dollar. Many children began working as young as 7, tending machines in spinning mills or carrying heavy loads. By the mid-1800s, child labor and its lasting effects on children's health and education came under the scrutiny of reformers. A United States Census report from 1890 showed that over 1.5 million children between the ages of ten and fifteen were employed. This number comprised almost 20 percent of all children in that age range. Just ten years later, the 1900 Census showed that over 1.75 million children between the ages of ten and fifteen were working in gainful occupations.[16]

According to Vaknin, the outcry against the use of children to sew soccer balls in Pakistan has led Nike and Reebok to relocate their workshops. Thousands of people lost their jobs as a result, including many women and some seven thousand of their children. Average family income, already barely enough to survive on, fell by 20 per cent. There are several other similar examples. According to Wasserman, garment manufacturers laid off fifty thousand children in Bangladesh in 1993 in anticipation of the passage of a US law against child labour (the *Child Labor Deterrence Act*, which never saw the light of day).[17]

Ending child labour without doing anything else could be very damaging to both families and the children themselves. Preventing them from working could force them into even more dangerous activities (including prostitution). Of course, we all agree that, ideally, these children would be in school, receiving an education that would lift them out of poverty. But to be relevant and socially responsible, this alternative must actually exist.

ESG should set attainable criteria for socially responsible child labour (and human rights) by establishing an analytical framework for regulating child labour. Abolishing and prohibiting child labour without attending to the fallout of such a ban, when real and credible alternatives are not present, is not socially responsible: it is primarily the responsibility of the governmental sector to encourage an increase in the opportunity cost of child labour – that is, to offer the children desirable alternatives such as school together with support for their family.

The Level and Breadth of Corporate Social Responsibility

Corporate social responsibility is a complicated matter. If we are to enable and encourage an increase in the level of socially responsible investment, then liability for major environmental and/or industrial accidents cannot lie exclusively with corporations.

A realistic framework is needed to properly manage the distribution of responsibility across companies, partners (bankers and insurers), and governments (representing society at large). This realistic framework must recognize the limits of a company's liability, the limited capacity for government intervention, and the limited ability of the courts to avoid type I errors (convicting an innocent firm) and type II errors (clearing a guilty firm). Furthermore, it must account for the existence of imperfect or asymmetric information (moral hazard, adverse selection, monitoring difficulties) between the main partners (governments, companies, their partners, including financial partners, and the courts). All of these factors come into play in determining the probability of environmental and industrial accidents.

In this context, the government, acting as a benevolent planner, must legislate shared responsibility and prevention standards. The following paragraphs are based on US case law (under CERCLA, the *Comprehensive Environmental Responsibility, Compensation and Liability Act*) and European regulations governing financial guarantees and compulsory insurance.[18]

Four key factors determine the proper level of socially responsible corporate liability: profitability, the cost and efficiency of measures to prevent accidents, the social cost of public funds, and the ability of the courts to avoid type I and type II errors. Interactions between these factors in the characterization of a socially responsible level of corporate liability are complex and not always intuitive, but, once properly understood, they make sense nonetheless. It is not appropriate to delve into those complex links between determinants here, but the interested reader can look at the references given in this endnote.[19]

THE PROTECTION OF THE ENVIRONMENT (EXTERNALITIES)

In a landmark speech to the Environmental Grantmakers Association[20] in 2001, the American journalist and public commentator Bill Moyers said,

> If you want to fight for the environment, don't hug a tree; hug an economist. Hug the economist who tells you that fossil fuels are not only the third most heavily subsidized economic sector after road transportation and agriculture but that they also promote vast inefficiencies. Hug the economist who tells you that the most efficient investment of a dollar is not in fossil fuels but in renewable energy sources that not only provide new jobs but cost less over time. Hug the economist who tells you that the price system matters; it's potentially the most potent tool of all for creating social change. Look what California did this summer in responding to its recent energy crisis with a price structure that rewards those who conserve and punishes those who don't. Californians cut their electric consumption by up to 15%.[21]

Ecological and environmental activists sometimes seem to believe that using and degrading natural ecological systems is inherently wrong and immoral. Economists disagree. Rather, they deem the use of ecological or environmental systems socially just and ethical if it results from decisions made by institutions or mechanisms, including regulatory ones, that emulate competitive markets.

Environmental protection raises complicated issues because environmental damage is an externality for economic agents, be they consumers, businesses, or others. Furthermore, this externality is not local, but global, creating an even greater incentive for free riding, or at the very least wastefulness. In general, companies tend to overuse environmental resources since they do not directly bear the costs of their degradation (tragedy of the commons): if a common good or property is not adequately managed (for instance, through community-based regulation, or pricing, or both), economic agents, whether co-operatives, private firms, trade unions, consumers, governments,

NGOs, or religious organizations, tend to over-exploit it and threaten its survival.

Two other aspects of the issue are, first, the inertia of climate change, and second, the uncertainty regarding the atmospheric accumulation of GHGs. Net GHG emissions (emissions minus absorption or uptake) accumulate every day, but their impacts are only felt after a number of years or decades. Uncertainty with respect to accumulation processes, impacts, and technological changes justifies the recourse to the precautionary principle and option valuation, and the choice to discount the future. The rising GHG stock has poorly understood bio-social impacts and must be managed in a fog to prevent it from rising above some threshold level. This is why, at the level of the nation-state, the governmental sector has a crucial role to play in seeking ways to protect the population from current and future inefficiencies in the use of this shared and global vital asset – namely, the environment.[22]

*Markets and Competitive Prices
at the Service of the Environment*

The design of any economic policy involves two phases: the first is devoted to defining goals, the second to choosing the instruments, mechanisms, and processes by which the goals will be pursued. In the event said goals are not fully attained, the second phase also defines the methods for evaluating the results and determining the provisions for corrective measures. There are two main types of instruments. On the one hand, there are those of the prescriptive variety (i.e., "command and control"), and on the other, there are market- or incentive-based instruments. Whatever the policy retained and the objectives pursued, it is essential that the means implemented pass the test of efficiency.

While the stage of defining policy and its objectives may be the subject of legitimate differences of opinion between various groups with divergent views, it is surprising to find so much discord at the policy-implementation stage, as if the means of applying a policy could itself be subject to any criteria other than efficiency.

The following belong to the class of prescriptive instruments: regulated design specifications; mandatory use of specific production or abatement technologies; and caps on how much pollution an identified source, whether corporate or otherwise, may emit or release.

In the category of market-based instruments we find the taxation and pricing of pollutants, such as pricing or taxation of garbage and waste water; refundable deposits on plastic or glass products, batteries, tires, etc.; user fees in the case of gasoline and motor oil, heavy vehicles, trucks and trailers; liability-insurance taxes on hazardous products;[23] the pricing of operating permits for polluting activities; differentiated negative taxation (subsidies) on less-polluting products such as methanol, natural gas, ethanol, wind power generation, public transit, etc.; the reduction or abolition of subsidies to polluting industries such as the coal and fossil fuel industries, intensive agriculture, industrial livestock farming, forestry, commercial fishing, industrial chemicals, etc.; and more current provisions for allocating tradable pollution permits.

We might include even more recent regulatory mechanisms for informing the public about the risks that companies' products and operations pose to their workers and citizens, thus impacting the reputation of polluters positively or negatively. In terms of mechanisms for regulating pollution through public information, it's worth drawing attention to the announcement by the US Environmental Protection Agency in February 2002 of the "Climate Leaders" program, which in turn led to the creation in 2012 of the Center for Corporate Climate Leadership, which helps organizations of all sizes measure and manage their GHG emissions.[24] This program, based on voluntary participation, seeks to challenge companies to reduce their emissions of such heat-trapping gases as carbon dioxide, methane, nitrous oxide, fluorinated hydrocarbons, fully halogenated fluorinated hydrocarbons, and sulphur hexafluoride. Through this program, the agency publicly acknowledges companies that work with it to develop aggressive, efficient, and credible programs to reduce GHG emissions. This public recognition, coupled with the public naming of major polluters, is intended to encourage reputation-conscious companies to implement cost-effective control programs.

This mechanism requires that the public have access to information (whether provided voluntarily or not) on businesses' self-protection (which reduces their probability of causing a major environmental disaster) and self-insurance programs (which reduces the loss in human lives and material wealth in the event of a major ecological or environmental industrial accident). Thus, those self-protection and self-insurance programs promote the accountability and liability of business leaders. They also encourage the creation of new markets by means of new information and communication technologies, such as combinatorial auctions with dozens or even hundreds of steps, which provide efficient market solutions to traditional problems of complementarities and externalities. They encourage research, the emergence of more effective solutions, and the pursuit of maximum transparency, such as applying the rules of strict, shared, or extended liability to all partners of the polluting company, especially in cases where the company's liability could lead to its bankruptcy.[25]

During a conference held at the University of Perpignan in October 2001, a participant asked me whether we should not protect consumers, especially the poorest, from the first type of market instrument: taxes and tariffs on polluting products. I replied that, on the contrary, they should not be protected, since the purpose of the policy is precisely to reduce the consumption of products whose production is particularly polluting. Very often the tax revenues thus generated are redistributed on a basis that is completely detached from the consumption of polluting products.[26]

This allowed me to point out the distinction between the issue of income and wealth distribution and the need for static and dynamic efficiency in the production and consumption of polluting goods and services that contribute to the population's well-being. The pervasive confounding of these issues of distribution and efficiency is an ongoing source of fruitless debate that undermines the prospect of genuine environmental protection.

As for tradable permit systems, several real-world experiments using permits for air pollution, toxic products, chlorofluorocarbon emissions (through the Montreal Protocol), sulphur dioxide and nitrogen oxide emissions (in the form of acid rain), and others have yielded conclusive results.

Another participant in Perpignan asked me whether these markets for pollution permits would not benefit the wealthiest countries at the expense of the poorest. I replied once again that, on the contrary, efficiency in attaining a level of environmental protection can only benefit poorer countries for whom the squandering of resources, environmental or otherwise, is particularly costly. Here again, it is important to separate efficiency issues from issues of wealth redistribution. Development assistance and the search for efficient (and therefore less costly) instruments for implementing policies must be two sides of the same coin, each finding an ally in the other.

It is important to bear in mind a major finding of the economic analysis of instrument choice. In a full-information situation – that is, a situation in which all partners have the same information, however incomplete it may be – market-based and command and control instruments can in theory achieve the same level of pollution abatement and the same level of innovation in pollution-control technologies. In this sense they can be considered equivalent. However, they may differ in the relative cost of achieving the targets set by the environmental protection policy, in their relative capacities to effectively capitalize on all the relevant information and expertise available, and in their respective risks of missing or exceeding these objectives.

The main difference between these two types of instruments is that market-based instruments do not explicitly tell the polluting companies what to do. They are regulatory tools that change behaviour via price signals rather than through explicit instructions on methods of pollution control. Decisions on the level of pollution abatement and the technologies to be used to achieve it are left to the companies themselves.

Pollution abatement is expensive. Thus, a firm will have to incur some costs in terms of labour, materials, and capital to reduce its pollution by one unit, whatever actual amount that unit represents. This minimum level of expenditure represents the marginal cost of pollution abatement to the firm. A first criterion for the efficient allocation of resources devoted to pollution abatement is that the pollution levels of individual firms should be such that the marginal cost of the reduction of one unit of pollution is the same for all firms.

Indeed, if two firms have different marginal costs of pollution control, it would be efficient to redistribute pollution (or pollution-abatement) levels by requiring the firm with the lower marginal cost to reduce its pollution more and the firm with the higher marginal cost to reduce its abatement, thereby saving resources overall and lessening the total social cost of environmental policy, while keeping the pollution level constant. Thus, if this first efficiency condition is not satisfied, the chosen instrument may be described as inefficient because it wastes scarce social resources that could be used in a different activity to increase social wealth.

In order to satisfy this first efficiency criterion, a command and control–type instrument (such as a system of pollution caps) must be such that the distribution of these caps across polluting companies ensures that the marginal costs of pollution abatement are the same for each. In order to achieve this, the agency responsible for setting and allocating these caps would clearly need to know the evolution of the marginal cost of abatement at the level corresponding to the cap for all companies – an impossible task.

On the other hand, a market-based instrument such as a tax per unit of pollution produced will ensure that each firm will have an incentive (i.e., maximizing its profits) to adjust its production and pollution level in such a way that the marginal cost of pollution abatement equals the tax imposed on the marginal unit of pollution. If the marginal cost of reducing pollution is lower than the tax payable on the marginal unit of pollution emitted, the firm will be able to increase its profit by reducing its pollution by one unit. It will have every incentive to reduce its emissions to the point where the marginal cost of abatement becomes equal to the tax payable on the marginal unit of pollution. Since all firms have an interest in performing these same calculations, equality of marginal costs is obtained in a decentralized manner.

Blanchard, Gollier, and Tirole characterize the virtues of a carbon levy or price as follows:

> A carbon price has at least five virtues:
> - It encourages those who can eliminate their pollution at a relatively low cost to do so ...
> - It boosts green innovation through the monetization of intellectual property associated with green R&D, which enables startups to receive financing from private investors to reach the necessary scale.
> - It requires measuring emissions (which is not always straightforward), but no other information and thus reduces bureaucratic red tape and discretion relative to other methods of reducing pollution.
> - It is simple, in that it empowers consumers to act for the climate as the price they pay for a product captures the cost of all emissions along the value chain ...
> - Although not its purpose, it generates fiscal revenue that can be used to compensate certain categories of economic agents or to fund the green transition, for example.[27]

But they add that "Carbon pricing has many virtues. Unpopular for good as well as bad reasons, it is nonetheless an essential piece of the puzzle. It has been poorly implemented: it has been too unambitious to have the desired impact, admitted many exemptions, given way to numerous fossil fuel subsidies, raised concerns about offshoring to countries practicing environmental dumping, and offered low visibility as to future levels of the carbon price. Insufficient compensation of low-income suburban and rural dwellers has also contributed to its unpopularity."[28]

On 16 January 2019, the *Wall Street Journal* published what is unquestionably one of the key points of agreement among economists – namely, the "Economists' Statement on Carbon Dividends," an initiative of the Climate Leadership Council.[29] This declaration reads as follows:

> Global climate change is a serious problem calling for immediate national action. Guided by sound economic principles, we are united in the following policy recommendations [note: the Climate Leadership Council used the terms "carbon tax" and "carbon price," meaning really "carbon levy," close to a price but not exactly a tax]:
>
> I. A carbon tax offers the most cost-effective lever to reduce carbon emissions at the scale and speed that is necessary. By correcting a well-known market failure, a carbon tax will send a powerful price signal that harnesses the invisible hand of the marketplace to steer economic actors towards a low-carbon future.
>
> II. A carbon tax should increase every year until emissions reductions goals are met and be revenue neutral to avoid debates over the size of government. A consistently rising carbon price will encourage technological innovation and large-scale infrastructure development. It will also accelerate the diffusion of carbon-efficient goods and services.
>
> III. A sufficiently robust and gradually rising carbon tax will replace the need for various carbon regulations that are less efficient. Substituting a price signal for cumbersome regulations will promote economic growth and provide the regulatory certainty companies need for long-term investment in clean-energy alternatives.
>
> IV. To prevent carbon leakage and to protect U.S. competitiveness, a border carbon adjustment system should be established. This system would enhance the competitiveness of

V. American firms that are more energy-efficient than their global competitors. It would also create an incentive for other nations to adopt similar carbon pricing.

V. To maximize the fairness and political viability of a rising carbon tax, all the revenue should be returned directly to U.S. citizens through equal lump-sum rebates. The majority of American families, including the most vulnerable, will benefit financially by receiving more in "carbon dividends" than they pay in increased energy prices.[30]

It remains for the responsible agency to set the right pollution-abatement level, and, by extension, the amount of the carbon levy. This is certainly a formidable task, but much less so than directly allocating pollution quotas to all companies.

There are sizable gaps between the proposed levels of the carbon levy. The rigorous analysis carried out in France by the Quinet Commission (2019) on the unit value of carbon led it to assert that this value should be €$_{2018}$250 (CAD$$_{2018}$375) in 2030.[31]

These values will probably need to undergo revision as we move toward 2030 and beyond. Nonetheless, with regard to the first criterion for the efficient allocation of effort and resources, it appears that market-based instruments largely dominate command and control instruments. The cost savings that can be attained by market instruments compared to command and control instruments are considerable, amounting to as much as several billion dollars per year.

Several criticisms have been levied at these market-based mechanisms, especially with regard to the carbon levy (wrongfully referred to as carbon tax). For instance, there are difficulties associated with obtaining accurate measurements of carbon emissions, setting the level of the levy, and implementing it across the entire economy. More often than not, these criticisms reflect a failure to understand basic economic principles regarding the roles played by prices and income in the decisions of economic agents.[32]

Efficiency in Terms of Expertise and Information: Extended Liability

It should be noted, however, that market-based instruments can be relatively inefficient when there is a desire to centralize information and expertise on optimal pollution abatement. This might be the case, for example, if the same information and expertise were used by a large number of companies. Sharing the costs of information and expertise requires a certain degree of coordination that is more difficult for market-based instruments than for command and control instruments to muster. At least at first blush, command and control instruments are amenable to capturing the benefits of centralized information more efficiently than would be possible under the conflicting interests between firms.

Market-based instruments provide greater incentives than command and control instruments for firms to research and implement technologically innovative pollution-abatement systems. This is because they allow firms to capture a significant share of the benefits of these innovations. Thus, market-based instruments such as taxes on emissions and tradable pollution permits are generally more dynamically efficient than regulations, mandated pollution technologies, and caps because they increase the intensity of incentives to innovate in pollution abatement. By increasing the incentives for firms to innovate in order to maximize not only their short-term profits but also their long-term valuations, market instruments are likely to lead to the emergence of more efficient and less socially costly "green" technologies.[33]

In a recent blog post, Matt Ridley wrote,

> In 2019 wind and solar between them supplied just 1.5 percent of the world's energy consumption. Hydro supplied 2.6 percent, nuclear 1.7 percent, and all the rest – 94 percent – came from burning things: coal, oil, gas, wood, and biofuels ... The world needs energy innovation if it is to reduce the use of fossil fuels ... Nuclear power could supply all our needs from a comparatively tiny footprint of land and steel, but we have made innovation in nuclear all but impossible by massively increasing the cost and time required to license a new design ... Molten-salt reactors will one day be more efficient, safer, and cheaper, but only if there is a revolution in regulation as much as one in technology ... There is renewed hope, however, that low-temperature superconductors and "spherical tokamak" designs may yet crack the problem of controlled fusion and that by 2040 we will have abundant, cheap, reliable energy on tap ... If that were to happen, through molten-salt fission or through fusion, imagine what we could do ... We could synthesize fuel for transport, dismantle wind turbines and

oil pipelines, stop burning trees in power stations, desalinate enough water to supply the human race without touching wild rivers, and suck carbon-dioxide out of the air. Above all, we could raise the standard of living of the poorest on the planet. It is surely worth a try.[34]

An important and often overlooked dimension of instrument choice is the analysis of the relative risks associated with different types of instruments. Indeed, whatever type of instrument is chosen, there is always a risk of falling short of the goals of the environmental protection policy, even if the instruments chosen would make it possible on average, or under normal conditions, to attain them.[35]

One of the objectives of instrument choice when implementing an environmental protection policy is to ensure that those who have the information are primarily responsible for the policy. Indeed, in light of the issue's complexity, the efficient use of information can yield considerable savings.

To illustrate, consider again CERCLA in the United States, the *Comprehensive Environmental Response, Compensation and Liability Act*. This law holds the "owners" and "operators" of companies that cause environmental disasters liable. Jurisprudence has evolved toward a growing recognition of the liability of the banks that finance said companies on the principle that a bank's involvement in these operations make them comparable to the "operators" recognized as liable in the law, despite the explicit recognition of banks' right to intervene to protect their interests as creditors.

It is useful here to cite the court's ruling in the case involving the financial institution Fleet Factors prosecuted under CERCLA:

> Our ruling today should encourage potential creditors to investigate thoroughly the waste treatment systems and policies of potential debtors. If the treatment systems seem inadequate, the risk of CERCLA liability will be weighed into the terms of the loan agreement. Creditors, therefore, will incur no greater risk than they bargained for and debtors, aware that inadequate hazardous waste treatment will have a significant adverse impact on their loan terms, will have powerful incentives to improve their handling of hazardous wastes. Similarly, creditors' awareness that they are potentially liable under CERCLA will encourage them to moni-

tor the hazardous waste treatment systems and policies of their debtors and insist upon compliance with acceptable treatment standards as a prerequisite to continued and future financial support ... We share the district court's conclusion that Fleet's alleged conduct brought it outside the statutory exemption for secured creditors. Indeed, Fleet's involvement would pass the threshold for operator liability. Fleet weakly contends that its activity at the facility from the time of the auction was within the secured creditor exemption because it was merely protecting its security interest in the facility and foreclosing its security interest in its equipment, inventory, and fixtures. This assertion, even if true, is immaterial to our analysis. The scope of the secured creditor exemption is not determined by whether the creditor's activity was taken to protect its security interest. What is relevant is the nature and extent of the creditor's involvement with the facility, not its motive. To hold otherwise would enable secured creditors to take indifferent and irresponsible actions towards their debtors' hazardous wastes with impunity by incanting that they were protecting their security interests. Congress did not intend CERCLA to sanction such abdication of responsibility.[36]

As one might expect, this ruling caused quite a stir, not only in the United States but also in Europe. The judge in the above case wanted to extend liability to all partners of the company at fault in order to give the institutions and agents with the greatest access to information the right incentives to use their inside information in the most socially beneficial way.

To the extent that the banks that provide funding to companies posing major environmental risks are well positioned to obtain inside information on the operations of these firms, it may be socially efficient to make them jointly liable with their clients for the environmental damage that the latter may cause. Making banks and other financial institutions liable for environmental damage caused by their corporate clients can thus generate the right incentives for production, self-protection, and self-insurance at a lower cost.

The Challenge of Adopting Market Instruments

In light of the clear relative efficiency of market instruments in terms of cost, information, R&D investment, proper incentivization, risk management, etc., it is fair to ask why their adoption by various government bodies is not more widespread.

First, it must be acknowledged that these instruments are gaining in currency, although most of those presently in use continue to be timid and prescriptive in nature. As the understanding of economics increases among politicians and actors with a specific interest in implementing effective environmental policy, market-based instruments are making significant inroads.

This development is to be welcomed as the costs of increasingly restrictive environmental policies are likely to rise substantially in the coming years. Thus, it can be expected that the efficiency of the instruments implemented to achieve environmental policy goals at the lowest cost will become a central preoccupation of policy-makers.

On the other hand, we also need to contend with pressure groups that may see these market instruments as a way for companies and governments to abdicate their responsibilities. They may prefer the status quo in environmental policy instruments and strive to block the quest for innovative solutions to environmental protection. These pressure groups – environmental activists as well as businesses that profit from the relative inefficiency of existing instruments – can derail the best intentions for environmental protection by their ignorance of the real challenges associated with combining economic growth with optimal environmental protection.

In concluding our discussion of competition and the environment, it may be worthwhile to reiterate that economic analysis is an important factor in environmental protection. Thus, it is misguided and misleading to present environment and economy, or environmentalists and economists, as being on opposing teams. In many instances, economists are strong and credible advocates for the environment. Indeed, economists are first and foremost experts in the efficiency of systems and instruments, whether the system is production, consumption, public policy, investment, or environmental protection. The economist's role is more to analyze a system's characteristics in terms of efficiency and effectiveness than to pass judgment on the objectives pursued.

In the context of environmental protection, the approach of economists is to identify shortcomings that are attributable to the absence of markets, leading to over-exploitation of environmental resources. This phenomenon is not new, nor is it limited to environmental issues. Economic theory provides a good explanation for environmental degradation when the absence of property rights prevents free negotiation and thus blocks the emergence of competitive equilibrium prices.

The barriers to the creation of markets and market institutions in a field like environmental protection should not be downplayed. Recurring challenges and the failure to reach an agreement on markets for carbon pricing and trading at the Madrid Conference of the Parties in 2019 – which followed on earlier meetings in Paris (2015) and Katowice (2017), and where the necessity of this type of agreement was highlighted – attest to the difficulties faced to date and going forward. Unfortunately, the economic solution to the difficulties and issues raised by environmental protection is ultimately sidelined by well-intentioned but idle chatter among those on the forefront who, sadly, have no understanding of the issue.[37]

Moreover, the presence of significant information asymmetries is likely to give rise to endless posturing and bickering in which all try to derive strategic advantage from their private information. The solution therefore lies in the definition of tradable property rights, on the one hand, and the use of environmental resource pricing, on the other.

In both cases, the goal is optimal environmental protection, and the best mechanisms for achieving it are primarily associated with free markets. These mechanisms make it possible to both clearly define the concept of optimal protection (equilibrium), and to achieve this level of protection efficiently – that is, by devoting the right level of social resources to it.[38]

PROTECTING AND SHARING WATER

Water is probably our most important resource. From a relatively abundant substance historically, water has become scarce with the explosive growth of the world's population and the phenomenal development of the world's economies.

To the extent that the distribution of water resources differs from the distribution of the population and water-intensive economic activities, there is a need to trade or even market water if we are to balance availability and needs. In this context, there are two main sets of issues related to water economics.

First, there is a need to improve water management with efficient instruments and institutions based on competitive markets, including appropriate pricing and well-regulated trade. Socially responsible management of water resources has become a global challenge and represents a major opportunity for development and wealth creation for all.

Second, there is a need to use available means to inform all stakeholders of the increasing value of water, including households and businesses, managers and operators of natural freshwater resources, industrial water service providers, operators of wastewater treatment plants or centres, and developers of technologies and equipment for the exploitation, transportation, and management of water resources.

The greatest danger on the horizon is that, through a lack of understanding, leadership, and open communication, the international community of developed and developing countries will lag in designing and implementing the governance mechanisms needed to manage our freshwater resources, however abundant or scarce. The global water crisis is imminent and much more critical than the climate crisis, but far fewer resources are devoted to it.

Water is both a human right and an economic commodity with very special characteristics: its consumption momentarily destroys the good (the glass of water I drink is unavailable to anyone else, so water is a private good in the economic sense of the term), but the water consumed regenerates and eventually finds its way back into nature to be consumed again in an unending cycle. Identifying and delivering the right balance between these two complementary visions – water as a human right and water as a commodity with special characteristics – involves untangling a Gordian knot that humanity must address today.

It is precisely because access to water is a human right that appropriate markets and commercial arrangements (pricing and control) must be designed to make this right a reality for all, rather than just a pipe dream.

We must ask questions that some still find extremely disconcerting: If water is considered a shared endowment, how can we prevent it from being over-exploited and over-consumed (the tragedy of the commons)? If water is assigned its due value, how can we avoid the opposite problem of it being underused because some rights holders may wish to withhold it from the market (tragedy of the anticommons)? How much should users pay for water (and wastewater treatment)? How to determine the "right" price? How is water scarcity managed in practice? How can trade transform a water-poor country into a country capable of managing its local water in a sustainable, if not self-sufficient, manner?

Market instruments can be developed and applied to water resources. This may be the most audacious challenge of all, as the creation of competitive water markets could be a first step toward a more prosperous era for everyone – individuals, the agricultural, and industrial sectors alike. At the forefront of the challenge are water-management technologies that can support the value chain, including dikes and dams, transportation, and de-salination plants.

Consumers of commodities, including water, respond to prices: lower prices lead to higher demand. When water is free, there is no reason to conserve or curb the amount of water used. Where water is scarce, providing water for free is a recipe for ensuring that demand exceeds supply.

Maintaining water markets can be difficult. Potable water distribution and wastewater collection systems are natural monopolies because it is not feasible to build several parallel networks of pipes, as competition would require.[39] However, monopolies, whether private or public, do not work well. They are rarely efficient, effective, or sensitive to the wishes of their customers, and they may overcharge because there is no competition to set a market price.

But going to the other extreme, setting the price of water at zero or artificially low also causes distortions. If there is no market to set the price, adequate regulation can ensure that the price reflects the opportunity cost and is thus the best possible approximation to the dynamics of supply and demand.

Whatever the case may be, the regulation of drinking water must be independent and free of conflicts of interest. In an ideal system, operation of water treatment plants and pipelines will be separated from the systems' oversight, which in turn will be separated from creation of the rules and standards with which the system must comply. We know how to do all of that, yet many books and documentaries, as well as political organizations, NGOs, and lobbies, present an apocalyptic and ultimately dystopian vision of the use of market and commercial mechanisms (pricing and markets) to help alleviate the impending global water shortage. To these authors and leaders, the commodification of water is nothing less than the embodiment of evil, a plot to enslave the world. In Canada, for example, water activist Maude Barlow and the Council of Canadians have taken on the mission of blocking any opening to market mechanisms. They claim that access to water is a fundamental human right, but at the same time, they refuse any opening to trade water, and hence to share it. Overabundant Canadian water is not for trade: "We demand that people everywhere and all governments reject the commodification of water and its sale on the open market and recognize that water is a public trust and a human right in law and practice for all time."[40]

They are oblivious to the fact that we are all increasingly in the same boat in the face of water shortages, and that the division should not be between those who have a surplus of water and those who suffer from shortages, but rather between those who advocate a reasoned use and an incentive-based protection of water and those who deny the reality of the urgent needs of humanity beyond their borders while proffering hollow platitudes.

The political lobbying of this self-righteous coalition borders on extreme forms of policy collusion. It has no other solution to offer than regurgitated clichés and falsehoods about competition and markets, caricaturing any market failure as indicative of markets' true nature, in order to virtually capture Canada's water resources and in so doing create a "tragedy of the anticommons" that hurts citizens both here and abroad.

6

Inequalities

The nature of the links between the creation, distribution, and redistribution of wealth is a recurring debate in democracies, whether of the social democratic persuasion or some other variant. While complex, these links are not necessarily incomprehensible if we carefully study their determinants.

Let us begin by recalling that wealth creation and increased productivity do not fall from heaven by divine grace; rather, they result from the actions, research, and thoughts of creators, innovators, and entrepreneurs who succeed in producing more goods and services of greater value with the available resources (labour, materials, environment, capital).

Moreover, the distribution of wealth is much more egalitarian in developed countries, having become even more so between 1920 and 1980 (six decades) before reversing course and becoming less egalitarian as of 1980 (four decades). Many analysts' and pundits' attention has been focused on this latter period of increasing inequality in income and wealth. However, if the reasons advanced to explain the increase in inequality since 1980 cannot explain the previous six-decade decrease, the explanation is incomplete or just plain wrong.

Recall that wealth created in an economy or society is allocated to wages and salaries, corporate profits, interest and investment income, net farm income, and taxes minus subsidies. Thus, we need to bear in mind that labour compensation as a share of GDP has sat around 50 per cent for several decades (in Canada), with only slight fluctuations. In real terms, labour compensation has therefore increased at the same rate as real GDP – some 141 per cent between 1981 and 2021. Moreover, employment in real terms come is only one source of revenues for individuals, since businesses ultimately belong to them too.[1]

The issue of inequality in a society, as well as its determinants and evolution over time, is the subject of perennial research efforts in academic and public policy circles. In addition to triggering calls for reforming capitalism, inequality never ceases to elicit commentary in the opinion pages of newspapers, magazines, and on social media.

Galvanizing elements are certainly the relative compensation of CEOs and artistic and sports celebrities, the evolution over time of income, wealth, and consumption inequalities, as well as the social role, or roles, if any, of inequalities in promoting higher levels of productivity, economic growth, and prosperity for all.

THE COMPENSATION OF CEOS AND CELEBRITIES

The relative earnings of CEOs are at the heart of discussions on inequality. In September 2017, the US Securities and Exchange Commission (SEC) implemented the CEO pay ratio disclosure mandated by the *Dodd–Frank Wall Street Reform and Consumer Protection Act* signed by President Barack Obama in July 2010.[2] This law requires companies to provide information on the total annual compensation of their CEOs and the median of the total annual compensation paid to their employees. The SEC gives companies limited leeway in determining whether the reported median pay covers all employees or only those based in the United States if they represent more than 95 per cent of employees.

The SEC rule allows companies to use reasonable estimates, assumptions, and methodologies. A company may use existing internal records, such as tax or payroll records, to identify the median employee and test to determine whether its workers are employees for purposes of the rule. Under the rule, employees of consolidated subsidiaries must be included and those of independent contractors must be excluded. Despite all the complexities facing companies, the information provided is very interesting.[3]

While many observers focus on the ratio of CEO to median employee total annual compensations, this is not the most informative and relevant figure. Other ratios, such as CEO pay per employee and the B ratio, equal to the ratio of CEO pay to the total payroll, may be more informative and relevant.

Data for the 500 largest US companies (the S&P 500 companies), as reported to the SEC as of the end of 2022, includes 10 companies with "outlier" data, 7 whose CEOs earned more than $100 million and 3 whose CEOs earned less than $1 million.[4] To avoid reporting biased results, those companies must be removed before computing average CEO pay ratios.

We observe that the CEOs of the 490 large companies so retained received on average a total compensation of $16.3 million in 2021–22.[5] This compensation is on average 291 times the median compensation of employees. To recognize the important differences in company size and compensation levels, a weighted average ratio, equal to the total CEO compensation over all companies divided by the total median compensation over the same companies, is more appropriate. We find that the CEO compensation is equal to a weighted average 193 times the median compensation of employees, to a weighted average of $310 per employee (total CEO compensation over the total number of employees), and yields a weighted B ratio of 0.5 per cent (total CEO compensation over the compensation of all employees, estimated by the median compensation times the number of employees, which is a conservative estimate of total compensation). Thus, the 25.8 million employees of these 490 companies "contributed" on average $310 to their CEO's compensation, or one-half of 1 per cent (0.5 per cent) of their respective annual compensation – in other words, $250 for a compensation of $50,000 and $500 for a compensation of $100,000. Viewed from a different angle, if we were to distribute the total compensation of all CEOs (US$8 billion) equally among all employees (25.8 million), the resulting average annual salary increase would be $310 per employee.

A majority of employees might consider inappropriate the fact that CEOs earn on average $16.3 million – that is, on a weighted average basis, nearly two hundred times (or nearly three hundred times on a raw average basis) the median compensation of employees in their companies. However, a majority might consider it appropriate to "contribute" 0.5 per cent of their annual compensation to hire the best possible CEO to run their company and ensure its profitability, sustainability, growth, and the protection of jobs. Even though both statements are similar, support may differ. Hence the need to frame the question correctly and to do the right analysis.

These measures – the CEO pay ratio, the CEO pay per employee, and the B ratio – vary across companies, sectors, and countries. There are a number of reasons for this variability, including the specificity of the role assumed and the scope and impact of the CEO's leadership and skill in designing and managing corporate strategies and activities. The strategic definition and exercise of the company's opportunities may impact differently the companies' performance and, by extension, the general well-being of employees, shareholders, and other stakeholders, including suppliers and customers.

Celebrities in Arts and Sports

Regarding the compensation of celebrities, Thomson shows that the top 1 per cent of groups and solo artists capture 77 per cent of all revenues from recorded music.[6] Krueger shows that the top 1 per cent of performers captured 26 per cent of all concert revenues in 1982 versus 56 per cent in 2003, while the top 5 per cent captured almost 90 per cent of all concert revenues.[7] Lunny states that in 2019, the top 1 per cent captured 60 per cent of revenues.[8]

In sports, according to Zingales, the purse earned by the winner of the Masters golf tournament in 2008 equaled 103 times the annual salary of a groundskeeper, compared to 3 times in 1948.[9] However, if this value is translated into expected earnings, it drops from 103 to 13 because the number of golfers has increased significantly and the competition has become global. Zingales adds,

> The golf example is illuminating because the same two phenomena that are driving the rise in golf prizes – enhanced competition and the increased value of being at the top – have also occurred in the corporate world, roughly at the same time. Increased integration of the global market makes it more difficult for companies to survive. In turn, a lot of executives who would have earned a decent living running mediocre companies are wiped out. At the same time, the most efficient firms can apply their advantage over the entire world market now. The value of being the best has increased disproportionately, and companies – just like the Augusta Golf Club – are not going to run the risk of losing the jackpot to save a few dollars on the executives.[10]

Stéphane Rousseau and colleagues write, "In the mid-twentieth century, Schumpeter examined the conditions needed for entrepreneurial innovation, and hypothesised that, owing to the deep uncertainty involved in invention and its low success rate, only exceptional gains would be able to encourage it. The gains should be much greater than the yield that attracts persons into ordinary commercial ventures."[11]

A possible contributing factor is the combined effect of an increase in the size and complexity of companies and the winner-take-all "tournaments" that have arisen under globalization: where there used to be two, three, or more CEOs, there is now only one, and where there were more winners in more (local) tournaments, there are fewer winners in fewer large tournaments.

We also read in Freeland that

> The average tenure of a Fortune 500 CEO has fallen from 9.5 years to 3.5 years over the past decade. That's true lower down the food chain, too. Thomas Philippon, the economist who documented the connection between deregulation and soaring salaries on Wall Street, also found that the jobs of financiers were very insecure. Nor does being your own boss protect you from the uncertainty of the markets. At a 2011 seminar at the Central European University in Budapest devoted to the psychology of investing, George Soros told the gathered academics that "the markets are a machine for destroying the ego."[12]

INEQUALITIES OF INCOME, WEALTH, AND CONSUMPTION

For several years now, researchers have tended to focus on the characterization of income and wealth inequalities and their evolution over several decades. Recently, we saw the publication of the World Inequality Lab's 2022 *World Inequality Report*, the fruit of a hundred researchers around the world.[13] We learn, among other things, that income inequalities at the global level (share of the top 1 per cent) have decreased for several decades (1910–70) but have increased since the late 1970s. As for wealth inequalities (share of the top 1 per cent), they also decreased from 1910 to 1980, then stabilized in western Europe and rose again in the United States. For Canada, we learn that income inequality (top 10 per cent share) has followed a similar path to that in the United States, although the increase since 1980 has been less pronounced, and wealth inequality has remained relatively stable since 1995.

A closer inspection is in order before becoming too excited about the increase in income and wealth inequalities. I will show in the next paragraphs that consumption inequalities decreased significantly in recent decades, for which relatively reliable data exist, and most probably for a much longer period of time.

The current fixation on income and wealth inequalities and the neglect of the more socially relevant consumption inequalities is a clear failure of public policy research by economists and other social scientists. Few researchers have looked at these consumption inequalities, although it is consumption, in kind and in expenditures, that determines the level and quality of life.[14]

The 2022 *World Inequality Report* remains silent on consumption inequalities. Besides this report, two recent important and well-publicized works totally neglect consumption inequalities. One is the UK Institute for Fiscal Studies' Deaton Review, led by Nobel economics laureate Angus Deaton.[15] The project aims to cover a broad set of issues related to inequalities, including

> which inequalities matter and why they matter; people's attitudes towards inequality; the political economy of inequality; the history of inequality; trends in economic inequalities; intergenerational inequalities; health inequalities; geographical inequalities; gender; race and ethnicity; immigration; early child development; education systems; families; social mobility; trade and globalisation; productivity, growth and innovation; labour markets; tax policy; and welfare policy.[16]

Angus Deaton himself writes, "We will think about inequalities broadly – note my use of 'inequalities' rather than 'inequality' – and will not be confined to the traditional economic concerns with measures of the distribution of income and wealth, important although those are."[17] In spite of those grandiose declarations, no mention is made of consumption inequalities besides consumption expenditures.

Another recent important work is the 2021 report *Major Future Economic Challenges*, produced by an international commission convened by the French government.[18] Chaired by Olivier Blanchard and Nobel economics laurate Jean Tirole, the commission aimed to address three long-term structural challenges: climate change, economic inequalities, and the demographic challenge. Surprisingly, the report's second chapter, "Economic Inequality and Insecurity: Policies for an Inclusive Economy" (authored by Dani Rodrik and Stefanie Stantcheva), remains totally silent on consumption inequalities. Moreover, the authors conducted a survey of French citizens' attitudes toward inequality, and found that "73% of respondents believe that inequality in income is a serious or very serious problem; 62% believe the same about inequality in wealth. 70% of our sample believes that inequality in opportunity is a big issue."[19] Again, no mention of consumption inequality.

On this subject, Watson writes,

> Our preoccupation with inequality is an error and a trap. It is an error because inequality, unlike poverty, is not the problem it is so widely presumed to be. Inequality can be good, it can be bad, and it can be neither good nor bad but benign ... Inequality is also a trap – not a trap anyone has set for us but one of our own making – because concern with it leads us to focus on the top end of the income distribution when our preoccupation should instead be the bottom where the bulk of human misery almost certainly resides.[20]

Amartya Sen for his part tells us to remember that

> Pervasive poverty and lives that were "nasty, brutish and short," as Thomas Hobbes put it, dominated the world not many centuries ago, with only a few pockets of rare affluence. In overcoming that penury, modern technology as well as economic interrelations have been influential. The predicament of the poor across the world cannot be reversed by withholding from them the great advantages of contemporary technology, the well-established efficiency of international trade and exchange, and the social as well as economic merits of living in open, rather than closed, societies. What is needed is a fairer distribution of the fruits of globalization.[21]

On the brighter side, inequalities in consumption have recently been the subject, under the aegis of the OECD, of a less popular but more important and admittedly more difficult research agenda. Statistics Canada is at the forefront of these developments and has recently published interesting, although still fragmentary, data on the subject.

An inclusive and realistic measurement of household consumption highlights the important redistributive effects not only of taxation and financial transfers but also of social transfers in kind (STiK). These correspond to individual goods and services provided to households free of charge or at insignificant prices by public administrations and non-profit organizations. We think, for example, of health, education, security, parks, free shows, help of all kinds offered to poor households, etc.[22]

In Canada in 2021–22, STiK represented about 75 per cent of the household disposable income (and about twice the employment income) of the lowest quintile (the lowest 20 per cent of income), and 13 per cent of the household disposable income (12 per cent of employment income) of the highest quintile. Globally, STiK have doubled (205 per cent) between 1999 and 2022. Together with net transfers in money (transfers received minus taxes paid), their impact on consumption inequalities is significant.

The main results for Canada are summarized in table 6.1. Between 1999–2000 and 2021–22, the employment income of the poorest quintile increased in real terms by 15.6 per cent, while it increased by 21.9 per cent for the highest quintile. The ratio of employment income of the highest over the lowest quintile increased by 5.7 per cent, while the difference increased by 22.4 per cent, indicating an increase in employment income inequality.

Net transfers in dollars, which subtract income taxes paid from transfers received, are positive for the poorest quintile and negative for the highest. For the poorest quintile, they increased in real terms by 89.2 per cent over the last two decades. For the richest quintile, net transfers fell further into the negative realm by 5.4 per cent. The difference in net transfers between the two quintiles (highest minus lowest) increased by 13.8 per cent from $64,175 in 1999–2000 to $73,020 in 2021–22. This translates into a significant reduction in overall income inequality.

STiK increased over the 1999–2022 period by 42.5 per cent for the lowest quintile and by 33.0 per cent for the highest quintile. But since STiK represent a much larger percentage of employment income for the lowest quintile than for the highest, the changes translate into a significant reduction in consumption inequality. This reduction in confirmed by the fact that the household actual final consumption (HAFC – that is, the sum of the household final consumption expenditures in dollars and STiK) increased by 46.8 per cent for those in the bottom quintile and by 12.8 per cent for those in the top. This translates into a significant decline of 23.2 per cent in consumption inequality, measured by the ratio of HAFC of the highest over the lowest quintile. As indicated in table 6.1, the difference in HAFC between the highest and lowest quintiles has decreased by 10.5 per cent between the two periods.

In table 6.1, an italicized positive percentage means that a negative value has become more negative. It is useful to remember that income quintiles are assigned based on equivalized household disposable income, which takes into account differences in household size and composition using a method proposed by the OECD. The "OECD-modified" equivalence scale assigns a value of 1 to the first adult, 0.5 to each additional person aged fourteen and over, and 0.3 for all children under fourteen.

In terms of taxation, tax progressivity in Canada has increased over the last two decades: the top quintile now pays around 60 per cent of all taxes, an increase of nearly 5 percentage points since 1999, compared to 1.1 per cent for the bottom quintile, a decrease of 0.3 percentage points. Tax progressivity, measured as the ratio of the share of taxes paid by the top quintile to the share of the bottom quintile, has increased by about 30 per cent over the past two decades.

Thus, for over twenty years, and most probably for a much longer period of time, consumption inequalities have decreased, unlike income and wealth inequalities. This is why the overwhelming emphasis placed on income and wealth inequalities gives us an incomplete picture – even a distorted one – of the reality of households, in particular less well-off households. This leads to needless clamouring about a (perceived) large and growing social divide and unnecessarily exacerbates social conflicts. Fuel is thrown on the fire of division and conflict when such studies are pursued, which, despite their interest, miss the most relevant social target of consumption inequalities.

THE SOCIAL ROLE OF INEQUALITY OF INCOME AND WEALTH

Income and wealth inequalities can be understood as responding to three social needs: to ensure an adequate level of savings and investment, to enable appropriate creative destruction through innovation and entrepreneurship, and to foster the development and acquisition of new skills that are socially necessary but individually costly. These three social needs require a certain level of income and wealth inequality, which thereby promote higher levels of productivity, economic growth, and prosperity for all.

Table 6.1
Employment income, net transfers, STiK, household actual final consumption (HAFC) by income quintile, Canada: 2021–22 vs 1999–2001 ($2012)

	1999	2000	2021	2022	Variation (2021–22)/(1999–2000)
			Employment income		
Lowest quintile L	8,894	9,195	10,140	10,774	15.6%
Highest quintile H	123,535	133,476	159,997	153,411	21.9%
Ratio H/L	13.9	14.5	15.8	14.2	5.7%
Difference H–L	114,642	124,281	149,857	142,637	22.4%
		Net transfers in $$ (NT: money transfers received minus taxes paid)			
Lowest quintile L	7,530	6,531	13,986	12,623	89.2%
Highest quintile H	–55,396	–58,892	–58,914	–60,518	4.5%
Difference	62,926	65,423	72,900	73,141	13.8%
			Social transfers in kind (STiK)		
Lowest quintile L	14,115	14,316	20,282	20,229	42.5%
Highest quintile H	14,104	14,543	19,339	18,771	33.0%
		Household actual final consumption (HAFC)			
Lowest quintile L	45,689	47,241	68,743	67,656	46.8%
Highest quintile H	112,620	116,157	126,812	131,147	12.8%
Ratio H/L	2.5	2.5	1.8	1.9	–23.2%
Difference H–L	66,931	68,916	58,069	63,491	–10.5%

Source: Statistics Canada 30-10-0587-01 as of 31 March 2023. Computations by the author.

The social role of higher income and wealthier groups are "to save and invest." This role has perhaps become more important in recent decades – since 1980, say – which would justify and explain the rise in income and wealth inequality. But who among us should be entrusted with this role, which comes with great responsibilities but also with considerable perks?

In the matter of inequality and wealth creation, a distinction must be made between the short and the long term. In times of accelerated wealth creation, the distribution temporarily skews to greater inequality before reverting to a more egalitarian level. New wealth is initially appropriated mainly by those who are primarily responsible for its creation. Next, a restructuring and reorganization of economic activities increases the productivity of human resources and promotes a more egalitarian distribution of wealth. Productivity is further enhanced by the development and acquisition of new skills, resulting in an even more egalitarian distribution. Developed countries, however, may have reached a peak in income and wealth inequality. Freeland reports that a group of economists interviewed by Alan Krueger in the mid-1990s cited technological change as the main factor in income polarization, followed by "unknown," and globalization.[23]

Incentives for creativity, innovation, and entrepreneurship are an essential factor in economic development and social well-being. They largely stem from the fact that the fruits of these talents and skills can be captured in the short term by those who are directly responsible for them – namely, creators, innovators, and entrepreneurs. Fruitful application and commercialization of the results of this creation requires human resources with extensive training and high skill levels. In a phase of accelerated wealth creation such as the one we may be currently experiencing, competitive pressure on these resources increases their value compared to the value of more basic human capital, which is less well trained and therefore less skilled in the use of new production and organizational technologies. This is a powerful incentive to acquire new skills.

When designing and implementing socially responsible redistribution policies, it must be kept in mind that redistributing income and wealth can only be achieved in an efficient and sustainable manner by enhancing individuals' skills portfolios to increase their value on markets, and thus to their fellow citizens. It is by implementing institutions and mechanisms that promote ongoing, rapid, and orderly adaptation of skill portfolios that governments can best combine wealth creation with responsible and incentivizing income redistribution.

This policy places greater demands on individuals and is thus less politically palatable. Nonetheless, it is the only policy that is socially responsible and compatible with sustained economic development and gains in well-being. The best way to redistribute wealth is to encourage everyone to participate in its creation.

INTERGENERATIONAL ISSUES: GRETA THUNBERG AND THE OCTOGENARIAN (MYSELF)

In a vibrant speech before the September 2019 UN Climate Action Summit in New York, Greta Thunberg, the young environmentalist who has become a spokesperson for her generation, claimed that the older generations of world leaders had stolen her dreams and childhood. Her words tell how angry she was, and indeed is.

Greta Thunberg's Passionate Speech

This is all wrong. I shouldn't be up here. I should be back in school on the other side of the ocean. Yet you all come to us young people for hope. How dare you!

You have stolen my dreams and my childhood with your empty words. And yet I'm one of the lucky ones. People are suffering. People are dying. Entire ecosystems are collapsing. We are in the beginning of a mass extinction, and all you can talk about is money and fairytales of eternal economic growth. How dare you!

For more than 30 years, the science has been crystal clear. How dare you continue to look away and come here saying that you're doing enough, when the politics and solutions needed are still nowhere in sight. With today's emissions levels, our remaining CO_2 budget will be gone in less than 8.5 years.

You say you hear us and that you understand the urgency. But no matter how sad and angry I am, I do not want to believe that. Because if you really understood the situation and still kept on failing to act, then you would be evil. And that I refuse to believe.

The popular idea of cutting our emissions in half in 10 years only gives us a 50% chance of staying below 1.5 degrees [Celsius], and the risk of setting off irreversible chain reactions beyond human control.

Fifty percent may be acceptable to you. But those numbers do not include tipping points, most feedback loops, additional warming hidden by toxic air pollution or the aspects of equity and climate justice. They also rely on my generation sucking hundreds of billions of tons of your CO_2 out of the air with technologies that barely exist.

So a 50% risk is simply not acceptable to us – we who have to live with the consequences.

To have a 67% chance of staying below a 1.5 degrees global temperature rise – the best odds given by the Intergovernmental Panel on Climate Change – the world had 420 gigatonnes of CO_2 left to emit back on Jan. 1st, 2018. Today that figure is already down to less than 350 gigatonnes.

How dare you pretend that this can be solved with just "business as usual" and some technical solutions? With today's emissions levels, that remaining CO_2 budget will be entirely gone within less than 8½ years.

There will not be any solutions or plans presented in line with these figures here today. because these numbers are too uncomfortable. And you are still not mature enough to tell it like it is.

You are failing us. But the young people are starting to understand your betrayal. The eyes of all future generations are upon you. And if you choose to fail us, I say: We will never forgive you.

We will not let you get away with this. Right here, right now is where we draw the line. The world is waking up. And change is coming, whether you like it or not.[24]

The Octogenarian Reply

In an op-ed published in the *Financial Post* in May 2022, I took the role of devil's advocate and challenged, with all due respect, Greta Thunberg's dismal vision.

This is unbelievable. I shouldn't be writing this. I should be retired in a bright calmative environment. And this, after expending sweat and tears contributing to a new age of civilization for future generations, i.e., you.

Yet you keep protesting in the streets like sheep. You pretend to be ignorant and unable to realize your dreams because of me. Empty and cheap words! How dare you!

You say you hunger for action. But limitless potential is already available. The ways and means are at hand for a better world. Yet you fail to put them to work. All you can do is blame others, i.e., me. How dare you!

You are wasting my heritage. For more than 40 years the science of economics has been crystal clear. The keys to growth and prosperity for all have been found. How dare you continue to protest, looking away, pretending that I did not do enough, when the economics and solutions are there at your disposal in plain daylight?

You say there is nothing you can see and nothing you can do. But no matter how sad and angry I am, I don't want to believe that. Because if you fully understood what you could be doing and still kept on failing to act, then you would be unworthy of the legacy your predecessors invested in you. And I refuse to believe that.

Economics is clear: Properly pricing the environment, through significant levies on carbon emissions, affecting all goods and services with no exceptions, is the only effective and efficient way to go. Effective in meeting the objective of a carbon-free world and efficient in minimizing its cost. Independently redistributing fiscal revenues to the lower quintiles of income-earners you so revere is the incentive-compatible way to allow them to support and benefit from this win-win reform while contributing to a cleaner world.

The objective of cutting our emissions in half or even more can be attained only if you decide to roll up your sleeves. And light up your brains. And support those leaders, policies and incentives that will force you and your neighbors to engineer sustainable growth paths. This can be done only if you resolutely demand that *you* do it, not cheaply demand that others do it for you.

You should ask yourself why our precious environment is not properly protected, why it is not already restored, and why the needed policies are not adequately financed? You should counter the Juncker curse – "We all know what to do but we don't know how to get re-elected once we have done it," as Luxembourg's former president Jean-Claude Juncker coined it. Political leaders fear that the pursuit of needed policies, which are necessarily demanding on you and your fellow citizens, will generate a backlash and prevent them from being re-elected. Let you defeat that curse. By urging your friends to be or to support those political leaders showing courage and leadership in setting significant across-the-board levies on carbon emissions. Levies that are demanding on everyone and everything that generates carbon emissions.

The future is bright and full of possibilities. A carbon-neutral world is within reach if you show courage and leadership to make it happen. How dare you pretend that your future is a dead-end bleakish road! You must show the maturity to shape it and then tell it like it can be, hence like it is.

Do not fail my generation. Do not fail my legacy, in you. Do not have blame as your middle name. All future yet unborn generations are looking at you. If you choose to fail us all, you will not be forgiven. You will not get away with this. Right here, right now is where you must draw the line.

        Let your hands shape the future.[25]

7

The Cost of Public Funds and the Governance of Public Projects

This brings us to another major fallacy that is frequently repeated by actors in both the private (competitive) and public (governmental) sectors. In its simplest form, the error appears as follows: since the cost of borrowing or financing is higher in the private sector than in the public sector, the cost of carrying out an activity (production, distribution, the provision of goods and services) will necessarily be lower in the public than in the private sector.[1]

Although it is generally accepted, and indeed observed, that governments can borrow at lower rates than private- or competitive-sector organizations, the error in the above argument is that part of the government's cost of borrowing is hidden from the casual observer of interest rates or yields.

THE REAL COST OF PUBLIC FUNDS

Let us consider two firms, one in the governmental sector and the other in the competitive sector, both of which produce, distribute, and supply the same goods and/or services. The cost to the governmental-sector firm of obtaining credit or capital is lower than that offered to the competitive-sector firm. This is because the former is less risky for lenders, who therefore require a lower rate of return. But why is the cost of financing lower for a governmental-sector firm compared to its competitive counterpart when both are engaged in the same processes and activities, presumably using the same technology and factors of production, and therefore exposed to the same risk factors?

This is because the governmental-sector enterprise belongs to the government, which is ultimately responsible for it and has the right and ability to raise additional taxes to reimburse its lenders if necessary – that is, if its activities and/or projects fail, or, more generally, fall short of expectations. Private- or competitive-sector firms do not have that option. That is why lenders or investors require a higher interest rate.

However, from the point of view of the citizens who are the ultimate customers and taxpayers, the right and power of the government to literally withdraw money from their bank accounts to cover financial distress situations does have a price: it is the option value today of the government right to require and obtain from them additional funds to cover what may, *ex post*, turn out to be bad or unprofitable projects.

Given this loan repayment guarantee, lenders will only require a small risk premium where appropriate, regardless of why or for what projects the government is borrowing and regardless of their contribution to the risk of the government's diversified portfolio of projects and activities. This guarantee allows the government to offer a transaction that is essentially risk-free for lenders, but potentially very risky for taxpayers. The error lies in the fact that this taxpayer-supported cost is dismissed and swept under the carpet.

The differential in interest rates on funds raised by governmental organizations, on the one hand, and private- or competitive-sector organizations, on the other, is fundamentally equal to the value of the government's right and ability to raise additional funds from taxpayers as lenders and investors, even without their "consent." In other words, if the citizens were to grant competitive-sector organizations in good financial standing the right and power to levy "taxes" should they find themselves in dire financial straits, these organizations would be able to raise capital on the same terms as the government. Hence, the claim that the public sector can produce at a lower cost because the government can pay lower interest rates on money it raises is a subtle but clear – and clearly widely held – error.[2]

Consider an example from the private sector. Bombardier president and CEO Pierre Beaudoin questioned the public-private partnership (PPP) model during a debate held at the Milken Institute in Santa Monica, California, in 2010. He was quoted as saying that it costs companies much more than governments to borrow large sums of money and that the private sector is well placed to manage project costs and meet project deadlines, but not, as a rule, to finance projects. He continued by saying that "over a 20-year period, a US$1 billion project is likely to cost an additional US$480 million if it is financed by the private sector rather than public authorities."[3] The error is flagrant.

An example from academia: Christina Pazzanese, in her article "Our Crumbling Infrastructure," writes, "Some observers, like the New York Times columnist Paul Krugman, a liberal economist, have criticized Trump's private investment strategy as unnecessary, given the government's unmatched ability to borrow money on the cheap."[4] Paul Krugman (2008 Nobel Memorial Prize in Economic Sciences) himself writes in a *New York Times* column, "To understand what's going on, it may be helpful to start with what we should be doing. The federal government can indeed borrow very cheaply; meanwhile, we really need to spend money on everything from sewage treatment to transit. The indicated course of action, then, is simple: borrow at those low, low rates, and use the funds raised to fix what needs fixing."[5] Again, the error is flagrant.

Examples from the political arena abound. Almost every day, politicians and business benefactors declare that the government can and should borrow money for private businesses because of the lower interest cost required by lenders. This policy is not only based on false arguments, as discussed above; it also ends up most of the time negatively impacting the economy in two ways. The first is that it tilts the balance toward national or regional "champions" at the expense of all other businesses, including current and future competitors of those champions. The second is that it reduces incentives for efforts, productivity, and growth, due to a perception of unfair competition, in firms that end up not being chosen by politicians and government officials. Crony capitalism is overwhelmingly bad for business.

If decisions must be based on a proper balancing of benefits and costs, it is crucial that the latter, as well as the former, be properly assessed. There is a large academic and professional literature on the social discount rate (SDR) to be used in cost-benefit evaluations of public investments and projects. The SDR blends the social rate of time preference, the average gross rate of return on capital in the economy, the interest rate on foreign borrowing, and an adequate risk assessment. There is an even larger and more general literature on the evaluation of public and private investments, including certainty-equivalent valuation and real-option valuation methodologies. Although related to those literatures, the current chapter puts the emphasis on the cost of money, and by extension, on the cost of public funds, which is a central element of investment and project evaluation.[6]

There is a large gap between the interest rates at which governments can borrow and *both* the weighted average SDR (generally estimated at around 7 to 8 per cent in real terms) and the private-sector cost of capital (generally estimated closer to 10 to 12 per cent in real terms). The argument that using the government's borrowing rate to evaluate projects and investments is wrong and will lead to too many projects, and too many long-term projects in particular (if recording and valuation of costs and benefits are done properly), being approved goes through whether you think the correct discount rate is the SDR or the private-sector cost of capital.

AUCTIONING GOVERNMENT BUSINESS ASSISTANCE PROGRAMS

For the same reasons, we can be suspicious of government grant, loan, and loan-guarantee programs, and even of public equity investments in private firms – particularly to the extent that they rely on the aforementioned rationale that the government faces lower financing costs than the private sector.

One transparent way to proceed in the context of this type of program would be to auction off specific government assistance projects, thus transferring to a local or international private financial consortium the responsibility for honouring the grant, loan, or capital injection. This consortium would assume responsibility for the outlays and the benefit from repayments at levels and under conditions determined by the government assistance project, in exchange for a premium received from the government.

As the conditions attached to these assistance, subsidy, and equity participation projects are naturally more favourable for the companies than similar funding obtained from financial markets, this premium would represent the compensation required by the consortium tasked with assuming the government's commitments.

From the government's perspective, the premium to emerge from the auction would be the best estimate of the public cost of the assistance or support project – this is, the expenditure to be recorded in the budget. Alternatively, the government could choose to take out an insurance policy with private insurers/investors, who would assume the risk of repayment of the assistance previously borne by taxpayers.

The government is neither mandated nor competent to play the market with taxpayers' money. The main advantage of auctioning government assistance is to cut out the ubiquitous risk of a creeping collusive capitalism at the expense not only of taxpayers, but also of the companies themselves, no matter how grandiloquent the intentions expressed by the government and other stakeholders may be. There are better ways to ensure the incentive-based development of successful businesses by providing them with tools to use in managing the real and systematic risks they face.

TOWARD A MORE RESPONSIBLE AND RIGOROUS MANAGEMENT OF PUBLIC FUNDS

But the problem in public finance (the wrongful evaluation of the cost of public capital, and the misevaluated business support programs) runs deeper. The management of public funds have been responsible or ethical to varying degrees in recent decades. Part of the problem lies with inefficient accounting practices. Government employee pensions are a good example. Many governments guarantee all or part of their pension payment obligations to their employees. The guaranteed portion is essentially risk-free for employees, unless the government declares bankruptcy.[7] If these guaranteed obligations are unfunded, best accounting practices (not an obligation) suggest governments record as expenses these future obligations using a fair market interest rate. But if the obligations are funded by taxpayers, accounting standards allow governments to discount them based on the expected rate of returns on risky investment. By expensing the government annual service cost at an inflated discount rate, governments undervalue their real annual compensation costs, which is a disservice to everyone: the taxpayers as well as the private-sector employers competing for the same employees. Best would be to expense the transactions at their real cost to taxpayers under accrual accounting, which does not prevent taxpayers from funding these obligations on a cash basis on the expectation of risky returns. Once risky returns materialized, taxpayers will be compensated through investment income. This way, taxpayers are compensated for the financial risks they bear, and transactions are recorded at their real value, leading to better policy decisions.

In recent years, due to the COVID-19 pandemic, all governments increased their deficit considerably in order to mitigate the pandemic's disastrous effects on activity and employment in various sectors of the economy. In Canada, for example, a projected deficit of some $25 billion in 2020 has risen to an astonishing level of nearly $400 billion for the federal government alone, and much higher at the national level when provincial and municipal deficits are counted. The prevailing wisdom is that this does not really matter because the interest rate charged on government borrowing is, apparently, very low. Another flagrant error.

The real or true interest rate is much higher than it appears, even in these "non-economic" times. Most of these loans to governments were from central banks, effectively meaning that money is being printed. This is because private lenders, who are generally eager to profit from the generous terms of government lending (irrespective of any uncompensated risks transferred to taxpayers), are not tripping over themselves to buy government bonds. Why? Because, first, the risk is too high and, second, letting central banks print money for the government eliminates the bad publicity suffered by lenders for calling in this government debt. Central banks are not true lenders, because they could simply erase government debt from their ledgers.

The enormous increase in government debt may be sending the signal that this debt is safe and, apparently, cheap. If governments can allow themselves to incur such massive debt to fight COVID-19, why could they not do the same to fight climate change, to invest more in health care and education (at all levels), to meet our crying need for revamped infrastructures, etc.? Recall the warning: economics is the dismal science par excellence – needs are infinite, but resources are limited. Rather than resulting in a more co-operative world, the decline in fiscal discipline is laying the groundwork for a future of aggressive political battles and social upheaval, at the expense of social democratic ideals.

The way to achieve an optimal public investment portfolio is to follow evaluation methodologies that are rooted in sound economics and finance and to apply them as rigorously as possible. Unfortunately, too many government departments and para-public agencies suffer from the same disease: they are political entities with a high aversion to the rigour of financial analysis. One thing is certain: hiding costs by transferring risks onto the backs of docile taxpayers without providing or at least assessing adequate compensation one way or another is not the right way to go.

The mismanagement and fallacious analysis will eventually backfire. One recent example of this dire predictive statement can be found in the report on the tragic financial situation of (bankrupt) Newfoundland and Labrador after years of blatantly negligent management of public finances.[8]

THE EVALUATION AND GOVERNANCE OF PUBLIC PROJECTS

Governance of private and public organizations and companies lies at the core of the competition-based social democracy model. The scope of this subject is vast, but the central argument is that good governance is the outcome of competition between organizations once their different mandates have been taken into account. Let us consider here the application of this matter to the choice between GOC (government operations control), IOC (internal operations control – in the case of a private project), and PPP (public-private partnership or private-private partnership) for the delivery of a major project. Putting aside the finer details, we must bear in mind that a large project will necessarily be delivered in a situation of imperfect and incomplete information.

Once we have characterized the process of deciding whether to proceed with a project and have chosen between the GOC/IOC and PPP modes, we turn our attention to the role of competition in these decisions. For the sake of simplicity, let us consider a public investment project.

Information relevant to a project, or more broadly to an organization, may be perfect or imperfect, and imperfect information may be complete or incomplete. Information is imperfect if the realization of possible situations, or "states of nature," at various times or periods is partly random. Information is imperfect but complete if all participants have the same imperfect knowledge of the relevant elements, and hence share the same probability distribution over states of nature. The realized state is ultimately observed by all participants. What makes a contract complete is the knowledge of all future events (in the short and long term) which could, if they occurred, trigger actions or reactions as provided in the contract on the part of the principal or contracting authority (public sector) and the agent or contractor (private partner). If this knowledge is unavailable or too costly, the contract will necessarily be incomplete.

There are, therefore, two conceptions of incompleteness or incomplete information, both of which are very important in the context of major projects, whether they are carried out in PPP or in conventional mode. First, the information may be asymmetric, that is, not available to all partners, some of whom are better informed than others as to certain aspects relevant to the progress of the project. Second, events that are not anticipated or provided for by the contract may trigger opportunistic behaviour on the part of one partner or the other.

For all intents and purposes, any contract spanning several decades is necessarily incomplete. Moreover, if there are asymmetric information structures, then, by definition, not all relevant variables are observed or observable by both parties. Incentive mechanisms as an integral part of contracts not only ensure effective risk management, but also and mostly serve to counteract the negative effects of information asymmetries by raising the congruence of the stakeholders' interests.

Incentive mechanisms will cover the entire duration of the project, from the design and construction to the operations and maintenance activities. In fact, when these two sets of activities are linked, the PPP contract comes into its own. Outlays on operation and maintenance will be burdensome if design and construction do not satisfy the contract's performance requirements. There is therefore a great interest in ensuring that the private partner exercises maximum diligence during the design/build phase to adequately meet these requirements.

Imperfect information is also incomplete if it is impossible to predict or too costly for the contract to cover all states of nature that may occur in the future. Follow-through for this type of unforeseen or excluded event is therefore problematic, as certain events may engender renegotiations that are advantageous to one party, or both. In these cases, it is necessary to assign a form of decision-making authority (property rights, or residual property rights) specifying the partner who decides what action is to be taken and/or identifies a process of (re)negotiation. This assignment and the conditions for exercising residual decision-making rights must be carefully delineated in order to best curb potentially opportunistic behaviour (holdup) by the partners.

This second type of incomplete information also refers to unforeseen contingencies, a concept used in the economic analysis of information, insurance, and contracts. Incomplete information of the second type should certainly be considered when drafting contracts, but not to the exclusion of incomplete information of the first type.

With regard to unforeseen events, the European Council has stated that

> The solvency margin is the additional capital reserve that insurance companies have to create as a buffer against unforeseen events. The general aim of the proposals is to provide improved protection for policyholders by increasing the capital resources of insurance companies and by ensuring more efficient state supervision of insurance companies. Higher solvency margins or risk buffers not only increase confidence in the performance of insurance companies, they also generally reduce system-related risks on financial markets. Efficient, viable insurance companies do much to enable the opportunities of the single market to be perfected and exploited to the full.[9]

We may also quote Donald Rumsfeld, who, as US secretary of defence, gave a popular definition of the concept of unforeseen events or unknown elements in February 2002: "There are known knowns. There are things we know we know. We also know there are known unknowns. That is to say we know there are some things we do not know. But there are also unknown unknowns, the ones we don't know we don't know ... And if one looks throughout the history of our country and other free countries, it is the latter category that tend to be the difficult ones."[10] Unforeseen events that are not included in the contract are those "unknown unknowns" that Rumsfeld is talking about.

The organizational or contractual problems posed by imperfect information, particularly when it is also incomplete of the first and/or second type, are similar in all organizations, whether their implementation mode is one of the various conventional GOC types or PPP.

In the short term, a well-formulated PPP contract must account for the presence of incomplete information of the first type (private, confidential, asymmetrical). For instance, the level of effort and behaviour invested by the private partner in carrying out the work, while it is known only to the private partner, is of great interest to the principal.

The contract must also account for the presence of incomplete information of the second type because characterizing the evolution of all possible situations or states of nature, in particular over a period of several decades, could be very complex, making it too costly or even impossible to draw up a contract covering all possible contingencies.[11]

From the outset, this type of contract should envision the actions, commitments, and responsibilities of each party in all possible situations in the short and long term. Rather than drawing up such a contract (if that were even possible), the parties could agree on either a decision-making authority (residual property rights) granted to one of the parties in situations not explicitly provided for in the contract, or on an arbitration process for any conflicts that these unforeseen situations might create.[12]

In the case of well-defined contingencies, the contract stipulates the actions, rights, and responsibilities of the partners. For example, a partnership agreement could explicitly provide that payment to the private partner only begins once the project has been provisionally accepted and that this date is established by an independent certifying body, a third party chosen by both parties whose mandate is to certify that the building and facilities meet the requirements set out in the partnership agreement. Since the term of the contract is predetermined and fixed, any delay in delivering the work reduces total payments to the private partner.

A partnership contract normally provides that payments from the public to the private sector be made over the term of the partnership and that they are conditional on the verified attainment of the established performance criteria and requirements (incentive mechanisms). The contract also provides mechanisms and conditions for renegotiation and dispute resolution if unforeseen events occur.

Again, it is important to stress and understand that these contractual problems are not specific to the PPP mode but are also present in the conventional or GOC mode, albeit in a somewhat different form. It must also be borne in mind that the whole exercise is about how the project is to be delivered, and not about the project itself, which is the same regardless of the delivery mode.[13]

This is where we see the full power of competition among private partners, agents, or contractors, and where the PPP contract comes into its own. A private partner's inclination to exaggerate the level of risk and thus inflate the risk premium may cause it to lose the project to a competitor. And the contract binds the private partner by imposing severe constraints on any attempt to demand *ex post* compensation not provided for in the contract in order to meet both expected yields to shareholders and timely repayment to the bank.

A *holdup* situation may even arise when one of the parties to a transaction or relationship must make costly efforts and investments, such as skills development, that are specific to the relationship, while the other party has the opportunity to benefit without assuming, or even contributing to, the costs. An investment is said to be specific to a given relationship when there is little or no possibility of earning a return on that investment outside of the relationship. Indeed, once specific efforts or investments have been made by one party, the other party could take advantage to redefine the terms of the relationship and under-compensate its partner for the latter's specific investments, since by definition these investments have little or no value outside the relationship between the two parties involved.

But it is precisely the role of contracts to protect the party responsible for the efforts or investments in question from the opportunism of the other party to under-compensate, *ex post*, the party responsible for these investments. For this reason, there is a provision that the partner responsible for the efforts will be compensated if a given level of performance is achieved. The contract protects this party against opportunistic behaviour by the other party. This *holdup* situation may affect either partner in a relationship, the principal or the agent.

Thus, three major factors come into play when comparing GOC to PPP. First, under PPP a call for tenders for a project is normally structured on the basis of a performance specification, whereas for conventional contracts, the proposal is made on the basis of detailed plans. As a result, the main PPP contractor has direct control over the design and conception and can therefore influence the direction of the project and ensure that it does not impose undue cost constraints during the delivery phase. In the traditional mode, project design and the drafting of plans are typically independent of project implementation. The builder and other companies involved in delivering and managing the asset cannot participate in this phase. Second, the structure of the private consortium ensures that the main subcontractors are generally known at the time of the proposal and chosen on a number of criteria that go well beyond the lowest price, which is the general rule in public contracts. Third, PPP project managers are generally free to adopt risk-mitigation measures that are unavailable to public-sector managers.

It is also important to note here the extent of the financial framework incentives the PPP consortium must put in place to guarantee its performance. In addition to the contractual requirements of the partnership agreement, the financing structure offers oversight guarantees that have no equivalent in the conventional GOC mode.

Once again, it is competition between partners, agents, or private contractors that encourages them to properly assess the risks, challenges, and pitfalls of the project. They can define the most appropriate governance structure and formulate a winning proposal. Competition is of particular importance here, revealing the full power of a PPP contract.

There is a persistent misunderstanding of the importance of risk and risk sharing in society and about how competitive markets price these through risk premiums. As with the other alleged virtues or vices of competition, this is a complex issue.

One such aspect of risk sharing, which is particularly relevant in the context of the CSD model, is undoubtedly the sharing and pricing of risk in private finance initiatives for public infrastructure or PPPs. While the terms "private finance initiative" and "public-private partnership" are well-known, it is more appropriate to speak of competitive-governmental partnership in the context of the CSD model.

Risk refers to the randomness and probability distribution of results, more precisely to the volatility of results around their average value: more volatility implies a greater probability that the actual result will be relatively far from the expected result, and more volatility means more risk. More rigorously, total risk is composed of diversifiable risk, which does not need to be compensated since it is relatively easy to eliminate through diversification, and systematic risk, which cannot be eliminated and therefore represents a cost requiring compensation. It is important but very challenging, if even possible, to understand the sources of volatility and to manage those risks.[14]

It is a fundamental role of financial markets to measure risks – for example, through measures of correlation or co-variance (beta) between the various risk factors – and to price these risks as a premium on top of the time preference, or risk-free, rate. In a risk-transfer agreement, one party assumes the risk – that is, the possibility that the outcome will be significantly lower or higher than the expected outcome – in exchange for a risk premium paid by the other party, which can then consider its outcome to be certain or almost certain.

What does optimal risk sharing mean in a competitive-government partnership?[15] Optimal risk sharing is partly a matter of transferring risk from the most risk-averse to the least risk-averse agents, and partly a matter of transferring risk from the agents least able to manage it to those most able. Managerial ability here refers to competencies, capabilities, and incentives to either increase the probability of positive outcomes and reduce that of negative outcomes or to increase the benefits and reduce the losses incurred whatever the outcome.

In the CSD model, the party assuming the risk will normally be the competitive sector and the party divesting the risk will be the governmental sector. In other cases, however, when the governmental sector acts as an insurer (as in the cases of unemployment insurance, education, and health care), it assumes risks that individuals cannot assume. In each transaction, the buyer and the seller share the gain from realizing the transaction, in other words the transfer of risk: the seller who sheds risk avoids the risky outcome in exchange for a premium paid to the buyer, who then faces a larger part of the outcome uncertainty or volatility.

In risk-sharing arrangements, both parties to the transaction will bear a share of the systematic risk and will receive competitive compensation accordingly. The important point to understand here is that, like other goods and services, risks are traded at a competitive price. An efficient competitive transfer or exchange of risks is a major source of welfare gains. Hence the significant efforts to innovate and the substantial resources allotted to risk management, risk transfer, and risk sharing in modern societies. It is central to the CSD model.

MODULARITY, MULTI-SOURCE PROCUREMENT, AND INNOVATION

To overcome the adverse effects that the status quo has on the welfare of populations that end up bound by it, we require competition and modularity. Competition, modularity, and innovation are interrelated processes.

Modularity is a broad concept that can be applied to many situations: modularity in design, production, and use. The underlying idea is to decompose the final product into several subsystems that can be designed and built independently. These subsystems or components are less complex than the system as a whole.

Modular production has two dimensions: the first refers to the design and production of a given good and the second to the organizational aspect. As a concept, modularity is relatively old. Modular production organizations can be found in the vast industrial standardization movements that occurred in the automotive and railway industries over a century ago.

A modular product often gives rise to modular organization. The relationships between the components of the finished products are mediated by their interfaces. An architecture is said to be perfectly modular when the interfaces are perfectly decoupled (i.e., a modification to one of the modules connected by the interface does not necessitate a modification to the other elements connected by this interface) and perfectly standardized (i.e., accepting connection with a wide variety of components). At the opposite end of the spectrum are integrated finished products. In terms of cost and efficiency, a perfectly modular architecture is ideal.

Modularity in the production of PSGS makes it possible to foster the optimization of the production and distribution of these goods and services. Once again, the goal is to adhere to an organizational structure that guarantees the right to raise economic challenges and the expression of economic freedom. Those guarantees emerge from competition between producers and distributors of public and social, as well as private, goods and services.

With modularity comes multi-source procurement and innovation. Innovation, not only technological but also organizational, must be based on an explicit process in which experimentation and change are seen as normal, even frequent or continuous. In order to reduce the costs of implementing innovations, and by extension, of promoting the emergence of an innovative society, the governmental sector must explicitly develop a multi-source policy for the attribution of contracts.

Multi-source procurement means that an organization in the competitive sector cannot acquire a monopoly or the power to significantly dominate the production, distribution, and/or provision of a PSGS over an extended span of time. In order to foster competition among suppliers and to identify those capable of achieving outstanding results in the production, distribution, and delivery of PSGS, a certain level of modularity and experimentation must always be present. This allows for the evaluation of new means and modalities, so that best practices can be updated and implemented as often as possible.

Multi-source procurement can be put into practice at the level of contract policy between the governmental sector and the competitive sector, but the management of such a portfolio of contracts by the governmental sector is problematic, and, more often than not, it can be delegated to the principal competitive contractor. The governmental sector then manages a general contract with one or more partners from the competitive sector who must put in place a multi-source procurement process at the level of contract performance for the production and distribution of the basket of PSGS provided for in the contract.

These developments suggest that there is a fundamental difference between the adoption of a new technology and its successful implementation,[16] while sharply delineating the significant risks and uncertainties inherent in switching from one technology to another as well as from one organizational mode to another. Clearly, innovations are quite unpredictable, and their adoption are even more inherently risky or uncertain. In light of the fact that many economists consider innovations, both technological and organizational, to be the main drivers of economic growth,[17] their inherently risky nature is both interesting and disconcerting.

A plethora of examples illustrate how hard it is to recognize the value of inventions.[18] Consider, for instance, the case of the laser. In addition to its uses in measurement, navigation, chemistry, music, surgery, and printing, it has also revolutionized the telecommunications industry with fibre optics. However, when it was invented at Bell Labs, the company's lawyers and patent agents did not initially deem it worthy of a patent application. There are similar stories about other major inventions, such as the telephone, radio, and transistor. In 1876, Western Union rejected an option to buy Bell's telephone patent at a low price, considering that its long-term interest was to focus on the telegraph, the core of its business and market at the time. Marconi believed that his invention, radio, would only be useful when communication by wire was impossible, such as for ship-to-ship or ship-to-shore transmission. One journalist even suggested that its main and probably only use would be to transmit Sunday sermons. IBM considered getting out of computers in 1949, reasoning that the global computer market would be saturated with some fifteen units. The inventor of the transistor thought that his invention could be useful in improving hearing aid systems. More recently, Matt Ridley recalls that Ken Olsen, founder and president of Digital Equipment Corporation, a pioneering company in minicomputers (which merged first with Compaq and then HP), said in 1977, "There is no reason for any individual to have a computer in his home."[19] And Steve Balmer, CEO of Microsoft, said in 2007, "There's no chance that the iPhone is going to get any significant market share. No chance."[20]

There are many more examples of the challenges of delivering an invention, an innovation, or, more generally, a technology that has been poorly understood or assessed. All the examples given above illustrate the difficulty of predicting future technological advances, which is itself a generic concept that should be understood as covering both the adoption (or dissemination) and application of inventions and innovations in organizations.

The multi-source procurement applied in the production and delivery of PSGS can be understood as follows: during a first stage, the governmental sector has recourse to a call for tenders to award a contract (to provide college education, for example). It is likely that, even in the presence of a policy explicitly encouraging the emergence of firms in the sector, relatively few suppliers will be able to submit a tender (say, ten or so). It would be a mistake to allocate the entire contract to the firm with the lowest price or best value for money. Indeed, this situation would echo the familiar scene of a public monopoly, while competition, modularity, and experimentation would be relegated to the status of a pipe dream.

During the second stage, the governmental sector must allocate and distribute contracts to a relatively large number of bidders (the best bidder, however, receives the lion's share). Whenever possible, analysis and inspection of the production and supply methods used by the successful bidders will increase the competitiveness of the other bidders. The governmental sector thus provides support to its suppliers, even if it does not have a direct interest in doing so, at least in the short term. However, incentive mechanisms could be used to ensure that the best suppliers transfer their innovations to competitors without fear and in exchange for an appropriate level of compensation.

The multi-source procurement system will, in some cases, create a trade-off between economies of scale and benchmarks of suppliers' performances, sustaining a strong level of competition over the long term and ensuring that prices are on average low and quality high. In short, this system will ensure that the production and distribution of

PSGS remain fluid and in a state of perpetual change – and that they do not fall into the hands of a private monopoly.

Modularity and multi-source procurement is a central feature of the CSD model. The golden rule is to determine the objectives of the program or contract and let the competitive-sector provider or contractor determine by what means the objectives will be pursued, met, or surpassed.

8

Free Trade and National Security

We briefly discussed the role of free trade when discussing policy 6 in the ten-point model for NCC proposed in chapter 3. We will not repeat here the elements raised there.

The globalization of markets and the internationalization of cultures are often held responsible for destroying jobs in developed countries due to outsourcing, offshoring, and imports; for encouraging the exploitation of workers in developing countries by unscrupulous entrepreneurs for the benefit of businesses, investors, and consumers in developed countries; and, finally, for undermining food security with food imports, environmental security through transportation-related GHG emissions, and, more generally, national security by the forging of global, and therefore multilateral, supply chains.

All of these claims are fundamentally misguided, founded as they are on ignorance and misunderstanding of three of the most important elements of modern economic history: the trustworthiness of competitive prices and their coordinating and incentivizing nature, opportunity costs, and comparative advantage.

Beneath these criticisms is the confusion between the impacts of free trade policies and those of other, variously flawed economic policies whose impacts are too often incorrectly attributed to the expansion of free trade. Similarly, the impacts of phenomena not explicitly accounted for, such as technological change and evolving competitive pressures, are too quickly laid at the feet of free trade. In other words, it is easy to blame free trade for "negative" outcomes that are due not to trade policy but to other policies or phenomena, the unfavourable effects of which parallel and often predate it. These parallel effects reverse the changes brought about by free trade. Sometimes, the pre-existing harms to the economy can be exacerbated by free trade. The counterfactual – What would have happened in the absence of changes to the conditions of free trade? – is often poorly modelled, setting the stage for free trade to be the scapegoat for damages that are actually attributable to ill-advised crony capitalism.

While empirical studies are currently all the rage in economics, we must never forget that an empirical study is only as good as its theoretical underpinnings. The theoretical model must be rigorous and appropriate – including a transparent counterfactual model in which causality is explicitly defined.[1] We might even coin the term "empiriness" to mirror the "mathiness" described and denounced by Paul Romer: "Mathiness [or empiriness, in our usage] lets academic politics masquerade as science. Like mathematical theory, mathiness uses a mixture of words and symbols, but instead of making tight links, it leaves ample room for slippage between statements in the languages of words as opposed to symbols, and between statements with theoretical as opposed to empirical content. Because it is difficult to distinguish mathiness from mathematical theory, the market for lemons tells us that the market for mathematical theory might collapse, leaving only mathiness as entertainment that is worth little but cheap to produce."[2]

Confounding the impacts of various phenomena and policies is a common error, frequently agenda driven and intentional. This is a sophisticated variant on the *post hoc, ergo propter hoc* error, a sophism or cognitive bias that consists of treating as a cause of a given phenomenon that which merely precedes it. We encounter this error under various guises in a number of academic contributions, in which a change in the conditions of free trade – typically a new agreement or a significant shift in international trade with a strong emphasis on imports – is identified as the cause of various changes in the economy (transitions in employment and wages, factory closures, changes in some tax revenues, societal transformations, child labour, and other calamities, etc.).

Popular misconceptions commonly arise from this error. A cause-and-effect relationship is inferred without due consideration of the potential impact of other aspects of economic policy, which may be poorly designed with the socio-economic challenges that existed prior to the "opening to free trade" event, or even concurrent with it.

Associating these undesirable, even disastrous, effects with trade policy is clearly indicative of a flawed representation (theoretical model) of reality. Too often, alleged measures of the impact of free trade in fact reflect the combined effects of correlated causal factors with insufficient attention being paid to the appropriateness of the underlying theory. This yields empirical results that, while "statistically significant," are specious, misleading, and fundamentally of little value.

Often, any difficulties or negative effects associated with free trade in a given country can be attributed to some relatively anomalous and unexplained situation in that country. Therefore, these analyses should not be used to detract from free trade, but rather to learn about and identify economic policy recommendations to reform the existing policies responsible for the undesirable situation. To summarize, in order to produce all potential benefits, a free trade policy may often require changes to some current economic policies that are impeding a given country's ability to profit from it. Not realizing this is a symptom of popular misconception.[3]

THE GOAL OF FOOD SECURITY OR SOVEREIGNTY

In developed countries particularly, the goal of food security or sovereignty translates into various supply management programs and/or generous farm subsidies to the detriment of consumers and taxpayers. To bolster their arguments, proponents of food sovereignty argue that it kills two birds with one stone by also reducing GHG emissions.

Boyer and Charlebois estimated that, in 2007, supply management cost Quebec families some $575 million per year, or $300 per family of four.[4] The argument for food sovereignty has a certain appeal, but it is nonetheless fallacious and dangerous.

The desire to purchase local goods is a matter of taste and a choice any consumer has the right to make. Similarly, there is nothing wrong with producers, whether collectively or individually, promoting their products by playing up their homegrown character. It's a matter of marketing and competition. Issues arise, however, when "buying local" becomes economic policy. This is especially true in that the reactions of trading partners could be very negative.

Proponents of buying local trumpet their desire to support the local economy and claim they are willing to pay more for some locally produced goods, even if similar products are available for less. Would it not make more sense for them to choose the cheaper alternatives and allocate their savings to purchasing other local goods, such as cultural products, for example, or even supporting local charities? These unrealized expenditures represent the opportunity costs of buying local at a higher price than necessary.

Every economic production activity or consumption decision carries an opportunity cost that must be properly evaluated: the opportunity cost of buying local must always be compared with the value of an alternative purchase, including the social and economic value of the alternative and the potential savings.

THE GOAL OF ENVIRONMENTAL SECURITY

This type of fallacy also besets the pursuit of environmental security. We have known the solution to environmental destruction for a long time: define and impose an appropriate competitive price on pollution and eliminate pet projects as well as regulations and other micropolicies or control measures that pop up left and right and are systematically designed to impose the bulk of their cost on others.[5]

We often hear that our lifestyle depends on perpetual growth, while the planet's resources are limited. This is false. This belief has risen repeatedly throughout history, only to be repudiated each time. In 1865, William Stanley Jevons, one of the best economists of his time, expressed concern about the disappearance of forests – and later, about the depletion of England's coal reserves.[6] This was also the discredited position taken by the Club of Rome during the 1970s.[7] Innovation, markets, and competitive prices have successfully dealt with all the threats of natural resource depletion confronting humanity in the past. Growth is driven by humanity's capacity for invention and innovation, scientific and technological progress, and improvements to old and new products and services – our scope for action is immense and continues to expand.

We saw above how free trade and climate change policies can be not only compatible, but mutually reinforcing. There is still a need for rigorous analyses to identify barriers erected by cronyism and vested private and public interests, so we can deliver sound policies at a cost that is not inflated by "pet projects."

THE DYNAMICS OF FREE TRADE: COMPARATIVE ADVANTAGE AND (NASH) CHOICE EQUILIBRIUM

In every defence of a specific industry, whether well-intentioned or not, we always find a fundamental imbalance between the clearly identified and narrowly targeted interests of some, who are able to hire lobbyists to fight for their cases, and a greater but more diffuse interest spread across the entire economy and population. Ultimately, we observe the victory of populism over competence.

A serious effort must be made to consolidate domestic markets – as they are often splintered by intra-national barriers to the mobility of goods, services, and labour – and to open up as much as possible to the vast international market so that we can profit from opportunities created by free trade agreements. To do this, it needs to be said that international trade at competitive prices, just like intra-national inter-regional trade, can and must be expanded for the good of all. At the same time, it is necessary to promote intra- and international trade that is more secure against unilateral protectionist actions by governments.

It is not the interests of firms and workers in specific industries that are to be defended, but rather the principles and mechanisms of healthy competition that must underlie international trade – again, just as in the case of intra-national and inter-regional trade. Targeted and protectionist defences of the interests of businesses and workers in a particular industry are always detrimental to companies and workers in other industries. Similarly, subsidies to some industries or firms are taxes on other industries and firms.

Stand on a street corner and ask a hundred passers-by to explain the difference between nuclear fusion and nuclear fission; you'll be lucky if two understand the question. You might be right to conclude that 98 per cent know nothing about nuclear energy. The case of international trade is similar. Ask a hundred passers-by to explain the link between trade deficit, foreign investment, and the exchange rate; if even one can, it would be your lucky day. Economics may at times be as complex as nuclear physics.

To understand the link, you must first understand comparative (or relative) advantage, the role of the exchange rate, the concepts of trade deficit or surplus, and foreign (or cross-border) investment deficit or surplus.

Comparative Advantage

It is too often forgotten that international trade is simply a logical extension of inter-regional trade and interpersonal exchanges. The same arguments underly their positive effects on the development and enhancement of social wealth and well-being. We all have an interest in specializing in the production of goods in which we have a comparative advantage and trading with others for the rest.

For two centuries, the understanding of comparative advantage, as formulated by the English economist David Ricardo in 1817,[8] has been at the heart of trade liberalization, phenomenal wealth creation, exceptional and inclusive economic and social growth, striking improvements in human welfare, and sweeping poverty eradication. This is the most compelling and powerful argument against the private interests of anti-trade groups at the regional, inter-regional, and international levels, no matter how eloquent their arguments.

By reallocating production, the well-being of both countries involved in a trade can be increased when it is done by way of an exchange occurring at competitive prices. This argument, which is a fundamental result of modern economic analysis, is valid at all levels of competitiveness (or absolute advantage) in both countries. Even if one country were more efficient than the other in producing both goods, both countries would benefit from opening their domestic markets to international trade and allowing their respective economies to adjust to international prices. The implications of this theory are immediate, but relatively counter-intuitive. It is not the absolute advantages of a country that matter, but rather its comparative (or relative) advantages. It is important to emphasize that all countries benefit from this trade, regardless of their absolute levels of competitiveness. These same countries will also benefit from opening their domestic markets to trade and allowing their respective economies to adjust to internationally competitive prices.

The argument that a trade deficit in one product or basket of products will generate net payments that leave the country to primarily benefit foreigners reflects a serious misunderstanding of how international trade works. Some people generally fear the application of competitive processes to the production and distribution of public and social, as well as private, goods and services, not only at the domestic but also at the international level.

However, the significant growth in international trade in recent decades has been a major contributor to improvements in collective economic well-being and to cultural and social development. Recall Amartya Sen's characterization of *social inclusion* in chapter 2 as a shared social experience, an active participation, an equality of opportunities, and a basic level of well-being for all citizens. The same reasoning applies to intra-national trade between regions.

In response to the mathematician Stanislaw Ulam, who challenged him to "name a proposition, from the social sciences, that would be both true and non-trivial," Paul A. Samuelson, the 1970 Nobel laureate in economics, countered by invoking the notion of comparative advantage: "That [comparative advantage] is logically true need not be argued before a mathematician; that it is not trivial is attested by the thousands of important and intelligent men who have never been able to grasp the doctrine for themselves or to believe it after it was explained to them."[9]

(Nash) Choice Equilibrium

It is not easy to identify the comparative advantages of countries, regions, or individuals a priori. Furthermore, these advantages may change over time as countries and regions develop and individuals acquire new skills. In more technical terms, comparative advantages are expressed using national or regional production potential for reallocating resources between the production of different products and services and reflecting on the characteristics of a country's available natural, institutional, and human resources at a given point in time. Obviously, these resources evolve: human resources can migrate from one region to another, institutional resources can be imitated, and endowments in natural resources can change as a function of past and present prospecting efforts.

All things considered, comparative advantages depend on dynamic and adaptive prospecting efforts (investment), institutional developments (rule of law, property rights, contract law, human rights, social and physical infrastructure), and the acquisition and transferability of skills (education). Determining who (country, region, individual) decides to do what, given what others (countries, regions, individuals) are doing, is a complex process. We can well imagine that these decisions could yield a Nash equilibrium in which each country, region, or individual optimizes its development, given its perception of its partners' and competitors' development and of the resources available to it.

One thing is certain: rationality in a country's decision making requires a comparative evaluation of how to allocate scarce resources to the many potential consumption, training, and investment options available to it on the basis of its actual and potential comparative advantage. These actual and potential comparative advantages ultimately determine the comparative advantages of tomorrow. China's comparative advantages today are not the same as they were in 1950 (under Mao Zedong) or 1980 (Deng Xiaoping). This is true for all regions.

Analysis of these partly exogenous and partly endogenous shifts in economic plates can and must also account for concerted policy interventions from governments at the group level (countries and regions). However, international free trade is consistently a positive element of this analysis. We would not want to be obligated to cut ties with others in order to acquire one or several specific skills given the constraints we are under. Quite the opposite: this kind of isolation would simply impose more constraints. By the same token, we would not want to have to cut ourselves off regionally or nationally in order to develop our comparative advantage given the constraints we are under. Again, quite the opposite is true.

As is the case for individuals, the dynamic development of a region's comparative advantage can and should be grounded in an explicit and unreserved participation in the world of free trade. Ultimately, this type of development, which is simultaneously modern and ambitious, is attainable at any level (national, regional, individual, and transnationally). But to benefit from it, we need intelligence and courage. Intelligence in choosing programs, policies, modalities, and mechanisms – that is, the means that favour the achievement of our ambitions – and the courage to pursue these means.

TRADE DEFICIT, FOREIGN INVESTMENT, AND THE EXCHANGE RATE

Examining any country's international trade data always reveals some sectors or goods and services with a negative trade balance and others with a positive balance. No country has a positive trade balance for all goods and services, and no country should strive for that. Furthermore, the sectoral goods and services trade balance (positive or negative) must be considered jointly with the overall trade balance. This includes the balance of financial transactions (loans) and foreign direct investment, meaning both the balance of direct investment abroad (by nationals) and direct investment at home (by foreigners). Their sum constitutes the balance of payments, for which "equilibrium pressures" both determine and are determined by the exchange rate. In other words, the trade balance for a product or basket of products cannot be considered in isolation. As mentioned above, the argument that a trade deficit in one product or basket of products will generate net payments that leave the country to primarily benefit foreigners reflects a serious misunderstanding of how international trade works. Here is why.

Consider a trade deficit (imports higher than exports of goods and services, including tourism), on the one hand, and a foreign investment surplus (total inbound investment from abroad higher than total outbound investment), on the other. These two, taken together, form the head and tail of a coin. They are glued together with a special adhesive: the exchange rate. The exchange rate is the amount of, say, US dollars that you can buy with one Canadian dollar; it is also expressed as the amount of Canadian dollars that an American can buy with one US dollar. Obviously, each rate is the reciprocal of the other.

The trade balance, the foreign investment balance, and the exchange rate are intimately connected and cannot be analyzed independently. In other words, any one of them cannot be explained in isolation without reference to the other two. They are always systematically in equilibrium and their respective values are determined jointly. Here is how.

Let us assume for simplicity that there are only two countries, the United States and Canada. When Canadians visit the United States, they must "buy" US dollars and "sell" Canadian dollars. Similarly, the Canadian importer of US goods and services (exported from the United States) must buy US dollars by selling Canadian dollars. When Canadians invest in the United States (buying a condo, a factory, treasury bills, or stocks), they must buy US dollars by selling Canadian dollars. If we were to reverse these three examples, the same would be true of American visitors, importers, and investors.

Thus, there is a supply and demand for Canadian and US dollars that determines the equilibrium exchange rate, which is nothing more than the equilibrium relative price of the currencies: if the supply of US dollars increases (Americans want to sell more of their dollars to buy Canadian ones), there is downward pressure on the price of the US dollar and the amount of US dollars you can buy with one Canadian dollar increases, while the amount of Canadian dollars you can buy with one US dollar decreases.

It's very similar to the tomato market: too many tomatoes supplied for sale relative to demand drives the price of tomatoes down; too few tomatoes supplied for sale relative to demand drives the price up.

One simply has to remember that the supply of US dollars (and therefore the demand for Canadian dollars) comes from Americans who want to buy Canadian goods and services (including tourism) or invest in Canada, while the demand for US dollars (and therefore the supply of Canadian dollars) comes from Canadians who want to buy American goods and services or invest in the United States.

The observed exchange rate is the result of demand and supply pressures in the currency market. Total demand for US dollars consists of the expenditures incurred in US dollars by Canadians for buying US goods and services ($G\&S_{CA}$) and investing (INV_{CA}) in the United States. The supply of US dollars is composed of the expenditures incurred in US dollars by Americans for their purchases of Canadian goods and services ($G\&S_{US}$) and their investments in Canada (INV_{US}), and similarly for the demand and supply of Canadian dollars.

At the observed, and thus equilibrium, exchange rate (supply = demand), the total quantity demanded in US dollars by Canadians ($G\&S_{CA} + INV_{CA}$) is necessarily equal to the total quantity of US dollars supplied by Americans ($G\&S_{US} + INV_{US}$). Therefore, $G\&S_{CA} + INV_{CA} = G\&S_{US} + INV_{US}$, which can be rewritten as follows: $G\&S_{US} - G\&S_{CA} = INV_{CA} - INV_{US}$, where all values are expressed in US dollars. The left-hand-side term in the last equation is the trade deficit/surplus, and the right-hand-side term is the investment surplus/deficit. At the observed exchange rate, the above equalities necessarily hold true.

The above equations do not require that $G\&S_{CA} = G\&S_{US}$ (trade equilibrium), or that $INV_{CA} = INV_{US}$ (foreign investment equilibrium). If the United States has a trade deficit with Canada (so $G\&S_{US} < G\&S_{CA}$), it necessarily follows that it has a foreign investment surplus of the same magnitude (so $INV_{CA} > INV_{US}$).

Thus, the exchange rate, the trade deficit, and the foreign investment surplus are all determined simultaneously: at the observed exchange rate, the trade deficit (surplus) is necessarily associated with a foreign investment surplus (deficit) of the same magnitude. If $G\&S_{CA}$ + $INV_{CA} \neq G\&S_{US} + INV_{US}$, there is an imbalance, and the exchange rate will adjust to re-establish equality between the supply of, and demand for, Canadian and US dollars.

A foreign investment surplus in the United States (meaning that Canada is investing more in the United States than Americans are investing in Canada) contributes to the growth of the US economy. This foreign investment surplus, which offsets the trade deficit, creates jobs in the United States, increases the productivity of the US economy, and contributes to US economic growth. Similarly, a trade surplus offsets a foreign investment deficit.

Any attempt by the United States to reduce its trade deficit (through the imposition of tariffs, for example) can only have some combination of the following potential impacts: a shift in the trade deficit from industries that are protected by the tariffs to unprotected industries with no significant reduction in the total trade deficit, a reduction in its foreign investment surplus, or an appreciation of the exchange rate between US and Canadian dollars.

On 20 July 2018, the *New York Times* reported the following (reminder: Larry Kudlow was President Donald J. Trump's chief economic adviser): "Larry Kudlow, the chairman of the White House's National Economic Council, said in an interview that the president strongly believed that his policies would increase investment and draw workers into the labor force. 'The United States is the hottest economy and investment destination in the world right now,' thanks largely to Mr Trump's policies, Mr. Kudlow said. 'Money is flowing in from everywhere and that's terrific.'"[10]

Larry Kudlow (and his president) should understand that the foreign investment surplus necessarily corresponds to the trade deficit, which it directly mirrors. Kudlow seemed to ignore this fact. What's more, the second part of his assertion is completely synonymous with the following statement: *"The United States is the hottest economy and export destination in the world right now, thanks largely to Mr Trump's policies. We incur a large trade deficit with everyone and that's terrific."*

Anne O. Krueger demonstrates how the ill-informed drive to cut the trade deficit that pursued after the election of Donald Trump has hurt the US economy. She states that international trade increased from approximately 20 per cent of global output in the immediate postwar period to 39 per cent in 1990, and then to 58 per cent in 2018. American consumers now pay more for many products from

China. Also, the United States had to pay out some $28 billion in compensation to US farmers.[11]

She adds that many US companies have had to pay more for their inputs, and have consequently lost market share to foreign competitors who benefited from a cost advantage. By pulling the United States out of the Trans-Pacific Partnership (TPP) the president succeeded in raising tariffs on US exports almost everywhere. Under the TPP, US wheat producers would have been spared the 38 per cent tariff that Japan imposes on all wheat imports. Now that the TPP has been replaced by the Comprehensive and Progressive Agreement for Trans-Pacific Partnership (CPTPP), a free trade agreement between eleven countries – Canada, Australia, Brunei, Chile, Japan, Malaysia, Mexico, New Zealand, Peru, Singapore, and Vietnam – Canadians and Australians exporting wheat to Japan are subject to lower tariffs than their US counterparts.

According to Krueger, high customs duties on US imports of steel and aluminum (that initially included those of its trading partners in the United States–Mexico-Canada Agreement) have only hurt American industries that use aluminum and steel, and employment in those industries has indeed declined in the past two years.[12]

THE WIN-WIN SOLUTION OF FREE TRADE

But why and how do countries benefit from international trade? It is for the same reason that regions benefit from inter-regional trade (Quebec-Ontario, Pennsylvania-Ohio, Finistère-Gironde, etc.) and individuals benefit from exchanges among themselves. The answer lies in the specialization of labour and production that trade allows – a key contributor to productivity. This specialization reflects the comparative (or relative) advantages of each and increases the well-being of all, regardless of their absolute advantages or disadvantages.

Dynamic or inter-temporal analysis applied to a multilateral world (with each country having its own monetary policy) certainly renders the analysis more complex, but the basic principles are the same. Three complementary factors have allowed international trade to expand to the benefit of all: a decline in transportation and travel costs, greater efficiency of financial markets, and the development of the important social capital of trust between trading partners through open and transparent treaties and the rule of law. These three factors work together to reduce transaction costs for the good of all.

It should be re-emphasized, however, that a more efficient economy will be able to export and import more, invest more abroad, and receive more foreign direct investment, irrespective of the trade and foreign investment deficit or surplus and exchange rate fluctuations, and thus benefit from a higher welfare level.

Rising productivity owing to a workforce that is better trained and highly motivated; public and private technological investments that have undergone more rigorous scrutiny, selection, and implementation processes; and institutions that are more efficient, are all important contributors to a country's or region's welfare gains, especially against the backdrop of an economy that is more open to international trade.

The current international challenges require a more informed, stronger, and resilient spirit of international co-operation able to stand up to antiglobalization trends. Focusing on local or domestic food and health-care clusters, for example, would negatively impact developing countries, among others, and thus increase the risk of pandemics in developed countries. More than ever, we humans are all in the same boat – but it's such a big boat that some seem unable to recognize it as such.

Let us hope that the march toward more co-operation, more globalization, more international treaties, and more competition – in other words, the march toward a more integrated, inclusive, and civilized world – will survive the current challenges and the protectionist policies of some governments.

CONCLUSION

Sweeping but Not Utopian Reforms

What I have been calling the NCC and CSD models – the new competition-based capitalism and the competition-based social democracy – together encapsulate major and far-reaching economic and social policy and program reforms. These policies and programs are mutually reinforcing. In reality, the reforms envisaged amount to a sweeping and ambitious, but attainable and pragmatic, socio-economic revolution.

They will elicit vehement opposition and criticism and will be resisted tooth and nail by many interest groups on all sides of the issues. This is because these reforms focus their cost-benefit analysis on citizens, not producers, pressure groups, or politicians.

The NCC and CSD models are based on intellectually coherent behavioural and informational foundations having concrete policy implications and applications. The foundations, tools, and instruments required for their implementation are for the most part already in place. A thorough revamping of governments' activities and priorities is certainly necessary, but the NCC and CSD models make this paradigm shift possible.[1]

Innovation and the commercialization of new technologies and organizations are major contributors to significant shifts in economic activity (changes in goods and services, in the organization of work, in job displacements, in trade, and in contractual relationships). They may generate sudden depreciation of the value of capital, qualifications, and skills (human capital).

The financial crisis of 2007–10 spread confusion about many of these risk-management market instruments. But we have to acknowledge that all significant technological progress carries with it the potential for good and bad applications. It is unfortunate that the bad applications often eclipse those that are good. Examples of technological advances with both good and bad applications include hammers, explosives, financial derivatives, and cyberspace.

A major source of opposition to socio-economic change, even when this change seems desirable from a social welfare perspective, is the lack of effective mechanisms or institutions to help individuals, as well as firms and organizations, reduce their direct costs of adapting to the change.[2] When society is confronted with changes to its socio-economic environment, its adaptability becomes crucial to maintaining or increasing its citizens' well-being.

This ability to adapt to an unstable environment must become a feature of all sectors that produce and distribute PSGS. Flexibility runs against inertia, inertia is born of fear, and fear comes from change. Unless people are equipped with the tools they need to deal with change, they will resist it economically and politically, at a significant cost to society. In any situation, resisting change is a very poor substitute for adapting to it.

Social flexibility in the face of socio-economic change will depend on the existence of institutions (tools and means, organizations and markets) that enable individuals, firms, and different tiers of government to manage risks effectively, to limit their exposure to downside risks while increasing their exposure to upside opportunities. An indispensable core policy of CSD is to foster the creation and implementation of tools, channels, and means (insurance, financial derivatives, lifelong learning) for individuals, businesses, and different tiers of government to effectively manage the risks and opportunities arising from the innovation and commercialization of new technologies and organizations. A proper set of risk-management mechanisms and institutions is necessary for a flexible society in which innovation, both technological and organizational, thrives.

Uncertainty is a source of opportunities. Thus, we need to extend and apply the scientific framework that has developed over the last decades for the analysis of financial risk and insurance to encompass a wider set of issues and to develop a quantitative approach to the management of risk and uncertainty at the individual, corporate, social, and policy levels.

Considerations of risk attenuation or risk management are not part of the current discourse surrounding public policy-making as social programs are usually evaluated according to criteria such as equity, accessibility, universality, and efficiency. These criteria are important and certainly relevant, but it is also desirable to place issues of risk front and centre in public policy debate.

Financial economics as a discipline has contributed in an essential way to the development of financial markets and has enhanced individuals' ability to deal with the uncertainties of economic life. The models developed by economists use concepts and methods from probability theory in an equilibrium setting. An important goal of CSD is to contribute to better social policies through a deeper understanding of how individuals react to uncertainty, and to propose and develop specific instruments and institutions to better manage such uncertainty and risks.[3]

We should seek to protect the movement toward globalization and the increasing liberalization of markets. Some people fear competitive processes not only at the national level but also in the international context. Globalization of markets is often viewed as responsible for destroying jobs (outsourcing and offshoring) in the developed economies and as favouring the exploitation of workers in underdeveloped countries. However, the substantial growth of international trade in the last half century has been a major factor in the enhancement of collective economic well-being and in cultural and social development.

Among the broadest and most encompassing challenges we face, one must mention in particular the ultimate danger of resorting to protectionist and "buy local" measures in efforts to spur demand for local products and services, to the detriment of the cost of living and the general well-being. There exists a real danger of seeing a vicious circle of protectionism appear in our societies, plunging economies into a de-growth morass. NCC and CSD models and reforms may be part of the answer to those fears.

IMPLEMENTATION: CHALLENGES AND PITFALLS FOR BOTH THE CSD AND NCC MODELS

The CSD model is a model of social organization based on the belief that PSGS are essential to ensuring economic growth and social cohesion. Among the necessary conditions for these PSGS to optimize the well-being of all, two are indispensable to competition-based social democracies: the goods and services delivered must meet the needs of citizens, and they must be supplied in an efficient manner. The first condition relies on the democratic electoral process, and the second on a systematic recourse to competitive processes, be they old and familiar or new and yet to be imagined and created.

The objective of the CSD model is to trigger a profound restructuring of the governmental sector in order to meet these challenges. For this purpose, I have laid out above ten generic programs and policies that constitute the basis of the CSD model, as well as ten generic programs and policies that constitute the basis of the NCC model. These programs and policies call for a major upheaval.

In the area of infrastructure (roads, waterworks, parks, airports, etc.), the governmental sector defines the goods and services to be offered to the population, solicits tenders from the competitive sector, and manages the resulting contracts and partnerships, whether public-private partnerships or other forms. This method of procurement provides adequate incentives for performance in the best interests of citizens, users, and taxpayers.[4] In the fields of education and health care, processes are similar, given the particular requirements that may be involved in the various upstream (investment) and downstream (service provision) activities. Again, the governmental sector defines the goods and services to be offered and the goals to be attained, in terms of quantity and quality. It then issues calls for tenders from the competitive sector and manages the resulting contracts and partnerships, ensuring adequate performance incentives in the best interest of citizens, users, and taxpayers. The quantity and quality of services rendered must be measured independently as specified by the contract. The compensation paid out to the competitive-sector partner will be in part determined by the result of this evaluation.

Competition and a performance requirement (incentive) are thus at the heart of the PSGS production and distribution system – all with due respect for competitive-sector suppliers and in the best interest of citizens, consumers, and taxpayers.[5]

Modularity and multi-source procurement is a central feature of the CSD model. The golden rule is to determine the objectives of the program or contract and let the competitive-sector provider or contractor determine how, and by what means, these objectives will be met. This allows for better identification and implementation of best practices through incentives to meet the objectives. The multi-source procurement system may, in some cases, create a trade-off between capturing economies of scale and generating more benchmarks from suppliers' performances. Multi-sourcing would induce a strong level of competition over the long term and make sure that prices are low and quality is high on average.

The present discussion does not claim to provide turnkey solutions to all issues raised by the implementation of the CSD and NCC models. Recall Ostrom's statement that "getting the institutions right is a difficult, time-consuming, conflict-involving process ... that requires reliable information about time and place variables as well as a broad repertoire of culturally acceptable rules ... Institutions are rarely either private or public – 'the market' or 'the state.' Many successful ... institutions are rich mixtures of 'private-like' and 'public-like' institutions defying classification in a sterile dichotomy."[6] The CSD and NCC models are examples of such mixtures of "private-like" and "public-like" institutions, somewhere between self-organization, self-governance, and bottom-up formulas and centralized, autocratic, and top-down ones. The roles of the governmental (public) sector and the competitive (non-governmental, private) sector in the CSD model are redefined to make the co-operation between those institutional set-ups compulsory and unavoidable, for the benefits of all citizens.

My goal here is to convince the reader that the reforms proposed by the CSD and NCC models are not the stuff of utopian dreams. Clearly, for such models to be fully operational, it will be necessary to invest important resources to design the explicit processes underlying each model. For the CSD model, such processes will draw on its fundamental principles – individual rationality, the power of incentives, the efficiency of competitive processes, and the value of modularity and experimentation – as well as the ten generic CSD policies and programs discussed above. However, the returns on these investments could be tremendous. Similarly, for the NCC model, such processes will draw on its fundamental principles – the separation of the public and private spheres, equal opportunity based on merit, entrepreneurial freedom, social and economic mobility based on performance in wealth creation, competitive price signals (and competition-emulating institutions) for input factors and products and services – as well as the ten generic NCC policies and programs discussed above. Again, the returns on these investments of resources could be tremendous.

The remainder of this chapter deals mainly with the implementation of the CSD model.

Let us consider in more detail the two most prominent and important sectors having an immediate impact on the well-being of citizens and in which the government is, directly or indirectly, a major player:

education and health care. In both cases, we can make matters a bit simpler without sacrificing general applicability by considering local schools and local clinics or hospitals.

Implementing the wrong solutions to the challenges we face in these sectors could cause the social fabric, on which the success of our growth and welfare policies depend, to tear and unravel. A successful resolution of the challenges in these sectors could propel social democratic societies to achieve even greater goals, such as eradicating poverty and creating a renewed sense of security – in a word: a better world for all.

Aside from the two sectors discussed here, there exist others for which the organizational micro-structure of the production, decision, and implementation processes makes a difference. And there are, of course, other matters of concern to citizens, governments, and competitive sectors that exceed the scope of the present discussion. However, on the basis of the methodological constructs in the previous chapters, and of the discussion of the two key sectors of education and health care, the reader will be able to imagine what the CSD model would imply for the sectors not explicitly addressed here.

Education and Health Care

Countries and regions must efficiently develop their stock of human capital in order to fully benefit from the accelerated growth opportunities offered by the globalization of markets, new information and communications technologies, and the internationalization of cultures. This means that formal education, lifelong learning and training, and workers' employability are all aspects of an integrated human capital development process – a portfolio of PSGS.

Similarly, health-care systems not only represent the largest service sector in many countries, but also make a crucial contribution to the flourishing of social cohesion and inclusion. Their efficiency, their impact on public finances, and their ability to rise to the challenges posed by aging populations and rising life expectancy depend on creative policy approaches, both to control rapidly increasing costs and to obtain the most out of the resources invested.

Many commentators and politicians claim that the problems of the education and health-care sectors could be solved by an injection of additional funds. The competition-based social democracy model does not a priori lean in that direction. The difficulties facing the education and health-care systems in our societies are not, in general, due to an overall lack of financial resources, but rather to their inherent organizational inefficiencies. Indeed, it is the organizational structure of the education and health-care systems that must be re-examined. There is a need to reform existing models, which are often based on a co-management framework hammered out between governments and labour or professional unions, whose interests (implicitly if not explicitly) take precedence over those of students and patients. A better use of the resources presently dedicated to providing education and health-care services to citizens could go a long way toward solving the problems that are endemic to centralized systems.

Unfortunately, the current governance systems are characterized by weak, if not absent or even counterproductive, incentive mechanisms and by inefficient allocation of resources, leading to significant waste. Education and lifelong training as well as health-care services have become sectors in which wastefulness is ubiquitous. Bureaucratic micromanagement of inter- and intra-organizational affairs hobbles institutional responsiveness to change and provokes fierce resistance to transparent and credible evaluation of the performance of the system. This is characteristic of sclerotic centralized systems.

A successful implementation of CSD features and policies in education and health-care rests on a set of factors, some internal and some external, to use the Ostrom's terminology. Internal factors (such as the capacity to communicate directly with one another, the possibility to develop trust, and the shared sense of a common future) are always relevant. The implementation will be facilitated if two features of the CSD model are present. First, if the objectives pursued – namely, the proper education of children and the proper health-care services to be offered to citizens, as determined by the political identification of the basket of local and well-identified PSGS – are locally formulated and widely shared. Second, if there is an explicit and open search for the best competitive-sector organizations to take responsibility for meeting the relevant objectives. One possible plus here would be to add representatives of local communities in the evaluation of bids from competitive-sector organizations.

Moreover, we can expect that the competitive-sector organizations that will participate in the call for tender will be strongly induced to reach out to the relevant communities and obtain a strong social acceptability for the ways and means they propose. Hence the participating organizations will find it in their best interest to bring aboard the school's or health-care facility's stakeholders (parents, pupils, patients, teachers, medical personnel, other personnel, local businesses, etc.). One effect of such a strategy will undoubtedly be to generate a grassroots movement, as a critical appraisal feature of the responsible organization's approach and leadership. As for external factors (the autonomy, the constraints), they may be considered under control also, insofar as the roles of the public and competitive/private sectors are well-defined and circumscribed.

Competitive mechanisms stand a much better chance of successfully providing more room for modularity, for freedom (the right to economic contestation), for robust incentive mechanisms, and for more efficient allocation and coordination processes. This increases the probability of success by fostering a better overall yield from the systems. Education and health care are services that are too complex and too diversified, from the demand as well as the supply side, to be efficiently produced and distributed in a centralized fashion.

In education and health care, as in other PSGS sectors, a better use of resources requires a more efficient division of responsibilities between the governmental and the competitive sectors (policy 1 in the ten-point CSD model proposed in chapter 2), as well as a systematic recourse to competitive processes and prices (policies 2, 3, and 4) to guide individual choices and social investments.

In a CSD world, the entire structure of the education and health-care sectors would be organized completely differently. The key words of this initiative are *competition, modularity, experimentation, accountability* (for the results), *effectiveness* (the measure of how close the results are to the objectives), and *efficiency* (the measure of how costly the delivery of the results is).

For instance, the objective in the education sector is to provide all students, no matter their age, with a high-quality education/training. Consequently, the centrality of the students to the organization's mission must always be pre-eminent. A new principle of equality must be applied. Equality in the field of education and lifelong learning does not consist in putting groups of twenty-five pupils in front of a teacher for a fixed number of hours per year. Equality does not mean that everyone is treated the same, but rather that they all have the same chances of success. The CSD model calls for an education system that creates equality of opportunity, implying that a lower-quality social or family environment must be compensated by a higher-quality formal education. It is therefore necessary for us to rebuild the education system by taking into account the diversity of individual needs in achieving a common set of objectives.

Returning the child and student to the centre of the debate does not necessarily mean that the other actors, such as teachers, will be downgraded. The CSD model recognizes the essential role played by teachers as well as parents, medical staff, psychologists, and others (including security personnel) in children's development and education. The CSD model can in fact prop up the dignity of the teaching profession by incorporating competition and incentive mechanisms. "Good" highly motivated teachers, who clearly represent a significant majority of their profession, will benefit from this organizational revolution. The handful of sub-par teachers who might loiter in our schools, colleges, and universities will find themselves motivated to quit the system and to take up other careers.

Similarly, the objective of the health-care sector is to provide all citizens, whether young or old, healthy or sick, with high-quality health services. But needs differ across individuals. It is not hard to fathom why age and health-care spending are linked. Older people consume far more health-care resources than the young, particularly at the end of their lives. Other factors also play a role in this increase in health-care spending. First, health care is a superior good, which means that income or GDP growth will be accompanied by an increase in health-care expenditures at all ages and for all social groups. Second, the higher costs of new drugs and treatments are in large part due to advances in knowledge and new technologies that expand the treatment possibilities available to the population. This expansion in the palette of treatments allows more people to be covered for more problems and for longer periods, thereby improving the health of the population but at a non-negligible cost.

The current education and health-care models, jointly administered by governments and labour and professional unions, are fundamentally inimical to the objectives they should pursue. There are many who await reform: the CSD model can satisfy the population's expectations, not by specifying the exact features of the education/training and health-care systems, but rather by identifying the processes that will give them life and adaptability.

The participation of competitive-sector organizations as education and health-care providers is very controversial. This controversy is often exacerbated by use of the term "privatization," which evokes fear in some circles. It is often incorrectly used to describe nothing more than delegated management, multi-source procurement, or incentive contracts. In the CSD context, it means subcontracting certain services or functions to the competitive sector in order to increase productivity or flexibility. In this case, the governmental sector retains responsibility for the quantity and quality of PSGS offered, even if they are contracted out to for-profit or not-for-profit organizations. In other cases, the term "privatization" may reflect an increase in the financial burden directly assumed by individuals, even if in the end all costs are assumed by citizens.

Education K–12 Services

Let us now sketch out the main features of these new CSD organizations. My admittedly cursory examination will primarily focus on the reorganization of K–12 education systems. But CSD ideas can and must also be applied to sectors of higher education (colleges and universities) and institutions of lifelong learning. The objective here is not to describe in narrow detail the full complexity of existing educational establishments. The model presented in the next few paragraphs is a simple illustration of the main principles of the CSD model as they could apply to the education sector, and by extension to other PSGS sectors.

One important characteristic of the education systems under CSD would be a sweeping decentralization of established processes: clear competency objectives to be met by the provider, but no more uniform working conditions, no more centralized labour contracts, no more labour union monopolies, and no more governmental officials dictating specific salary conditions for education professional and support staff.

To keep matters as simple as possible, let us consider that there are six main agents or actors in education establishments: (1) the students; (2) the governmental sector; (3) competitive-sector suppliers of educational goods and services; (4) competitive-sector suppliers of ancillary goods and services such as catering, student support, recreational activities, security services, construction/upgrading and maintenance of facilities; (5) competitive-sector suppliers or managers of evaluation methodologies and procedures; and (6) the overall integrator firm responsible for managing the interrelated responsibilities of the other actors.

The last four actors, potentially sourced from one single competitive-sector organization, would operate under incentive-compatible contracts signed with the governmental-sector authority (municipal, regional, or national) with the explicit objective of meeting the needs of the primary stakeholders: the students. The architecture of such a CSD model can be summarized as follows: the student must be educated, trained, guided, and evaluated by competitive-sector organizations under contractual arrangements with the governmental sector.

We see that the CSD model would replace public schools as we know them with a competitive school system in which competitive-sector organizations (private corporations, co-operatives, not-for-profit organizations, social economy organizations, organized labour–backed collectives, etc.) would compete to show their superior competencies and efficiency in order to obtain performance-based education contracts.

Hence, we would move from the current system of low-accountability and low-performance public schools and health centres toward a system of strictly accountable (to students and parents; to patients and their families), high-performing (payments made on the basis of objectives attained), publicly financed (with possibly complementary private or personal contributions), competitive (private, co-operative, associative, etc.) schools or health centres, operating under limited-term incentive contracts with the governmental sector, which ultimately remains responsible for the quality of the education and health-care systems.

In the CSD education system, the governmental sector has redefined responsibilities. The first is to determine the quantity and quality of education goods and services by defining competence thresholds that students must attain or surpass at different stages of their education. Only these targets need to be set. The pedagogical methods to be used to reach these objectives could be specified by competitive-sector organizations in their respective bids, being adequately incentivized by their contracts to deliver on their promises and commitments. This should ensure sufficient modularity and experimentation in the search for and implementation of best practices (for example, for the role of remedial education programs for students, in particular those lagging behind in basic literacy and numeracy skills[7]). The governmental sector's second responsibility is to manage contracts with these competitive-sector organizations in the education system. Though constrained by these new and limited responsibilities, the governmental sector retains considerable leeway.

The governmental sector will draft and sign contracts with education businesses. These contracts integrate incentive mechanisms, and their application is subject to rigorous, transparent, and regular control and evaluation. The contracts will be awarded to those firms that propose the best services at the best costs, the best value for money. Companies that outperform the objectives will receive bonuses, while those that fall short will be penalized, but may receive special assistance to help them improve their performance. They may also be sanctioned and, in the worst-case scenario, replaced on short notice.

Let us consider the tendering process to be implemented (the reader can adapt the processes for other PSGS sectors). The tendering process will be run in a clear and transparent way in order to support the development of competition between competitive-sector firms in the education sector in accordance with the ten generic policies described in chapter 2. The two most important policies at this stage are the promotion of open and transparent competitive mechanisms in the attribution of contracts for the provision of education PSGS, and the promotion of efficient competitive-sector organizations with a capacity to bid efficiently for those contracts. This system will, first and foremost, guarantee the quality of the education sector. Competitive-sector suppliers of educational goods and services will be able to promote their competencies on the vast education market.

Let us consider a particular procedure in order to better illustrate these ideas. Within each school or institution, three "lines of business" could be assigned to competitive-sector organizations on the basis of a competitive tendering procedure: teaching, broadly defined, and supervisory services; ancillary goods and services (catering meals, security, and recreation); and construction/upgrading and maintenance of facilities. The competitive-sector organizations in each of these lines of business will be in competition and the ones with the best proposals will obtain a contract for a limited term, let's say for five years. Accountability for the results and performance will replace prescribed processes.

In order to ensure coordination within the school and to clearly delineate the responsibilities of each stakeholder, a single firm will be in charge of each line of business in any given school. Each of the three competitive-sector organizations retained within the institution will appoint a director to oversee its activities. These directors will, in turn, be under the authority of a director general (typically a DG firm) responsible for integrating their services across the whole establishment. This integrator of services will normally be an expert in human resources management and/or in education system management. The DG firm will also receive incentive-based compensation, be responsible for the school's performance, and, in the event of failure by one of the partners, be able to recruit other suppliers on short notice. The DG firm's most important task will be to manage relationships between service providers in the best interest of the students. The DG firm will be evaluated and compensated on this basis.

Facility maintenance/construction firms as well as suppliers of ancillary goods and services already exist in the economy, and they only need to be integrated into schools. Other (new) firms will be created from the human resources already existent in the educational sector. Clearly, the most important area of activity will be teaching and supervision. It will consist of competitive-sector firms mainly made up of teachers, but also including supervisory and specialized services staff (psychologists, social workers, medical personnel, etc.). Like the other two service providers and the integrator, these companies will be selected by a competitive tendering process launched by the government and will be subject to incentive contracts. The contract term will reflect the complexity of the services. Nothing would prevent a DG firm from integrating as subsidiaries the other three lines of business operators.

The agent or actor in charge of evaluating the performance of the other actors will intervene at a more global level and will not be integrated into schools. This actor will assume a threefold task. First, ensure that the government-set standards, outlined in the contract, relative to teacher qualifications and the curriculum are adhered to. Second, design methods and procedures (exams) allowing an evaluation of the pupils' progress throughout the duration of the contract to verify if stated objectives are met. Third, provide students with vocational guidance to help them choose an educational path commensurate with their interests and aptitudes and offering them the best career opportunities.

It is important that the education sector not fall into the hands of too few competitive-sector organizations. Particular attention will have to be paid to how contracts are drafted and awarded to ensure that competitive pressures are maintained.

The CSD model requires implementing mechanisms to encourage innovation. The use of multi-source procurement mechanisms, together with a system for collecting and sharing information, must be generalized in order to support competitive pressures and induce innovation, modularity, and experimentation in the discovery of best practices. The term of the contracts should be neither too long nor too short. Contracts of optimal duration will stimulate performance and preclude any company being shielded from competition for too long. Competitive-sector firms will understand that a bad evaluation of their services will lead to the cancellation of the contract and their replacement with more efficient organizations. With the modular architecture in place, the threat of contract cancellation or non-renewal will be quite credible.

Let us briefly mention some of the major benefits associated with this new structure. First, the level of student supervision and counselling will not be identical in all schools. In order to properly educate students from underprivileged environments, competitive-sector firms (being accountable for results achieved) will offer the services of more qualified and thus generally better-paid personnel to meet the students' specific needs. In order to learn how to read, a child from a family whose parents do not speak the language of instruction will need more coaching than one whose household does and whose parents are resource rich and highly educated. This obvious fact cannot be denied anymore, and the CSD competitive mechanisms will naturally account for this reality. In this way, an equality of opportunities will be ensured by market mechanisms.

The three different modules we identified above are present in each school. Each firm is a module that can be removed and replaced quickly without affecting the other two. It seems highly likely that companies from various sectors will naturally tend to organize their activities in a modular way to reduce their service costs. Even under the broad constraints of government policies and targets (as specified in the contracts), competitive-sector organizations will have a lot of leeway in how they pursue the goals they have been assigned and are committed to. This freedom will undoubtedly give rise to many experiments as regards teaching methods. Only a wide array of methods tailored to the local situation can meet the need of a diverse population of pupils.

The organizations in charge of providing educational and training services will manage any internal problems that arise within their own teaching staff. Wage policy based on quality, competence, or performance rather than seniority will keep teachers eager to provide high-quality instruction. Proper career planning and development should align the expected contribution to the level of experience. The CSD mechanisms will free teachers from the administrative straightjackets that often curb their ability to shine as teachers. Top-tier teachers will become important members of competitive-sector teaching services firms. Wages and other contract clauses will no longer necessarily follow a set pay scale, but the best teachers will be rewarded more while the worst ones will be encouraged to leave the school and the company. Appropriate incentive pay systems will foster updated and improved teaching, in terms of both skills and curriculum.

As stated above, the structure of instruction/education will not be identical in all schools. The evaluations carried out prior to the tendering process by the responsible competitive-sector evaluation firms and governmental authorities will make it possible for education services firms to determine the optimal level of supervision, reflecting the challenges present in the establishment and not the number of pupils. In underprivileged districts, where violence may be more prevalent, this new structure will make it possible to ensure the education and the safety of the students with the help of psychologists, medical personnel, and security personnel necessary to meet the objectives. Remember: firms are accountable for education outcomes.

Parents often complain about the mental fatigue experienced by teachers. Once again, standards set by contracts will help alleviate this problem. Competitive-sector organizations will be incentivized to make sure they have a pool of highly qualified substitute teachers to call on if necessary. Being accountable for the results gives the competitive-sector education services firms a strong interest in ensuring that the development of students is shielded from occasional, but unavoidable, absence or fatigue among teaching staff.

Application of CSD principles will make it possible to educate our children in a well-adapted and more efficient way. Competition, freedom (including the right to confront and replace if necessary the people and organizations responsible for providing educational services), and modularity, in conjunction with the systematic application of the relevant generic policies and programs discussed above, are the tools that will make it possible to achieve this goal.

And similarly, *mutatis mutandis*, for the health-care and other sectors of PSGS.

WHAT COULD GO WRONG?
LOTS, BUT NOTHING INTELLIGENCE AND COURAGE CAN'T COUNTER

The crucial challenge facing social democratic institutions (including citizens and their governments) is to clearly demonstrate the intelligence and courage of their ambitions: the intelligence to design the ways and means whereby the reforms necessary to systematically achieve social democratic objectives are to be implemented (the CSD and NCC models), and the courage to deliver and persevere with these reforms.

One big danger on the horizon is that, through lack of understanding, lack of leadership, and lack of power and willingness to think outside of the box, the international community of social democratic societies may fail to design and implement in time the governance mechanisms needed to efficiently manage our PSGS systems. This will require both high-level and on-the-street communications to generate the necessary degree of social acceptability. Other major challenges are the implementation process by which the new roles of the governmental and competitive sectors will materialize, the design of proper gaming-free incentive contracts, the most effective information gathering to evaluate the performance of those organizations in delivering PSGS as specified in their respective contracts, and the enablement of a sufficient intensity of competition throughout the economy. I look at those challenges below.

The dominant liberal meritocratic capitalism has lost some of its virtue and moved away from its foundational principles: the separation of the public and private spheres, equal opportunity based on merit, entrepreneurial freedom, social and economic mobility based on performance in wealth creation, competitive price signals (and competition-emulating institutions) for input factors and products and services. The current brand of capitalism has diverged into a high and misunderstood level of income and wealth inequality with an emerging upper class managing to resist challenges from new talents and skills and from new entrepreneurs. A significant challenge in liberal meritocratic capitalism is to prevent this upper-class oligarchy from succeeding in becoming immune to competition, thereby undermining the principle of equality of opportunity based on merit. Hence the importance of revisiting and re-founding capitalism (the NCC model), as we revisit and re-found social democracy (the CSD model).

The alternative is that the portfolio of PSGS will be subtly abandoned, maybe not in terms of quantity but certainly in quality. In many countries, the movement has already begun, and this in spite of the fact that those societies have become richer, more educated, and better able to face up to the challenges, as if a new tragedy of the commons has emerged. More and more people chasing limited resources in the education, health-care, and other sectors of PSGS. The common good is taking a back seat as individuals and governments are riveted to the notion of protecting and reviving a bygone world. The top-down managerial style and monopolistic one-size-fits-all model governing the production and delivery of PSGS may have been appropriate at some point in the past, but these are not the best policies anymore.

The efficient ways and means by which PSGS should be provided in the future will differ from what we have seen in the past. As suggested above (introduction, observation 4), those ways and means must adapt to cultural changes, educational attainment, entrepreneurial capabilities, and technological developments. The CSD model makes this adaptation continuous and explicit through a modular and diversified portfolio of ways and means to attain the objectives pursued. Competition and modularity were anathema for the PSGS system till the recent past. People are now better educated and more affluent, hence capable of and maybe ready for taking a larger part of responsibility as producers and benefactors of PSGS.

Challenge 1:
The New Roles of the Governmental and Competitive Sectors

The first challenge identified above – namely, the implementation process by which the new roles of the governmental and competitive sectors will materialize – is basically a political challenge: a political party needs to show up, propose the changes, and, once elected, introduce them in a sequential manner. The CSD and NCC models represent significant departures vis-à-vis current ways and means, although some of those changes are already in place in different sectors, contexts, countries, and regions. Reforms will be demanding, but they have the advantages of both clearness and operationality.

As mentioned above in the policy 1 of the CSD model (see chapter 2), the role of the governmental sector is fourfold: to identify citizens' needs for PSGS, both in terms of quantity and quality; to determine the characteristics of PSGS; to arbitrate, as required, between different baskets of PSGS and between different coalitions of citizens, given the available resources; and to manage contracts and partnerships for the production, distribution, and delivery of the chosen basket of PSGS. Each of these roles is replete with challenges and pitfalls. But the first three are already being assumed by the public sector. The fourth one is new in terms of scope but not totally so given the numerous contracts that the public sector already design and manage with competitive-sector businesses. The main challenge here is with the draft and management of incentive contracts for the provision of PSGS, explicitly discussed below as challenge 2.

One difficult obstacle will be the resistance of labour and professional unions to such a profound redesign of their roles, from simply demanders of guaranteed compensation (global wage and benefits) to active partners with other stakeholders, all in the same boat, whose fate depends on the effort and collaboration of all. Another difficult obstacle will be the reduction of the public central bureaucracy. Most so-called civil servants will be asked to enter the down-to-earth workforce in competitive-sector organizations responsible, under contract with the governmental sector, to produce and deliver PSGS. But none of these obstacles can be qualified as impossible to counter.

Challenge 2:
The Design of Gaming-Free Incentive Contracts

The second challenge identified above – the design of proper gaming-free incentive contracts – is a more technical and difficult task. But successful contracts of this type exist already in both the public and private sectors, in particular throughout supply chains and networks in different fields and contexts. There is no reason to expect that the new governmental sector, whose main task will be to design and manage such contracts, will be unable to rise up to the challenge. Some may fear that gaming-free incentive contracts will in some cases be *very* complicated and comprehensive if they are to leave no gaps. Some may also argue that previously productive people (e.g., teachers and doctors) will be sucked into just managing them. But there is little if any probability of seeing such movement given that the compensation of stakeholders will depend, in part, on the performance of the organization. The better teachers (and support staff) and doctors (and support staff), as essential performance-related service providers, will most likely remain teachers and doctors, while professional managers will manage the organization. There is also every reason to believe that management expertise in contract negotiation and enforcement, which has been proven over many years in many fields and contexts around the world, will be up to the challenge (on both sides, governmental and competitive).

In spite of those checks and balances, there is always a possibility that incentives will be derailed. Unfortunately, no system is perfectly immune to cheating and gaming. One significant historical experience with faulty incentive systems and their trust-destroying impacts is the subprime financial crisis of 2007–10.[8] It is instructive to recall some of the errors and corrections made as a result. Confidence (or trust, as discussed in chapter 1) is an especially important type of social capital. Consequently, the *loss of confidence within the financial system*, and particularly in interbank financial relations, helped precipitate the financial crisis and subsequent economic recession. To re-establish and maintain confidence, four issues had to be tackled then, and then addressed again and again thereafter: the manipulation or even falsification of information provided by public organizations (governments and government-sponsored enterprises) and private companies; faulty risk measurement; political intervention in publicly owned or regulated companies and the indulgent attitudes of regulators toward these companies (the US cases of Fannie Mae and Freddie Mac being the most notorious, with banks bowing to political pressures in their lending decisions coming close);[9] and flaws in performance incentive programs, which too often neglect and thereby promote reckless risk taking.

The incentive mechanisms used in the financial services industry rewarded income generated almost regardless of risk, with negligent and faulty risk measurement and unjustified risk taking as predictable results. A number of economists warned companies against these practices, reminding them that, in designing incentive mechanisms, it is necessary to account for the risks taken or incurred to avoid what economists and insurers call "moral hazard." Economists specializing in performance incentives have been suggesting for a number of years that bonuses be made conditional on risk audits to penalize, rather than reward, exceptional financial results relying on reckless risk taking.[10] These suggestions have been mostly ignored with disastrous effects.

If a major failure exists in the management-compensation consulting industry, with its many so-called professionals and gurus, it must be the compensation packages in the financial industry. Whether these compensation packages stem from sheer incompetence or ignorance of basic incentive issues, blatant conflict of interest within the board's compensation committees, or all of the above, one fact remains: the elementary principles of incentive pay were forgotten. Another blatant conflict of interest comes from rating agencies. These agencies gained significant income from rating structured products. There was thus a risk of a conflict of interest because the agencies received lump sum payments from the issuing institutions to establish ratings for products while advising these institutions on the issuing of the same products.

But there is light at the end of the tunnel. In the rescue of Fannie Mae and Freddie Mac, the managers, shareholders, and bondholders of these government-sponsored enterprises, which were overly dominant in mortgage credit and were protected by indulgent regulators, have received a large share of negative attention and blame. The government will be paid back first, and these companies seem no longer able to benefit from their political relationships to hide mismanagement: the door is closing! While the horse may be gone, at least the colt will be kept in the stable. Other examples could be given. But in the end, the significant bailouts of financial institutions, as well as industrial corporations, rightly left the previous (irresponsible) stockholders, bondholders, owners, and lenders with huge losses.

The problem was recognized by the chairman of the Federal Reserve Board: "Prospectively, we are committed to promoting an environment that supports the homeownership goals of creditworthy borrowers. To this end, the Federal Reserve Board has proposed new regulations to better protect consumers from a range of unfair or deceptive mortgage lending and advertising practices. To help ensure that the rules are broadly enforced, we are engaging in a program with other federal and state agencies to conduct consumer compliance reviews of non-depository lenders and mortgage brokers. These reviews are targeting underwriting standards, risk-management strategies, and compliance with consumer protection laws and regulations."[11] That statement and the policy it announced are from March 2008 – much too late. Why wasn't this policy in place in 2005 or 2006 when the system failure was already in the making? Where was the Fed then?

Banks, investment banks, and other financial institutions were quick to rely on choices made by their competitors or partners while assuming that those competitors and partners must have checked the risk characteristics of such securities, hence saving themselves from making "redundant" and costly verifications. This is a well-known free-riding problem in common agency contexts. In the end, a global web of individually rational actions and policies, based on others' supposedly individually rational actions and policies, ended up creating a huge but unnecessary and ultimately avoidable systemic risk that by definition must eventually be confronted: the chips will fall where they may!

This blatantly faulty incentives and control system allowed mortgage brokers to pursue high-risk (not for them) mortgage loans. Where was the Fed, whose mission includes promoting "the stability of the financial system," seeking "to minimize and contain systemic risks through active monitoring and engagement," promoting "the safety and soundness of individual financial institutions and monitors their impact on the financial system as a whole," and promoting "consumer protection and community development."[12]

The main lesson learned from the financial crisis of 2007–10 is that things may go wrong, especially when failures are aligned in a perfect storm. The specific lessons – namely, the faulty incentive systems, the endemic presence of conflicts of interest, the ill-advised political interventions in GSEs (government-sponsored enterprises such as Fannie Mae and Freddie Mac), the failure of regulators to abide by their commitments, and the free-riding behaviour of major partners (banks) – are important assets in our tool box today. One may hope that they will be kept in mind for a long time.

Challenge 3:
Information Gathering and Performance Evaluation

The third challenge identified above – the proper information gathering to evaluate the performance of competitive-sector organizations in delivering PSGS as specified in their respective contracts – is a key element. In schools, there are many examples of students' knowledge level and progress evaluation in different countries and contexts. In the CSD context, the governmental sector will define what level of knowledge in different subjects is expected at different stages of the curriculum, and these proficiency requirements will be part of the contract with a particular competitive-sector organization in charge of a specific school or group of schools. The evaluation itself will be conducted by independent organizations, with results determining in part the compensation of the organization responsible for the school performance, as set in the contract.

Although the independence of the evaluator firm is crucial, that should not create particular problems. Nevertheless, the governmental sector must make sure that this independence is real. Moreover, the ways and means by which the organization responsible for a school's performance aim to satisfy and even surpass the competency level defined in its contract is expected to vary from school to school, as a function, among other things, of a given school's characteristics. The information gathered through these evaluations across the school system should allow the identification of best practices, through a form of field experiments.

The evaluation firm could be explicitly mandated to conduct such "field experiments," in one form or another. In its commendation for the 2019 Nobel laureates in economic science, Abhijit Banerjee, Esther Duflo and Michael Kremer, the Royal Swedish Academy of Sciences tells us that

> field experiments have shown that the primary problem in many low-income countries is not a lack of resources. Instead, the biggest problem is that teaching is not sufficiently adapted to the pupils' needs. In the first of these experiments, Banerjee, Duflo et al. studied remedial tutoring programmes for pupils in two Indian cities. Schools in Mumbai and Vadodara were given access to new teaching assistants who would support children with special needs. These schools were ingeniously and randomly placed in different groups, allowing the researchers to credibly measure the effects of teaching assistants. The experiment clearly showed that help targeting the weakest pupils was an effective measure in the short and medium term.[13]

Challenge 4:
Enabling a Proper Intensity of Competition

The fourth challenge identified above – the enablement of a proper intensity of competition throughout the economy – questions the mandate and ways and means of the different competition bureaus and antitrust authorities, and not only their current state of intervention in the economy with regards to anti-competitive conduct and mergers and acquisitions, but also their implication in PSGS markets and labour unions. The PSGS sectors are typically public monopolies (protected by law). Labour unions are also typically monopolies, which fall outside the application of the *Competition Act*. In the CSD and NCC models, these legal exemptions are abandoned. Clearly, this move, intended to protect citizens against abuses of market power and to give them the power to contest and displace current providers of PSGS through competitive markets and institutions, will be fought tooth and nail by those who profit from these protections on the backs of citizens.

The challenge these fights may represent for CSD and NCC policies and programs is mainly a matter of developing a strong and convincing communication on the foundations and principles of social democracy. There is no reason to expect that the opponents of this transformation will be easily convinced (or defeated) through electoral processes. NCC policies 2, 7, 8, 9, and 10 (chapter 3) are all directly related to the development and implementation of this proper intensity of competition.

Notes

PREFACE

1 Stakeholder capitalism claims that since corporations rely on a multitude of stakeholder contributions (from employees, customers, suppliers, communities, and, more broadly, society and the environment at large) to operate effectively and create value, businesses should focus on maximizing returns not only to owners but also to various stakeholders. As for ESG capitalism, it is a loose and subjective concept used for a wide range of causes, from climate policies to diversity initiatives. Considering that there are numerous ESG reporting frameworks around and that they are rather vague in nature, it is possible for a CEO to claim almost anything creates stakeholder value for some groups.
2 This point is very well developed in Paul Seabright, *The Company of Strangers: A Natural History of Economic Life* (Princeton, NJ: Princeton University Press, 2010); Matt Ridley, *The Rational Optimist: How Prosperity Evolves* (New York: Harper Perrenial, 2011); and Yuval Noah Harari (2014), *Sapiens: A Brief History of Humankind* (New York: Harper, 2014).
3 A compelling example is Leonard E. Read, "I, Pencil," *The Freeman*, December 1958, 32–7. Another one is Paul Seabright's account of the shirt's worldwide supply chain, which for some reason works well despite the fact that nobody manages, or even would know how to manage, it. Seabright, *Company of Strangers*, 17–19.
4 According to the *Merriam-Webster* dictionary, "Both *manifest* and *manifesto* derive ultimately from the Latin noun *manus* ('hand') and *-festus*, a combining form of uncertain meaning that is also found in the Latin adjective *infestus* ('hostile'), an ancestor of the English *infest*. Something that is manifest is easy to perceive or recognize, and a manifesto is a

statement in which someone makes his or her intentions or views easy for people to ascertain. Perhaps the most well-known statement of this sort is the *Communist Manifesto*, written in 1848 by Karl Marx and Friedrich Engels to outline the platform of the Communist League." *Merriam-Webster Online*, s.v. "manifesto," accessed 28 March 2023, https://www.merriam-webster.com/dictionary/manifesto.

INTRODUCTION

1 From Karl Marx and Friedrich Engels, *Manifesto of the Communist Party* (English edition of 1888), chapter 1: "Modern bourgeois society with its relations of production, of exchange and of property, a society that has conjured up such gigantic means of production and of exchange, is like the sorcerer, who is no longer able to control the powers of the nether world whom he has called up by his spells." The authors are alluding here to *The Sorcerer's Apprentice* (1797) by Johann Wolfgang von Goethe. Marx and Engels's manifesto is available online at Project Gutenberg, https://www.gutenberg.org/cache/epub/61/pg61-images.html.

CHAPTER ONE

1 Incentive structures or frameworks, however complex and diversified, aim to achieve a sense of belonging and a form of congruence in the behaviour of agents or members of an organization, individuals in a given firm, or firms in a given value chain. Incentives need not be financial but, when appropriate, must relate to the agent's impact on the performance of the organization. Behaviour is a matter of preferences and incentives and so the two sets of factors must be conjointly considered. For more on incentives and organizations, see Jean-Jacques Laffont and David Martimort, *The Theory of Incentives: The Principal-Agent Model* (Princeton, NJ: Princeton University Press, 2002); Paul Milgrom and John Roberts, *Economies, Organization and Management* (Englewood Cliffs, NJ: Prentice-Hall, 1992); and Marcel Boyer, "The Twelve Principles of Incentive Pay," *Revue d'Économie Politique* 121, no. 3 (2011): 285–306.
2 For striking differences between static and dynamic analyses of market power, see Marie-Laure Allain, Marcel Boyer, and Jean-Pierre Ponssard, "The Determination of Optimal Fines in Cartel Cases: Theory and Practice," *Concurrences – Competition Law Review*, no. 4-2011, art. no. 63260

(2011): 32–40, and Marie-Laure Allain, Marcel Boyer, Rachidi Kotchoni, and Jean-Pierre Ponssard, "Are Cartel Fines Optimal: Theory and Evidence from the European Union," *International Review of Law and Economics* 42 (June 2015): 38–47.

3 Consider the fact that UK bank notes carry the message "I promise to pay the bearer ..." and the signature of the cashier at the Bank of England. This says so much about what money is, and also about the fact that the whole edifice of money rests on a huge amount of (rarely scrutinized) trust. At the end of the day a fifty-pound note is just a small piece of paper and nothing else unless trust gives it value.

4 The 2022 Nobel Memorial Prize in Economic Science, more precisely the Sveriges Riksbank Prize in Economic Sciences in Memory of Alfred Nobel, awarded to Ben S. Bernanke, Douglas W. Diamond, and Philip H. Dybvig for their research on banks and financial crises, is directly related to this responsibility. See Committee for the Prize in Economic Sciences in Memory of Alfred Nobel, "The Laureates Explained the Central Role of Banks in Financial Crises," Popular Science Background, Royal Swedish Academy of Sciences, accessed 15 April 2023, https://www.nobelprize.org/uploads/2022/10/popular-economicsciencesprize2022-2.pdf.

5 Raghuram G. Rajan, *Fault Lines: How Hidden Fractures Still Threaten the World Economy* (Princeton, NJ: Princeton University Press, 2010), claims that private institutions, assuming that Freddie Mac's and Fannie Mae's involvement in the subprime market would significantly reduce the danger of high-risk loans, ended up taking too much risk by extending cheap credit. The problem is not with the economics and financials of the banking sector per se, but with the faulty incentive schemes promoted by government interventions in favour of cheap credit.

6 The mark-to-market accounting rule is the major one coming to mind.

7 During the financial crisis and recession of 2007–10 these factors were dominant.

8 For an insider view of the crisis, see Ben S. Bernanke, Timothy F. Geithner, and Henry M. Paulson, *Firefighting: The Financial Crisis and Its Lessons* (New York: Penguin Books, 2019). See also my own "Growing Out of Crisis and Recessions: Regulating Systemic Financial Institutions and Redefining Government Responsibilities," chapter 24 in Marcel Boyer et al., *Advanced Methods of Investment Evaluation: Information, Value Creation and Real Options*, CIRANO Monograph 2017MO-03 (Winter 2017), http://cirano.qc.ca/files/publications/2017MO-04.pdf.

9 Luigi Zingales, "Plan B," *Economists' Voice* 5, no. 6 (2008),

https://doi.org/10.2202/1553-3832.1446.

10 See chapters 8, 12, and 20 in Boyer et al., *Advanced Methods of Investment Evaluation*.

11 See S. Verguet, S.T. Memirie, M.T. Tolla, and D.T. Jamison, "Extended Cost-Effectiveness Analysis," in *Global Health Priority Setting: Beyond Cost-Effectiveness*, ed. O.F. Norheim, E.J. Emanuel, and J. Millum (New York: Oxford University Press, 2019), 87–102.

12 For a particularly informative analysis, see Yann Algan, Elizabeth Beasley, Sylvana Côté, Jungwee Park, Richard E. Tremblay, and Frank Vitaro, "The Impact of Childhood Social Skills and Self-Control Training on Economic and Noneconomic Outcomes: Evidence from a Randomized Experiment Using Administrative Data," *American Economic Review* 118, no. 8 (2022): 2553–79.

13 See Martin Boyer, Philippe De Donder, Claude Fluet, Marie-Louise Leroux, and Pierre-Carl Michaud, "Long-Term Care Insurance: Information Frictions and Selection," CESifo Working Paper Series No. 6698 (24 November 2017), https://ssrn.com/abstract=3075158; Boyer, De Donder, Fluet, Leroux, and Michaud, "A Canadian Parlor Room–Type Approach to the Long-Term Care Insurance Market," *Canadian Public Policy* 45, no. 2 (2019): 262–82; Boyer, De Donder, Fluet, Leroux, and Michaud, "Long-Term Care Risk Misperceptions," *Geneva Papers Issues and Practice* 44, no. 2 (2019): 183–215.

14 See "Flooding," Insurance Bureau of Canada, accessed 28 March 2023, https://bac-quebec.qc.ca/en/insurance-issues/flooding/.

15 "The Wimbledon tennis tournament had the foresight to buy around £1.5 million (US$1.9 million) per year in pandemic insurance following the SARS outbreak in 2003, said GlobalData in a recent bulletin. Paying out roughly £25.5 million (US$31.7 million) in premiums over that 17-year period, Wimbledon is set to receive an insurance payout of around £114 million (US$142 million) for this year's cancelled tournament." "Wimbledon Shows How Pandemic Insurance Could Become Vital for Sports, Other Events," *Insurance Journal*, 13 April 2020, https://www.insurancejournal.com/news/international/2020/04/13/564598.htm.

16 Wikipedia, s.v. "EllisDon," last edited 12 September 2022, 16:10, https://en.wikipedia.org/wiki/EllisDon.

17 Kavita Sabharwal-Chomiuk, "EllisDon to Become 100 Per Cent Employee-Owned," *Electrical Business*, 16 March 2020, https://www.ebmag.com/ellisdon-to-become-100-per-cent-employee-owned/.

18 The ownership of an IP, whether as a patent, copyright, or trademark, may be a bit tricky. If the IP was developed under an employment status, it is likely owned by the employer, but not necessarily.
19 See, for instance, Emma Woolacott, "Lessons from History's Worst CEOs," *CEO Magazine*, 18 July 2018, https://www.theceomagazine.com/business/management-leadership/lessons-from-historys-worst-ceos/.
20 In "The Retail Gasoline Price-Fixing Cartel in Québec," *Canadian Competition Law Review* 35, no. 1 (2022): 134–63, I report on a cartel of gas service stations between 2001 and 2006 in Quebec (the largest cartel case in the history of the Canadian Competition Bureau). While controlling about 90 per cent of one of the relevant markets (Sherbrooke), the cartel could raise prices by 1–5 per cent above the estimated competitive price. One restricting factor was the presence of competitive market cities not too distant for the relevant markets.
21 J.A. Schumpeter, *Capitalism, Socialism and Democracy*, 3rd ed. (1942; New York: Harper, 1975), 82: "The opening up of new markets, foreign or domestic, and the organizational development from the craft shop and factory to such concerns as U.S. Steel illustrate the same process of industrial mutation ... that incessantly revolutionizes the economic structure *from within*, incessantly destroying the old one, incessantly creating a new one. This process of Creative Destruction is the essential fact about capitalism."
22 "Business Employment Dynamics – Second Quarter 2022," news release, US Bureau of Labor Statistics, 25 January 2023, https://www.bls.gov/news.release/archives/cewbd_01252023.htm:

> The Business Employment Dynamics data measure the net change in employment at the establishment or firm level. These changes come about in one of four ways. A net increase in employment can come from either opening units or expanding units. A net decrease in employment can come from either closing units or contracting units. Gross job gains include the sum of all jobs added at either opening or expanding units. Gross job losses include the sum of all jobs lost in either closing or contracting units. The net change in employment is the difference between gross job gains and gross job losses ... Establishments are used in the tabulation of the BED statistics by industry and firms are used in the tabulation of the BED size class statistics. An establishment is defined as an economic unit that produces goods or services, usually at a single physical location, and engages in one or predominantly one activity. A firm is a legal business, either

corporate or otherwise, and may consist of several establishments. Firm-level data are compiled based on an aggregation of establishments under common ownership by a corporate parent using employer tax identification numbers. The firm level aggregation, which is consistent with the role of corporations as the economic decision makers, is used for the measurement of BED data elements by size class. Because of the difference in the unit of analysis, total gross job gains and gross job losses by size class are lower than total gross job gains and gross job losses by industry, as some establishment gains and losses within a firm are offset during the aggregation process. However, the total net changes in employment are the same for not seasonally adjusted data and are similar for seasonally adjusted data.

For the full series from 1993.3 to 2022.2, see "Table 1. Private Sector Gross Job Gains and Job Losses, Seasonally Adjusted," US Bureau of Labor Statistic, accessed 15 April 2023, https://www.bls.gov/web/cewbd/table1_18_ind3.txt.

23 See Marcel Boyer and Molivann Panot, "Obamacare: Enjeux économiques et constitutionnels," CIRANO Cahier Scientifique 2020s-60 (November 2020), http://cirano.qc.ca/files/publications/2020s-60.pdf.

24 See Marcel Boyer, "A Habit Forming Optimal Growth Model," *International Economic Review* 19, no. 3 (1978): 585–609; Boyer, "Rational Demand and Expenditures Patterns under Habit Formation," *Journal of Economic Theory* 31, no. 1 (1983): 27–53; Gary Becker and Kevin Murphy, "A Theory of Rational Addiction," *Journal of Political Economy* 96, no. 4 (1988): 675–700.

25 Garrett Hardin, "The Tragedy of the Commons," *Science* 162, no. 3859 (1968): 1244. Hardin was concerned with uncontrolled population growth under a laissez-faire policy of reproduction. He was contesting Adam Smith's invisible hand precept that "decisions reached individually will, in fact, be the best decisions for an entire society."

26 Michael A. Heller, "The Tragedy of the Anticommons: Property in the Transition from Marx to Markets," *Harvard Law Review* 111, no. 3 (1998): 677.

27 Elinor Ostrom, *Governing the Commons: The Evolution of Institutions for Collective Action* (Cambridge: Cambridge University Press, 1990), 21.

28 Ibid., 14.

CHAPTER TWO

1. For more about the principles of social democracy, see (among many other sources) J. De Beus and T. Koelble, "The Third Way Diffusion of Social Democracy: Western Europe and South Africa Compared," *Politikon*, 28, no. 2 (2001): 181–94.
2. See Stuart White, "'Rights and Responsibilities': A Social Democratic Perspective," in *The New Social Democracy*, ed. Andrew Gamble and Tonight Wright (Oxford: Blackwell, 1999), 166–79.
3. Amartya Sen, *Development as Freedom* (Oxford: Oxford University Press, 1999).
4. A.O. Hirschman, *Exit, Voice, and Loyalty: Responses to Decline in Firms, Organizations, and States* (Cambridge, MA: Harvard University Press, 1970).
5. Simon Kuznets, "How to Judge Quality," *New Republic*, October 20, 1962, 29.
6. James Gardner March, "Bounded Rationality, Ambiguity and the Engineering of Choice," *Bell Journal of Economics* 9, no. 2 (1978): 587–608.
7. Marcel Boyer, "A Habit Forming Optimal Growth Model," *International Economic Review* 19, no. 3 (1978): 585–609; Boyer, "Rational Demand and Expenditures Patterns under Habit Formation," *Journal of Economic Theory* 31, no. 1 (1983): 27–53.
8. See Marcel Boyer, "The Twelve Principles of Incentive Pay," *Revue d'Économie Politique* 121, no. 3 (2011): 285–306. See also chapter 7 below.
9. In more technical terms, adverse selection is a problem of pre-contractual opportunism, while moral hazard is a problem of post-contractual opportunism.
10. Boyer, "The Twelve Principles of Incentive Pay."
11. In a column for the *Financial Times* entitled "When It Comes to Foreign Workers, Some Ideas Aren't So Crazy" (26 September 2008), Tim Harford writes,
    > Shortly after the Soviet Union collapsed, a Russian bureaucrat travelled to the west to seek advice on how the market system functioned. He asked the economist Paul Seabright to explain who was in charge of the supply of bread to London. He was astonished by the answer: Nobody ... Earlier this month, the Migration Advisory Committee presented a list of professions that would qualify migrants for entry, broadly on the grounds of UK skills shortages ... Perhaps the previous patchwork of immigration restrictions was even worse. Yet nobody now thinks that a government-appointed committee, no mat-

ter how wise or diligent, could plan how many memory chips the UK should import, or how much beef, or how many copies of Jay-Z's latest album. The exercise is no simpler when the imports are workers. If anything, the opposite is true ... This is not an argument about what the limits on foreign workers should be; it is an argument about how laughable it is to rely on a centrally planned list of what sort of work foreigners should be allowed in to do.

The bread story is told by Seabright himself in his book *The Company of Strangers: A Natural History of Economic Life* (Princeton, NJ: Princeton University Press, 2010), 19.

12 William J. Baumol, John C. Panzar, and Robert D. Willig, *Contestable Markets and the Theory of Industry Structure* (New York: Harcourt Brace Jovanovitch, 1982).

13 Wikipedia, s.v. "Modularity," last edited 15 November 2022, 12:01, https://en.wikipedia.org/wiki/Modularity.

14 There are obvious links between income- and wealth-support policies and optimal taxation. The theory of optimal taxation studies the design and implementation of a tax system that minimizes the distortions caused by taxation while achieving desired levels of redistribution and revenue. For a relatively general discussion of optimal taxation, see Florian Scheuer and Iván Werning, "Mirrlees Meets Diamond-Mirrlees," NBER Working Paper 22076 (March 2016), https://www.nber.org/system/files/working_papers/w22076/w22076.pdf.

15 See Marcel Boyer, "A Pervasive Economic Fallacy in Assessing the Cost of Public Funds," *Canadian Public Policy* 48, no. 1 (March 2022): 1–10, https://www.utpjournals.press/doi/full/10.3138/cpp.2021-035.

16 In more technical terms, efficiency requires that consumers' marginal rate of substitution between A and B is equal to producers' marginal rate of transformation/substitution between A and B. If both are equal to the same relative prices (including the taxes), the efficiency condition is met in a decentralized way. Efficiency therefore depends on us not tampering with the relative prices on which consumption decisions and production decisions are made.

17 The World Health Organization designed a recommended code of practice that was ratified by its 193 member states in 2010. Its goal is "to provide ethical principles applicable to the international recruitment of health personnel in a manner that strengthens the health systems of developing countries ... to mitigate the negative effects of health personnel migration on the health systems of developing countries ... to consider the legal responsibilities of health personnel to the health

system of their own country... and not seek to recruit them." See World Health Organization, WHO Global CODE of Practice on the International Recruitment of Health Personnel, Sixty-third World Health Assembly – WHA63.16 (May 2010), https://www.un.org/en/development/desa/population/migration/generalassembly/docs/globalcompact/WHA_RES_63.16.pdf.

CHAPTER THREE

1 Other criticisms, analyses, and movements to reform capitalism take more from the "democratic socialism" mould, contemporary business management, and the impacts of technological change, in particular automation and information technologies. Consider the work of Peter Drucker, especially *Post-capitalist Society* (New York: Harper Business, 1994), who maintains that we have passed into a post-capitalist production system in which capital has lost its centrality because it is less entrepreneurial and more the property of financial companies, such as insurance firms, investments funds, banks, etc. As the owners of capital, citizens have thus become virtual owners of large enterprises. This does not destroy, but does alter, the nature of capitalism. Drucker predicts that post-capitalist society will become a society of organizations in which social classes will be divided into knowledge and service classes. He expected the transformation to post-capitalism to be completed by 2010–20. He also argues in favour of a reform of intellectual property by the creation of a universal licensing system. Consumers would subscribe at a given cost, and producers could use, reproduce, and distribute protected works freely.
2 Branko Milanovic, *Capitalism, Alone: The Future of the System that Rules the World* (Cambridge, MA: Harvard University Press, 2019).
3 Tianlei Huang and Nicolas Véron, "The Private Sector Advances in China: The Evolving Ownership Structure of the Largest Companies in the Xi Jinping Era," Working Paper 22-3, Peterson Institute for International Economics (March 2022), https://www.piie.com/publications/working-papers/private-sector-advances-china-evolving-ownership-structures-largest.
4 Luigi Zingales, *A Capitalism for the People: Recapturing the Lost Genius of American Prosperity* (New York: Basic Books, 2012).
5 "Updated Estimates of the Subsidies to the Housing GSEs," Congressional Budget Office, 8 April 2004, https://www.cbo.gov/sites/default/files/108th-congress-2003-2004/reports/04-08-gse.pdf.

6 Marcel Boyer, "Growing Out of the Crisis and Recessions: Regulating Systemic Financial Institutions and Redefining Government Responsibilities," CIRANO Scientific Series 2015s-01 (January 2015), https://cirano.qc.ca/files/publications/2015s-01.pdf. Despite a 2002 study released by Fannie Mae that argued that it was very unlikely that the two government-sponsored enterprises would ever require a government bailout. See Joseph E. Stiglitz, Jonathan M. Orszag, Peter R. Orszag, "Implications of the New Fannie Mae and Freddie Mac Risk-Based Capital Standard," *Fannie Mae Papers* 1, no. 2 (March 2002): 1–10.

7 The worst collusive, or crony, capitalists are those who can drape their requests for protection and subsidies in the flag of a noble cause, such as the pursuit of a common good or the defence of the national interest. Thus, Zingales identifies academics (professors and administrators of schools, colleges, and universities) as among the worst crony capitalists around. We might add farmers and national champions or treasures, among others.

8 An example is provided by Claude Montmarquette, "Le Remboursement Proportionnel au Revenu (RPR): Un système pour les prêtes d'études alliant efficacité et accessibilité," CIRANO Rapport de projet 2006RP-08 (April 2006), https://cirano.qc.ca/files/publications/2006RP-08.pdf.

9 Jean Tirole, *Économie du bien commun* (Paris: Presses Universitaires de France, 2016).

10 Jean-Jacques Laffont, "Étapes vers un État moderne: Une analyse économique," in *État et gestion publique: Actes du Colloque du 16 décembre 1999* (Paris: La Documentation Française, 2000), 117–49, https://www.cae-eco.fr/Etat-et-gestion-publique.

11 "A Manifesto for Renewing Liberalism," *The Economist*, 13 September 2018, https://www.economist.com/leaders/2018/09/13/a-manifesto-for-renewing-liberalism.

12 "Competition: Trustbusting in the 21st Century," *The Economist*, 15 November 2018, https://www.economist.com/special-report/2018-11-17.

13 Joseph E. Stiglitz, *People, Power, and Profits: Progressive Capitalism for an Age of Discontent* (New York: W.W. Norton, 2019).

14 Joseph Stiglitz was a key player in these developments. In 2001, he was awarded a Nobel Prize for his contributions to information economics.

15 Philippe Aghion, Céline Antonin, and Simon Bunel, *The Power of Creative Destruction: Economic Upheaval and the Wealth of Nations* (Cambridge, MA: Harvard University Press, 2021).

16 Mariana Mazzucato has written three influential books on capitalism: *The Entrepreneurial State: Debunking Public vs Private Sector Myths* (Lon-

don: Anthem Press, 2013); *The Value of Everything: Making and Taking in the Global Economy* (London: Allen Lane, 2018); and *Mission Economy: A Moonshot Guide to Changing Capitalism* (London: Allen Lane, 2021).

17 Thomas Piketty, *Capital and Ideology*, trans. Arthur Goldhammer (Cambridge, MA: Belknap Press of Harvard University Press, 2020), 967–8.

18 Ibid., 989.

19 Marcel Boyer, "L'économie des organisations: Mythes et réalités," Conférence présidentielle, Société canadienne de science économique, St-Sauveur, QC, May 1996, published in *L'Actualité économique* 96, no. 4 (2020): 471–98, https://www.erudit.org/en/journals/ae/2020-v96-n4-ae06831/1087014ar.pdf.

20 Justin Y. Lin, "Collectivisation and China's Agricultural Crisis in 1959–61," *Journal of Political Economy* 98, no. 6 (1990): 1228–52; Justin Y. Lin and D.T. Yang, "Food Availability, Entitlements and the Chinese Famine of 1959–61," *Economic Journal, Royal Economic Society* 110, no. 460 (200): 136–58. Also see Ezra F. Vogel, *Deng Xiaoping and the Transformation of China* (Cambridge, MA: Belknap Press of Harvard University Press, 2011), who writes, "The misguided Great Leap Forward caused devastation throughout China. Starvation was widespread. After peasants were organized in huge communes with mess halls so that more of them could work on large, poorly planned construction projects or in the fields, they could see that those who performed no work were fed as well as the others and they lost any incentive to work, causing a great drop in the size of the harvests; many mess halls ran out of food" (41).

21 See World Business Council for Sustainable Development, *Vision 2050: The New Agenda for Business* (Geneva: WBCSD, 2010), https://www.wbcsd.org/contentwbc/download/1746/21728/1, and *Reinventing Capitalism: A Transformation Agenda* (Geneva: WBCSD, 2020), https://www.wbcsd.org/contentwbc/download/10585/157859/1.

22 See the op-ed by Jamie Dimon (JPMorgan Chase) and Warren E. Buffett (Berkshire Hathaway), "Short-Termism Is Harming the Economy," *Wall Street Journal*, 6 June 2018, https://www.wsj.com/articles/short-termism-is-harming-the-economy-1528336801. The authors argue that short-termism harms companies, which should therefore abandon quarterly earnings per share targets in favour of annual or multi-year targets.

23 See "About Us," Business Roundtable, accessed 15 April 2023, https://www.businessroundtable.org/.

24 See also Raghuram G. Rajan, *The Third Pillar: How Markets and the State Leave the Community Behind* (New York: Penguin Press, 2019).

25 "Economists' Statement on Carbon Dividends," Climate Leadership Council, accessed 31 March 2023, https://www.econstatement.org/.

26 See Olivier Blanchard, Christian Gollier, and Jean Tirole, "The Portfolio of Economic Policies Needed to Fight Climate Change," Working Paper 22-18, Peterson Institute for International Economics (November 2022), https://www.piie.com/sites/default/files/2022-11/wp22-18.pdf.
27 Michael Patrick F. Smith, "The First Step Is Admitting You Have a Problem," *New York Times*, 5 February 2021, https://www.nytimes.com/2021/02/05/opinion/fossil-fuel-oil-climate-change.html.
28 Ibid.
29 Joint and several liability means that responsibility is shared by two or more parties. It makes all parties responsible for damages up to the entire amount awarded. That is, if one party is unable to pay, the others named must pay more than their share.
30 Readers with an interest in this matter can peruse Marcel Boyer, "The Twelve Principles of Incentive Pay," *Revue d'Économie Politique* 121, no. 3 (2011): 285–306.
31 For data on the total payroll for Big Tech companies, see table 3.1.
32 In the epitome of irony, we often see these same directors complain about similar behaviour in their trading partners. They see the mote in their brother's eye, but not the beam in their own.
33 "Business Employment Dynamics," US Bureau of Labor Statistics, accessed 31 March 2023, https://www.bls.gov/bdm/.
34 According to the avoidable cost criteria (Baumol), a price is predatory if it does not allow a company to cover the costs that it would avoid if it did not supply the good or service in question. See Lina Kahn, "Amazon's Antitrust Paradox," *Yale Law Journal* 126, no. 3 (2017): 710–805. In her highly influential article, Khan, who at thirty-two became chairperson of the US Federal Trade Commission, analyzes Amazon's growth strategy in terms of predatory pricing and common carrier responsibility regulation (see policy 9 in this chapter). See also Marcel Boyer, Thomas W. Ross, and Ralph A. Winter, "The Rise of Economics in Competition Policy: A Canadian Perspective," *Canadian Journal of Economics* 50, no. 5, 50th Anniversary Issue (December 2017): 1489–1524.
35 Keith McArthur, "Rivals Agree Competition Laws Flawed," *Globe and Mail*, 10 December 2001, https://www.theglobeandmail.com/report-on-business/rivals-agree-competition-laws-flawed/article18420014/; McArthur, "Air Canada Charged with Predatory Pricing," *Globe and Mail*, 6 March 2001, https://www.theglobeandmail.com/report-on-business/air-canada-charged-with-predatory-pricing/article1178833/.
36 See Marcel Boyer, "Challenges and Pitfalls in Competition Policy Implementation," Joint State of the Art Lecture (Canadian Economics Associ-

ation, Atlantic Canada Economics Association, CIRANO, Phelps Centre for the Study of Government and Business, and Rotman Institute for International Business), St Francis Xavier University, Antigonish, NS, 4 June 2017. Available at https://www.youtube.com/watch?v=u9LUdeYe4dQ&t=1560s&ab_channel=CanadianEconomicsAssociation. See especially 1:10:25.

37 See Marcel Boyer, "A Pervasive Economic Fallacy in Assessing the Cost of Public Funds," *Canadian Public Policy* 48, no. 1 (March 2022): 1–10, https://www.utpjournals.press/doi/full/10.3138/cpp.2021-035.

38 Boyer, Ross, and Winter, "The Rise of Economics in Competition Policy," 1489–1524.

39 See Marcel Boyer, Michel Moreaux, and Michel Truchon, *Partage des coûts et tarification des infrastructures* (Montreal: CIRANO, February 2006), https://cirano.qc.ca/files/publications/2006MO-01.pdf, and Marcel Boyer and Nicholas Marchetti, "Principes de choix d'une méthode économique d'allocation: Partage des coûts et tarification à Gaz de France," CIRANO Rapport de projet 2007-RP07 (March, 2006), http://cirano.qc.ca/files/publications/2007RP-07.pdf.

40 Marcel Boyer, "The Measure and Regulation of Competition in Telecommunications Markets," in *Regulation and the Evolution of the Global Telecommunications Industry*, ed. Anastassios Gentzoglanis and Anders Henten, 109–27 (Cheltenham, UK: Edward Elgar Publishing, 2010).

41 For an overview, see Marcel Boyer and Jacques Robert, "Competition and Access in Electricity Markets: ECPR, Global Price Cap, and Auctions," *Deregulation of Electric Utilities*, ed. George Zaccour (Amsterdam: Kluwer Academic, 1998), 47–74.

42 In technical terms, the business establishes a price structure suggested by Ramsey, reflecting its knowledge of demand and costs. It is no longer necessary for the regulator to find and measure these demand and cost conditions and elasticities.

43 David Card, "Who Set Your Wage?," NBER Working Paper 29683 (January 2022), 16–18, https://www.nber.org/system/files/working_papers/w29683/w29683.pdf.

44 For example, "economist" is not a reserved or certified title. Anyone can call him- or herself an "economist." A company or university may want to recruit an economist with a degree from a recognized university (branded), but nothing should prevent it from recruiting self-taught economists if it is satisfied with their pedigrees and can assess their quality.

CHAPTER FOUR

1 See Matt Ridley, *The Rational Optimist: How Prosperity Evolves* (New York: Harper Perrenial, 2011).
2 Serge Coulombe, Jean-François Tremblay, and Sylvie Marchand, *International Adult Literacy Survey: Literacy Scores, Human Capital and Growth across 14 OECD Countries*, Statistics Canada Catalogue no.89-552-MIE (Ottawa: Minister of Industry, 2004), https://publications.gc.ca/collections/Collection/CS89-552-11E.pdf.
3 Coulombe, Tremblay, and Marchand, 31. See also Helen Abadzi, *Efficient Learning for the Poor: Insights from the Frontier of Cognitive Neuroscience* (Washington, DC: World Bank, 2006).
4 Hernando De Soto, *The Other Path: The Invisible Revolution in the Third World* (New York: Harper and Row, 1989).
5 Ronald Coase, "The Nature of the Firm," *Economica*, new ser., 4, no. 16 (1937): 386–405. Coase acknowledges earlier contributions from, among others, Alfred Marshall, John Bates Clark, Frank Knight, and Lionel Robbins.
6 From Russ Krajec, "How Patent Pools Work," BlueIron IP, acessed 31 March 2023, https://blueironip.com/how-patent-pools-work/:

> Patent pools are sophisticated ways that companies can bring technology together, cross license them, and license that package of intellectual property to the market. For many major technologies, such as Bluetooth, MPEG, 3G, 4G, and even electric vehicle charging, companies have banded together to get their technology in wide adoption – and patent pools are the vehicle. Very few individual companies have the market power to dictate standards that are used across an industry. In almost all circumstances, an industry standard allows everyone to build to that standard. For example, a cellular telephone from any manufacturer can, in most cases, operate on any provider's network. The complex handshaking, data exchange, frequency allocation, and the rest of the industry standard makes this happen seamlessly. Patent pools are a way for standards essential patents to be shared, and in many cases, for the patent owners to be paid for their contribution. A patent pool minimizes transaction costs because in one transaction, a company can get the benefit of multiple patents from multiple patent holders. Licensees of a patent pool avoid patent litigation because they have access to all complementary patents in the pool. The key to a patent pool is that patents are essential to meet the standard. Patents that are not essential are (generally) not included in the pooled patents.

From Wikipedia, s.v. "Patent Pool," last edited 27 May 2022, 08:24, https://en.wikipedia.org/wiki/Patent_pool:

> In 1856, sewing machine manufacturers Grover & Baker, Singer, and Wheeler & Wilson, all accusing each other of patent infringement, met in Albany, New York to pursue their suits. Orlando B. Potter, a lawyer and president of Grover & Baker, proposed that, rather than squander their profits on litigation, they pool their patents. This was the first patent pool, a process which enables the production of complicated machines without legal battles over patent rights. In 1917, the two major patent holders for airplanes, the Wright Company and the Curtiss Company, had effectively blocked the building of new airplanes, which were desperately needed as the United States was entering World War I. The U.S. government, as a result of a recommendation of a committee formed by Franklin D. Roosevelt, then Assistant Secretary of the Navy, pressured the industry to form a patent pool, the Manufacturer's Aircraft Association. In a more modern example, in August 2005, a patent pool was formed by about 20 companies active in the Radio Frequency Identification (RFID) domain. The RFID Consortium picked Via Licensing to administer its patent pool in September 2006.

7 From "A Statement on FRAND Licensing of Standard Essential Patents," Apple, accessed 31 March 2023, https://www.apple.com/ca/fr/legal/intellectual-property/frand/, one reads the following:

> How standard essential patents are licensed affects competition, innovation, product compatibility, and consumer choice. When licensed on fair, reasonable, and non-discriminatory [FRAND] terms, everyone stands to benefit. On the other hand, when companies use the market power of a standard and standard essential patents to demand unfair, unreasonable, or discriminatory terms, consumers are harmed and fewer choices are available. Apple brings a balanced perspective to the promises and perils of standardization and outlines several core principles to promote fair, reasonable, and non-discriminatory licensing of standard essential patents, addressing transparency during negotiation, merits-based evaluation, portfolio licensing, use of a common royalty base and rate, and injunctive relief. Taken together, these principles provide a consistent framework for fair, reasonable, and non-discriminatory licensing of standard essential patents.

8 In the case of a pure public good, which by definition can be consumed in totality by everyone, additional consumers' consumption can be satis-

fied at no cost. Hence the marginal cost pricing principle would set the price at zero. But in such a case, production cost is not covered. To ensure efficiency in production and consumption, Lindahl pricing requires each individual to pay a price that reflects his or her marginal evaluation of the public good at the efficient quantity. This pattern of prices motivates each individual to consume all the public good supplied, with the sum of the prices motivating the efficient supply. See Dwight Lee, "On the Pricing of Public Goods," *Southern Economic Journal* 49, no. 1 (1982): 99–105. For a practical application of Lindahl pricing to copyrighted musical works and sound recordings, see Marcel Boyer and Anne Catherine Faye, "Music Royalty Rates for Different Business Models: Lindahl Pricing and Nash Bargaining," in *Encyclopedia of Law and Economics*, ed. Alain Marciano and Giovanni Ramello (New York: Springer, 2018), https://link.springer.com/referenceworkentry/10.1007/978-1-4614-7883-6_761-1.

CHAPTER FIVE

1 Joan Roughgarden, "Guide to Diplomatic Relations with Economists," *Bulletin of the Ecological Society of America* 82, no. 1 (2001): 85–6.
2 Forum for Sustainable and Responsible Investment, *Report on US Sustainable, Responsible and Impact Investing Trends 2020* (Washington, DC: US SIF, 2020), https://www.ussif.org/files/Trends%20Report%202020%20Executive%20Summary.pdf. The 2022 report was published on 13 December 2022; it is available at https://www.ussif.org/trends.
3 Jon Hale, *Sustainable Funds U.S. Landscape Report* (Chicago: Morningstar, 2020).
4 See European Sustainable Investment Forum, *European SRI Study 2018* (Brussels: Eurosif, 2018), https://www.eurosif.org/wp-content/uploads/2021/10/European-SRI-2018-Study.pdf; Forum for Sustainable and Responsible Investment, *Report on US Sustainable, Responsible and Impact Investing Trends 2020*.
5 "Business Roundtable Redefines the Purpose of a Corporation to Promote 'An Economy that Serves All Americans,'" Business Roundtable, 19 August 2019, https://www.businessroundtable.org/business-roundtable-redefines-the-purpose-of-a-corporation-to-promote-an-economy-that-serves-all-americans.
6 "U.S. Department of Labor Announces Final Rule to Protect Americans'

Retirement Investments," news release, Department of Labor, 30 October 2020, https://www.dol.gov/newsroom/releases/ebsa/ebsa20201030.

7   Vivek Ramaswamy, "The Stakeholders vs. the People," *Wall Street Journal*, 12 February 2020, https://www.wsj.com/articles/the-stakeholders-vs-the-people-11581552372.

8   See Diego Restuccia and Richard Rogerson, "The Causes and Costs of Misallocation," *Journal of Economic Perspectives* 31, no. 3 (2017): 151–74. The authors write,

> When Hsieh and Klenow (2009) apply their method to four-digit manufacturing industries in China, India, and the United States, they find large effects of misallocation on total factor productivity. In particular, if misallocation were eliminated, total factor productivity in manufacturing would increase by 86–110 percent in China, 100–128 percent in India, and 30–43 percent in the United States ... Kalemli-Ozcan and Sorensen (2014) study misallocation of capital among private manufacturing firms in 10 African countries. Their sample also includes firms from India, Ireland, Spain, and South Korea that can be used as benchmarks. Subject to the caveat of small sample sizes, they find that capital misallocation in Africa is significantly higher than in developed countries, though not as severe as in India. (156, 159)

9   Milton Friedman, "A Friedman Doctrine – The Social Responsibility of Business Is to Increase Its Profits," *New York Times*, 13 September 1970, https://perma.cc/TU2U-FJUE.

10 Oliver Hart and Luigi Zingales, "The New Corporate Governance," *University of Chicago Business Law Review* 1, no. 1 (2023): 197.

11 Alex Edmans, "Applying Economics – Not Gut Feel – To ESG," London Business School Working Paper (16 March 2023), 4, https://papers.ssrn.com/sol3/papers.cfm?abstract_id=4346646. Emphasis in the original.

12 International Labour Organization, *Global Estimates of Child Labour: Results and Trends, 2012–2016* (Geneva: International Labour Organization, September 2017).

13 "The Power of Publicity," *The Economist*, 3 December 1998, https://www.economist.com/special-report/1998/12/03/the-power-of-publicity.

14 Sam Vaknin, "Commentary: The Morality of Child Labor," United Press International, 4 October 2002, https://www.upi.com/Archives/2002/10/04/Commentary-The-morality-of-Child-labor/7691033704000/.

15 Miriam Wasserman, "Eliminating Child Labor," *Federal Reserve Bank of Boston Regional Review* 10, no. 2 (2000), https://www.bostonfed.org/home/publications/regional-review/2000/quarter-2/eliminating-child-

labor.aspx. For a collection of photographs of children's workplaces taken between 1908 and 1924 by Lewis Wickes Hine on behalf of National Child Labor Committee, see the National Child Labor Committee Collection, US Library of Congress, accessed 3 April 2023, https://www.loc.gov/pictures/search/?sp=1&co=nclc&st=grid. "The NCLC photos are useful for the study of labor, reform movements, children, working class families, education, public health, urban and rural housing conditions, industrial and agricultural sites, and other aspects of urban and rural life in America in the early twentieth century." From "About This Collection," National Child Labor Committee Collection, US Library of Congress, accessed 3 April 2023, https://www.loc.gov/pictures/search/?sp=1&co=nclc&st=grid.

16 Catherine A. Paul, "National Child Labor Committee," Social Welfare History Project, Virginia Commonwealth University, accessed 3 April 2023, http://socialwelfare.library.vcu.edu/programs/child-welfarechild-labor/national-child-labor-committee/. Also see US Bureau of the Census, Historical Statistics of the United States: *Colonial Times to 1970*, bicentennial ed. (Washington, DC: Bureau of the Census, 1975), https://www.census.gov/history/pdf/histstats-colonial-1970.pdf.

17 Wasserman, "Eliminating Child Labor."

18 On this subject, see Marcel Boyer and Jean-Jacques Laffont, "Environmental Risks and Bank Liability," *European Economic Review* 41, no. 8 (1997): 1427–59; Marcel Boyer and Donatella Porrini, "Modeling the Choice between Regulation and Liability in Terms of Social Welfare," *Canadian Journal of Economics* 37, no. 3 (2004): 590–612; Marcel Boyer and Donatella Porrini, "The Impact of Court Errors on Liability Sharing and Safety Regulation for Environmental/Industrial Accidents," *International Review of Law and Economics* 33, no. 1 (2008): 337–62. The application of extended liability for environmental damage under CERCLA has given rise to a very large literature in law and economics. CERCLA exempts from owner/operator liability any person who, without participating in the management of a facility, holds indicia of ownership primarily to protect the person's security interest in the facility. Holding a security interest means having a legal claim of ownership in order to secure a loan, equipment, or other debt. This exemption protects from CERCLA owner/operator liability those entities, such as private and governmental lending institutions (e.g., banks), that maintain a right of ownership in, or guarantee loans for, facilities that become contaminated with hazardous substances. Amendments to CERCLA in 1996 state that a lender participates in management and will not be protected by

the secured creditor exemption if it either exercises decision-making control over environmental compliance related to the facility, such that the lender has undertaken responsibility for hazardous substance handling or disposal practices; or exercises control at a level comparable to that of a manager of the facility, such that the lender has assumed or manifested responsibility with respect to day-to-day decision making regarding environmental compliance.

19 Marcel Boyer and Donatella Porrini, "Sharing Liability between Banks and Firms: The Case of Industrial Safety Risk," in *Frontiers in the Economics of Environmental Regulation and Liability*, ed. Marcel Boyer, Yolande Hiriart, and David Martimort (Aldershot, UK: Ashgate, 2006), 311–41; Boyer and Porrini, "The Impact of Court Errors on Liability Sharing and Safety Regulation for Environmental/Industrial Accidents." The following discussion is somewhat "wonkish." It is provided here to illustrate the complexity of responsibility rules by briefly developing the analysis of the four factors. First, a decrease in corporate profitability should reduce the company's socially responsible (ESG) liability and raise prevention (safety) standards. This will increase monitoring efforts, but prevention efforts will be reduced despite the heightened standards, increasing the likelihood of industrial or environmental accidents. The higher prevention standards combined with the decrease in prevention activities means that the company is more likely to be found guilty of negligence in the event of an accident (if prosecuted). Second, a higher cost of accident-prevention activities typically leads to a reduction in prevention efforts and thus an increased probability of accidents, leading in turn to a lower liability level for the firm, greater monitoring efforts, and a higher probability of being found guilty of negligence. Third, an increased effectiveness of prevention efforts in reducing the probability of accidents also affects first-order values (a reduced level of prevention combined with reduced probability of accidents), resulting in an increase in the company's liability followed by a decrease in standards of prevention, a decrease in monitoring activities, a decrease in the level of prevention, and a lower probability of accidents and of being convicted for negligence (which explains the decrease in the value of monitoring). Fourth, an increase in the social cost of public funds (reduced efficiency of government financing or increased transfer of risks onto the backs of taxpayers) will lead the benevolent government to reduce the ESG liability of businesses while increasing prevention standards. This will lead to an increase in monitoring efforts, a reduction in the level of prevention chosen, and thus an increase in the

probability of accidents, and an increase in the probability of conviction. Fifth, an increase in the efficiency of the judicial system (reduction of type I and II errors) will lead the benevolent government to reduce corporate liability and lower standards of prevention, giving rise to a decrease in monitoring efforts, an increase in the level of prevention chosen by the company and a corresponding reduction in the likelihood of accidents and of conviction for negligence.

20 On this association's website (https://ega.org/) we read, "The Environmental Grantmakers Association (EGA) was formed in 1987 with twelve member foundations from across the United States. Today, our members represent over 200 foundations from North America and around the world. Recognizing the importance of diverse perspectives, the organization values ecological integrity, justice, environmental stewardship, inclusivity, transparency, accountability, respect and balancing pragmatism with idealism. EGA will strive to 'walk the talk' with all of its resources and focus. The ultimate goal of EGA and its members is a world with healthy, equitable, and sustainable ecosystems, communities, and economies."

21 Bill Moyers, "After 9/11," keynote address to the Environmental Grantmakers Association Brainerd, MN, 16 October 2001, PBS.org, accessed 3 April 2023, http://www.pbs.org/moyers/journal/blog/2008/09/bill_moyers_after_911.html.

22 For a simple but illuminating account of green accounting, see William Nordhaus, laureate of the 2018 Nobel Memorial Prize in Economic Sciences, "Green National Accounting," *Project Syndicate*, 3 September 2021, https://www.project-syndicate.org/magazines/green-national-accounting-by-william-d-nordhaus-2021-09. Nordhaus writes, "Those who claim that environmental regulations harm economic growth are completely wrong, because they are using the wrong yardstick. Pollution *should* be in our measures of output, but with a negative sign. If we use green national output as our standard, then environmental and safety regulations have increased true economic growth substantially in recent years."

23 "Superfund" is the common name for the environmental remediation program that resulted from the 1980 *Comprehensive Environmental Response, Compensation, and Liability Act*. As explained above, CERCLA is a US federal law designed to ensure toxic waste sites are cleaned up.

24 The Center for Corporate Climate Leadership's website can be viewed at https://www.epa.gov/climateleadership.

25 For further discussion, see Marcel Boyer and Jean-Jacques Laffont, "Envi-

ronmental Protection, Producer Insolvency and Lender Liability," in *Economic Policy for the Environment and Natural Resources*, ed. Athanasios Xepapadeas (Cheltenham, UK: Edward Elgar Publishing, 1996), 1–29; Marcel Boyer and Jean-Jacques Laffont, "Environmental Risk and Bank Liability," *European Economic Review*, no. 41 (1997): 1427–59; Marcel Boyer and Jean-Jacques Laffont, "Toward a Political Theory of the Emergence of Environmental Incentive Regulation," *RAND Journal of Economics* 30, no. 1 (1999): 137–57; Marcel Boyer, Tracy Lewis, and W.L. Liu, "Setting Standards for Credible Compliance and Law Enforcement," *Canadian Journal of Economics* 33, no. 2 (2000): 319–40.

26 This is exactly the principle underlying the program announced by the Government of Canada in December 2020: A broad-based carbon levy (tax), the proceeds of which would be redistributed to citizens on a basis that is independent of their carbon-emissions generation.

27 Olivier Blanchard, Christian Gollier, and Jean Tirole, "The Portfolio of Economic Policies Needed to Fight Climate Change," Working Paper 22-18, Peterson Institute for International Economics (November 2022), 8–9, https://www.piie.com/sites/default/files/2022-11/wp22-18.pdf.

28 Ibid., 36.

29 "Economists' Statement on Carbon Dividends," *Wall Street Journal*, 16 January 2019, https://www.wsj.com/articles/economists-statement-on-carbon-dividends-11547682910.

30 "Economists' Statement on Carbon Dividends," Climate Leadership Council, accessed 31 March 2023, https://www.econstatement.org/.

31 See *The Value for Climate Action: A Shadow Price of Carbon for Evaluation of Investments and Public Policies*, report by the commission chaired by Alain Quinet (Paris: France Stratégie, February 2019), https://www.strategie.gouv.fr/sites/strategie.gouv.fr/files/atoms/files/fs-the-value-for-climate-action-final-web.pdf.

32 One example among many is the commentary by Ellen R. Wald, "The Climate Leadership Council's Devious Plan to Distract American Carbon Consumers," *Forbes Magazine*, 20 June 2017, https://www.forbes.com/sites/ellenrwald/2017/06/20/the-climate-leadership-councils-devious-plan-to-distract-american-carbon-consumers/?sh=53f5a3ac6ad6.

33 Adam B. Jaffe and Robert N. Stavins, "Dynamic Incentives of Environmental Regulation: The Effects of Alternative Policy Instruments on Technology Diffusion," *Journal of Environmental Economics and Management* 29, no. 3 (1995): 43–63.

34 Matt Ridley, "The Folly of Renewable Energy," *National Review*, 3

December 2020, https://www.nationalreview.com/magazine/2020/12/17/the-folly-of-renewable-energy/.
35 See Martin Weitzman, "Prices vs Quantities," *Review of Economic Studies* 41, no. 4 (1974): 477–91. This article sheds some light on the complexity of the analysis of the choice of instruments for environmental protection.
36 Extract of the ruling of the Eleventh Circuit Court in the case *US v. Fleet Factors Corp.*, available at https://casetext.com/case/us-v-fleet-factors-corp-3. Also see Kathy E.B. Robb and Christopher Sheehey, "Lender Liability for Contaminated Land," *Journal of Environmental Law* 4, no. 1 (1992): 145–58.
37 On this subject, see Christian Gollier, *L'environnement après la fin du mois* (Paris: Presses universitaires de France, 2019).
38 A recent example of a misguided step motivated by the right intentions but marred by a flawed analysis is the cancellation of the authorization of the Keystone XL pipeline by President Biden on the day of his inauguration. Rather than implement a competitive pricing scheme through a carbon levy, the US government is pursuing the right goals with the wrong means – clearly as a concession to its political base, which is more interested in symbolic gestures than genuine environmental protection. Unlike a well-designed carbon levy, the shutdown of the Keystone XL pipeline will have no effect on the consumption of fossil fuels. Similarly, Alberta premier Jason Kenney's criticism of President Biden's policy is unfounded as he pushes for the pipeline and against the carbon levy, a policy of brazen cronyism. The right policy mix is to go ahead with the pipeline and introduce an appropriate carbon levy.
39 But this does not necessarily apply to the providers of drinking water or water treatment.
40 "Vandana Shiva and Maude Barlow Decry Move to Trade in Water Futures," Blue Planet Project, 18 December 2020, https://www.blueplanetproject.net/index.php/vandana-shiva-and-maude-barlow-decry-move-to-trade-in-water-futures/.

CHAPTER SIX

1 In particular, portfolios of shares in public enterprises such as (in Canada) Caisse de dépôt et placement du Québec, Alberta Investment Management Corporation, and British Columbia Investment Management Corporation, as well as those of the Fonds de travailleurs (Fonds de soli-

darité FTQ and Fondation de la CSN), belong to taxpayers and workers who receive the dividends. It is the same in many countries.

2 See 17 CFR Parts 229 and 249 (Release Nos. 33-9877; 34-75610; File No. S7-07-13), Securities and Exchange Commission, accessed 3 April 2023, https://www.sec.gov/rules/final/2015/33-9877.pdf, and "Securities and Exchange Commission: 17 CFR Parts 229, 240, and 249, Pay Ratio Disclosure; Final Rule," *Federal Register* 80, no. 159 (18 August 2015), https://www.govinfo.gov/content/pkg/FR-2015-08-18/pdf/2015-19600.pdf.

3 Marcel Boyer, "CEO Pay in Perspective," *Journal of Leadership, Accountability and Ethics* 18, no. 3 (2021): 36–73.

4 The excluded S&P 500 companies (outliers) are the following (level and growth of CEO pay in 2022): Warner Bros Discovery ($246.6 million, +554 per cent), Amazon ($212.7 million, 12,546 per cent), Expedia ($296.2 million, 6,952 per cent), ServiceNow ($165.8 million, 560 per cent), Activision Blizzard ($154.6 million, 413 per cent), Oracle ($138.2 million, 1,200 per cent), Intel ($178.6 million, 698 per cent), Berkshire Hathaway ($373,653, 1.8 per cent), Tesla ($0, 0 per cent), Take-Two Interactive Software ($142,996, 3.4 per cent).

5 For the breakdown of individual CEO compensation structure as disclosed to the SEC (including salary, bonus, stock awards, options awards, change in pension value, and deferred compensation earnings, plus other compensation), see "Company Pay Ratios," AFL-CIO, accessed 3 April 2023, https://aflcio.org/paywatch/company-pay-ratios.

6 Derek Thomson, "The Shazam Effect," *The Atlantic*, 15 December 2014, https://www.theatlantic.com/magazine/archive/2014/12/the-shazam-effect/382237/. The author writes, "Even when offered a universe of music, most of us prefer to listen to what we think everyone else is hearing!"

7 Alan Krueger, "Land of Hope and Dreams: Rock and Roll, Economics and Rebuilding the Middle Class," Rock & Roll Hall of Fame, Cleveland (OH), 12 June 2013, https://obamawhitehouse.archives.gov/sites/default/files/docs/hope_and_dreams_-_final.pdf.

8 Oisin Lunny, "Record Breaking Revenues in the Music Business, but Are Musicians Getting a Raw Deal?," *Forbes*, 15 May 2019, https://www.forbes.com/sites/oisinlunny/2019/05/15/record-breaking-revenues-in-the-music-business-but-are-musicians-getting-a-raw-deal/?sh=7893050d7ab4.

9 Luigi Zingales, *A Capitalism for the People: Recapturing the Lost Genius of American Prosperity* (New York: Basic Books, 2012), 20–5. The data is from 2008. It probably kept increasing during the last decade and more.

10 These developments in the magnitude of purses in the area of sports reminds us of the spectacular prizes described by Joseph A. Schumpeter, *Capitalism, Socialism, and Democracy*, 2nd ed. (1942; Floyd, VA: Sublime Books, Floyd VA, 2014), Kindle (no page numbers available):

> Prizes and penalties are measured in pecuniary terms ... They are addressed to ability, energy and supernormal capacity for work; but if there were a way of measuring either that ability in general or the personal achievement that goes into any particular success, the premiums actually paid out would probably not be found proportional to either. Spectacular prizes much greater than would have been necessary to call forth the particular effort are thrown to a small minority of winners, thus propelling much more efficiently than a more equal and more "just" distribution would, the activity of that large majority of businessmen who receive in return very modest compensation or nothing or less than nothing, and yet do their utmost because they have the big prizes before their eyes and overrate their chances of doing equally well.

11 Stéphane Rousseau, Ejan Mackaay, Pierre Larouche, and Alain Parent, *Business Law and Economics for Civil Law Systems* (Cheltenham, UK: Edward Elgar, 2021), 107.

12 Chrystia Freeland, *Plutocrats: The Rise of the New Global Super-Rich and the Fall of Everyone Else* (Toronto: Doubleday Canada, 2012), 53.

13 See Lucas Chancel, Thomas Piketty, Emmanuel Saez, and Gabriel Zucman et al., *2022 World Inequality Report* (Paris: World Inequality Lab, 2021), https://wir2022.wid.world/www-site/uploads/2023/03/D_FINAL_WIL_RIM_RAPPORT_2303.pdf.

14 Marcel Boyer, "Inequalities: Income, Wealth, and Consumption," CIRANO Cahier Scientifique 2020s-26 (April 2020), https://www.cirano.qc.ca/files/publications/2020s-26.pdf. Among recent research on consumption inequalities, one may mention Sam Norris and Krishna Pendakur, "Consumption Inequality in Canada, 1997 to 2009," *Canadian Journal of Economics* 48, no. 2 (2015): 773–92; Bruce D. Meyer and James X. Sullivan, "Consumption and Income Inequality in the United States since the 1980s," *Journal of Political Economy* 131, no. 2 (2023): 247–84; Alan J. Auerbach, Laurence J. Kotlikoff, and Darryl Koehler, "U.S. Inequality, Fiscal Progressivity, and Work Disincentives: An Intragenerational Accounting," NBER Working Paper 22032 (February 2016), https://www.nber.org/system/files/working_papers/w22032/revisions/w22032.revo.pdf.

15 See in particular the series of publications gathered at https://ifs.org.uk/inequality/research-publications/?select-blog_post_types%5B0%5D=chapter&hidden-current-page=1&current-page=1#listing, as well as Pascale Bourquin, Mike Brewer, and Thomas Wernham, "Trends in Income and Wealth Inequalities," IFS Deaton Review, 9 November 2022, https://ifs.org.uk/inequality/trends-in-income-and-wealth-inequalities/.

16 Angus Deaton, "Inequality and the Future of Capitalism," IFS Deaton Review, 14 May 2019, https://ifs.org.uk/inequality/inequality-and-the-future-of-capitalism/.

17 Ibid.

18 Olivier Blanchard, Jean Tirole et al., *Major Future Economic Challenges* (Paris: France Stratégie, June 2021), https://www.strategie.gouv.fr/sites/strategie.gouv.fr/files/atoms/files/fs-2021-rapport-anglais-les_grands_defis_economiques-juin_1.pdf.

19 Dani Rodrik and Stefanie Stantcheva, "Economic Inequality and Insecurity: Policies for an Inclusive Economy," in Blanchard and Tirole et al., *Major Future Economic Challenges*, 195.

20 William Watson, *The Inequality Trap: Fighting Capitalism Instead of Poverty* (Toronto: University of Toronto Press, 2015), xi.

21 Amartya Sen, "If It's Fair, It's Good: 10 Truths about Globalization," *International Herald Tribune*, 14 July 2001.

22 STiK (social transfers in kind) correspond to expenditures made on behalf of households by governmental bodies or non-profit institutions serving households. STiK are complementary to notions of both consumption and income. We might want to conceptualize STiK as income in the form of services. Treating STiK as a supplementary form of income lets us calculate adjusted household disposable income (AHDI) – this allows us to report household income in different forms. Note that the concepts of HAFC (household actual final consumption) and AHDI are the internationally recommended measures of consumption and income.

23 Freeland, *Plutocrats*, 91.

24 "Transcript: Greta Thunberg's Speech at the U.N. Climate Action Summit," NPR, 23 September 2019, https://www.npr.org/2019/09/23/763452863/transcript-greta-thunbergs-speech-at-the-u-n-climate-action-summit.

25 "If Young People Forget and Fail Us, My Generation Will Never Forgive Them," *Financial Post*, 4 May 2022, https://financialpost.com/opinion/marcel-boyer-if-young-people-forget-and-fail-us-my-generation-will-never-forgive-them.

CHAPTER SEVEN

1 For a more in-depth investigation of this issue, see Marcel Boyer, Éric Gravel, and Sandy Mokbel, "The Valuation of Public Projects: Risks, Cost of Financing and Cost of Capital," Commentary No. 388, C.D. Howe Institute (September 2013), https://www.cdhowe.org/sites/default/files/attachments/research_papers/mixed/Commentary_%20388_0.pdf.
2 See Marcel Boyer, "A Pervasive Economic Fallacy in Assessing the Cost of Public Funds," *Canadian Public Policy* 48, no. 1 (March 2022): 1–10, https://www.utpjournals.press/doi/full/10.3138/cpp.2021-035. See also Christian Gollier, *Pricing the Planet's Future: The Economics of Discounting in an Uncertain World* (Princeton, NJ: Princeton University Press, 2013), who argues for a decreasing discount rate over time for very long-term projects.
3 See Sylvain Larocque, "Bombardier s'interroge sur la viabilité des PPP," *La Presse*, 5 May 2010, https://www.lapresse.ca/affaires/economie/quebec/201005/04/01-4277120-bombardier-sinterroge-sur-la-viabilite-des-ppp.php, and Marcel Boyer, "Financement des PPP: L'erreur de Pierre Beaudoin," *La Presse*, 7 May 2010, https://www.lapresse.ca/opinions/201005/07/01-4278358-financement-des-ppp-lerreur-de-pierre-beaudoin.php.
4 *Harvard Gazette*, 6 January 2017, https://news.harvard.edu/gazette/story/2017/01/our-crumbling-infrastructure/.
5 "Build He Won't," *New York Times*, 21 November 2016, https://www.nytimes.com/2016/11/21/opinion/build-he-wont.html.
6 William J. Baumol, "On the Social Rate of Discount," *American Economic Review* 58, no. 4 (1968): 788–802; Kenneth J. Arrow and Robert C. Lind, "Uncertainty and the Evaluation of Public Investment Decisions," *American Economic Review* 60, no. 3 (1970): 364–78; Arnold C. Harberger, "On Measuring the Social Opportunity Cost of Public Funds," *IDA Economic Papers* (January 1971); Edmond Malinvaud, "The Allocation of Individual Risks in Large Markets," *Journal of Economic Theory* 4, no. 2 (1972): 312–28; Malinvaud, "Markets for an Exchange Economy with Individual Risks," *Econometrica* 41, no. 3 (1973): 383–410. David F. Bradford, "Constraints of Government Investment Opportunities and the Choice of Discount Rate," *American Economic Review* 65, no. 5 (1975): 887–99; Marcel Boyer, "Le rôle du gouvernement dans la formation de capital," in *Économie du Québec et choix politiques*, ed. Claude Montmarquette, 189–210 (Montreal: Presses de l'Université du Québec, 1979); Glenn P. Jenkins, "Discount Rates for Eco-

nomic Appraisal of Public Sector Expenditures," *Canadian Public Policy* 6, no. 3 (1980): 549–55; Jenkins, "The Public-Sector Discount Rate for Canada: Some Further Observations," *Canadian Public Policy* 7, no. 3 (1981): 399–407; David F. Burgess, "The Social Discount Rate for Canada: Theory and Evidence," *Canadian Public Policy* 7, no. 3 (1981): 383–94; Claude Montmarquette and Iain Scott, "Taux d'actualisation pour l'évaluation des investissements publics au Québec," CIRANO Rapport de projet 2007RP-02 (May 2007), https://enavantmath.org/files/publications/2007RP-02.pdf; Luc Baumstark and Christian Gollier, "The Relevance and the Limits of the Arrow-Lind Theorem," *Journal of Natural Resources Policy Research* 6, no. 1 (2014): 45–9. Christian Gollier, Frederick van der Ploeg, and Jiakun Zheng, "The Discounting Premium Puzzle: Survey Evidence from Professional Economists," Department of Economics Discussion Paper Series, University of Oxford (2022); Treasury Board of Canada, *Canadian Cost-Benefit Analysis Guide – Regulatory Proposals* (Ottawa: Treasury Board Secretariat, 2022), https://publications.gc.ca/site/eng/9.910204/publication.html.

7 Wikipedia, s.v. "Illinois Pension Crisis," last edited 27 June 2022, 09:36, https://en.m.wikipedia.org/wiki/Illinois_pension_crisis; Raymond Scheppach, "COVID-19 Will Turn the State Pension Problem into a Fiscal Crisis," *The Conversation*, 16 June 2020, https://theconversation.com/covid-19-will-turn-the-state-pension-problem-into-a-fiscal-crisis-139262.

8 Dame Moya Greene et al., *The Big Reset: The Report of the Premier's Economic Recovery Team* (St John's: Government of Newfoundland and Labrador, 2021), https://thebigresetnl.ca/wp-content/uploads/2021/05/PERT-FullReport.pdf.

9 On this subject, see "Proposition de directive du Parlement européen et du Conseil modifiant la directive 73/239/CEE du Conseil en ce qui concerne l'exigence de marge de solvabilité des entreprises d'assurance non-vie," French Senate, accessed 4 April 2023, https://www.senat.fr/ue/pac/E1597.html, and "Les directives 'Solvabilité I' de l'Union européenne," Office fédéral des assurances privées OFAP (Switzerland), accessed 4 April 2023, https://www.finma.ch/Finma Archiv/bpv/f/dokumentation/00920/01218/index.html.

10 "DoD News Briefing – Secretary Rumsfeld and Gen. Myers," news release, US Department of Defense, 12 February 2002, https://archive.ph/20180320091111/http://archive.defense.gov/Transcripts/Transcript.aspx?TranscriptID=2636.

11 See Marcel Boyer, "Défis et embûches dans l'évaluation des PPP: Pour un secteur public efficace et efficient," CIRANO Cahier Scientifique

2020s-25 (April 2020), https://cirano.qc.ca/files/publications/2020s-25.pdf.

12 Though it is generally the case that residual decision-making, or property, rights are assigned to the principal (owner, contracting authority, senior manager), under some circumstances they may be assigned to the agent (employee, contractor, subordinate). On this subject, see Marcel Boyer and Jacques Robert, "Organizational Inertia and Dynamic Incentives," *Journal of Economic Behavior and Organization* 59, no. 3 (March 2006): 324–48.

13 Some twenty-five years ago I wrote the following in "L'économie des organisations: Mythes et réalités," Conférence présidentielle, Société canadienne de science économique, St-Sauveur, QC, May 1996, in *L'Actualité économique* 96, no. 4 (2020): 471–98, https://www.erudit.org/en/journals/ae/2020-v96-n4-ae06831/1087014ar.pdf (my translation):

> The *scientific* analysis of organizations and strategic behaviour has evolved significantly in the past fifteen or twenty years ... At the firm level, this relates to the scale (vertical and horizontal integration), the organizational structure (decision-making process, accountability, and incentive mechanisms), and supplier-company-customer networks and contracts. In the bigger picture, it's about the scale and organizational structure of governments as producers of goods and services and as providers of oversight and regulatory mechanisms, public and para-public institutions like hospitals and universities, and all other socio-economic organizations and institutions. Thus, the concept of organization we use here is very general: it encompasses private and public companies, business networks, and all institutions. (471–2)

14 Risk management generally means that one acts in a manner that reduces the probability and/or severity of bad outcomes without compromising good ones.

15 We need to distinguish between risk sharing and risk pooling. The latter refers mainly to insurance needs and contracts whereby, for example, it can be known that 1 per cent of a given population of a thousand people will incur a loss of magnitude L in the future. The members of this community can come together to pool this risk since, on average, ten of them will incur a loss and, in this case, if each contributes 1 per cent of L to the pool, there will be enough money to fully compensate the loss incurred by these ten members. In general, individuals prefer making a known contribution of 1 per cent of L to risking the loss of either 0 or L.

16 Marcel Boyer and Séverine Clamens, "Strategic Adoption of a New Technology under Uncertain Implementation," CIRANO Scientific Series 97s-40 (December 1997), https://cirano.qc.ca/files/publications/97s-40.pdf.
17 Paul Romer, winner of the 2018 Nobel Memorial Prize in Economic Sciences, developed an approach to continuous growth on the basis that inventions and innovations – in short, new knowledge – are "nonrival" and thus have the characteristics of informational goods and assets. Therefore, they are not subject to a finite potential use constraint. So growth is potentially unlimited.
18 Boyer and Clamens, "Strategic Adoption of a New Technology."
19 Matt Ridley, *How Innovation Works: And Why It Flourishes in Freedom* (New York: HarperCollins, 2020), 259–60.
20 David Lieberman, "CEO Forum: Microsoft's Ballmer Having a 'Great Time,'" *USA Today*, 29 April 2007, https://usatoday30.usatoday.com/money/companies/management/2007-04-29-ballmer-ceo-forum-usat_N.htm.

CHAPTER EIGHT

1 Sound modelling of causality in a situation with correlations and confounding factors is complicated in any area of science. In *The Book of Why: The New Science of Cause and Effect* (New York: Basic Books, 2018), Judea Pearl and Dana Mackenzie claim that causal analysis, in particular the new revolution in causality studies, makes it possible to go from correlation to causality, thus ending a century of confusion and placing the study of cause and effect on solid scientific footing. But even today, many statistical studies, artificial intelligence studies, and econometric studies do not go past measuring correlations and lack any credible statements about causality, whatever the claims of their authors.
2 Paul M. Romer, "Mathiness in the Theory of Economic Growth," *American Economic Review* 105, no. 5 (2015): 89–93.
3 The following academic papers, an impressive but by no means exhaustive list, all suffer to varying degrees of seriousness from this error: Ricardo Hausmann, Jason Hwang, and Dani Rodrik, "What You Export Matters," *Journal of Economic Growth* 12, no. 1 (2007): 1–25; Svetlana Demidova, "Productivity Improvements and Falling Trade Costs: Boon or Bane?," *International Economic Review* 49, no. 4 (2008): 1437–62; Erhan Artuç, Shubham Chaudhuri, and John McLaren, "Trade Shocks and Labor Adjustment: A Structural Empirical Approach," *American Econom-*

ic Review 100, no. 3 (2010): 1008–45; David H. Autor, David Dorn, and Gordon H. Hanson, "The China Syndrome: Local Labor Market Effects of Import Competition in the United States," *American Economic Review* 103, no. 6 (2013): 2121–68; Avraham Ebenstein, Ann Harrison, Margaret McMillan, and Shannon Phillips, "Estimating the Impact of Trade and Offshoring on American Workers Using the Current Population Surveys," *Review of Economics and Statistics* 96, no. 4 (2014): 581–95; Rafael Dix-Carneiro, "Trade Liberalization and Labor Market Dynamics," *Econometrica* 82, no. 3 (2014): 825–85.

4 Marcel Boyer and Sylvain Charlebois, "La Gestion de L'offre des Produits Agricoles: Un Système Coûteux Pour les Consommateurs," *Les Notes économiques*, Institut économique de Montréal (August 2007), https://www.iedm.org/sites/default/files/pub_files/agrio807_fr.pdf.

5 See the interesting interview with Christian Gollier, of the Toulouse School of Economics, on the television program Rendez-vous des entrepreneurs français in 2019: "La REF 2019 – Christian Gollier sur 'Le capitalisme à l'épreuve du réchauffement climatique,'" available at https://www.youtube.com/watch?v=ZS9Xx7hhw3c&ab_channel =Widoobiz.

6 William Stanley Jevons, *The Coal Question: An Inquiry Concerning the Progress of the Nation, and the Probable Exhaustion of Our Coal Mines* (London: Macmillan, 1865).

7 Donella Meadows, Dennis Meadows, Jørgen Randers, William W. Behrens, *The Limits to Growth*, report of the Club of Rome (Washington, DC: Potomac Assoiates, 1972).

8 David Ricardo, *On the Principles of Political Economy and Taxation* (London, 1817).

9 *Understanding the WTO* (Geneva: World Trade Organization, 2007), 16, https://www.wto.org/english/thewto_e/whatis_e/tif_e/utw_chap1_e.pdf.

10 Ana Swanson, Jim Tankersley, and Alan Rappeport, "Trump Blasts Fed, China and Europe for Putting U.S. Economy at a Disadvantage," *New York Times*, 20 July 2018, https://www.nytimes.com/2018/07/20 /business/trump-fed-china-economy.html.

11 Anne O. Krueger, "Trump's Spectacular Trade Failure," *Project Syndicate*, 22 September 2020, https://www.project-syndicate.org/commentary /trump-trade-policy-is-a-failure-by-anne-krueger-2020-09.

12 The same is true for farming, which will end up (as is usually the case for all industries and all countries) suffering from the trade war being waged by the US administration despite temporarily benefiting from compensation paid out by that same administration, generating a mas-

sive risk of "moral hazard" and, over time, a serious loss of competitiveness. See Dan Charles, "Farmers Got Billions from Taxpayers in 2019, and Hardly Anyone Objected," *The Salt* (blog), NPR, 13 December 2019, https://www.npr.org/sections/thesalt/2019/12/31/790261705/farmers-got-billions-from-taxpayers-in-2019-and-hardly-anyone-objected.

CONCLUSION

1 New ideas (such as the NCC and CSD models) usually go through three phases (as per the following, apocryphal statement usually attributed to Arthur Schopenhauer): First, they are mocked as utopian; then they are aggressively resisted; finally, they are acknowledged as self-evident.
2 Robert J. Shiller, *The New Financial Order: Risk in the 21st Century* (Princeton, NJ: Princeton University Press, 2013), is one such book. Shiller (winner of the 2013 Nobel Memorial Prize in Economic Sciences) brings up ideas for using modern economic and financial theory to help manage risks to the value of jobs and homes, to the vitality of communities, to the stability of national economies, to inequality insurance, to intergenerational social security, and to economic security, equity, and growth.
3 See chapter 1, where I reference Zingales's "Plan B."
4 Marcel Boyer, "Défis et embûches dans l'évaluation des PPP: Pour un secteur public efficace et efficient," CIRANO Cahier Scientifique 2020s-25 (April 2020), https://cirano.qc.ca/files/publications/2020s-25.pdf.
5 In *The Third Pillar: How Markets and the State Leave the Community Behind* (New York: Penguin Press, 2019), Raghuram G. Rajan writes about

> the three pillars that support society and how we get to the right balance between them so that society prospers. Two of the pillars are the usual suspects, the state and markets. It is the neglected third pillar, the community, the social aspect of society, that I want to reintroduce into the debate. When any of the three pillars weakens or strengthens significantly, typically as a result of rapid technological progress or terrible adversity like a depression, the balance is upset and society has to find a new equilibrium. The period of transition can be traumatic, but society has succeeded repeatedly in the past. The central question is how we restore the balance between the pillars in the face of ongoing disruptive technological and social change. (xiii)

6 Elinor Ostrom, *Governing the Commons: The Evolution of Institutions for Collective Action* (Cambridge: Cambridge University Press, 1990), 14.
7 Abhijit Banerjee, Shawn Cole, Esther Duflo, and Leigh Linden, "Reme-

dying Education: Evidence from Two Randomized Experiments in India," *Quarterly Journal of Economics* 122, no. 3 (2007): 1235–64. Alternatively, the identification of best practices might result from the search for factors explaining the improvements over time in the relative scores of schools in national evaluations. See Marcel Boyer and Mathieu Laberge, *Portrait of Quebec High Schools 2008* (Montreal: Montreal Economic Institute, 2008), https://www.iedm.org/sites/default/files/pub_files/portrait08_en.pdf.

8   For a more detailed analysis of the crisis, see "Growing Out of Crisis and Recessions: Regulating Systemic Financial Institutions and Redefining Government Responsibilities," chapter 24 in Marcel Boyer et al., *Advanced Methods of Investment Evaluation: Information, Value Creation and Real Options*, CIRANO Monograph 2017MO-03 (Winter 2017), http://cirano.qc.ca/files/publications/2017MO-03.pdf.

9   Fannie Mae published a study in 2002 by Joseph E. Stiglitz, Jonathan M. Orszag, and Peter R. Orszag ("Implications of the New Fannie Mae and Freddie Mac Risk-Based Capital Standard," *Fannie Mae Papers* 1, no. 2 [March 2002]: 1–10) in which the authors claimed that it was very unlikely that the two government-sponsored enterprises *would ever* require a government bailout. One can read in the US Financial Crisis Inquiry Commission (FCIC) report of January 2011, "Unfortunately, the balancing act ultimately failed and both companies were placed into conservatorship, costing the U.S. taxpayers $151 billion so far." Note: conservatorship is established either by court order (with regards to individuals) or via a statutory or regulatory authority (with regards to organizations). When referring to government control of private corporations such as Freddie Mac or Fannie Mae, conservatorship implies a more temporary control than outright nationalization.

10 See among others Bernard Sinclair-Desgagné, "How to Restore Higher-Powered Incentives in Multitask Agencies," *Journal of Law, Economics, and Organization* 15, no. 2 (1999): 418–33.

11 Ben Bernanke, "Mortgage Delinquencies and Foreclosures," speech delivered at Columbia Business School's 32nd Annual Dinner, New York, 5 May 2008, http://www.federalreserve.gov/newsevents/speech/Bernanke20080505a.htm.

12 "About the Fed," Board of Governors of the Federal Reserve System, accessed 12 April 2023, https://www.federalreserve.gov/aboutthefed.htm.

13 Committee for the Prize in Economic Sciences in Memory of Alfred Nobel, "Research to Help the World's Poor," Popular Science Background, Royal Swedish Academy of Sciences, 2–3, accessed 4 April 2023, https://www.kva.se/app/uploads/2022/06/popeken19.pdf.

Index

adaptation to change, 51
anti-competitive practices, 73, 79, 188; abusive non-compete clauses, 63, 82, 83; abusive no-poaching agreements, 83
avoidable cost criteria, 71, 79, 200n34

best practices: discovery of, 5, 23, 26, 28, 179, 187; implementation incentives of, 49–51, 149, 169, 176
business, decoupling from politics, 73, 96

capitalism: and democracy, 96; necessity of reform, 9–10; radicalism and disruption, 82; stakeholder/ESG capitalism, 199n1; state capitalism, 58–9
capitalism reform proposals: Aghion, 64–5; *The Economist*, 62–3; Mazzucato, 65–6; Piketty, 66–9; Stiglitz, 63–4; Tirole, 61–2; World Business Council for Sustainable Development, 69–70; Zingales, 59–61

carbon levy/tax, 72–4, 110–12, 134–5; Quinet Commission, 112
CEO, role of, 23, 73, 96
CERCLA: exemptions from, 206n18; Fleet Factors prosecuted under, 114–15; liability under, 104, 114
certification, abusive use of, 63, 82, 83
child labour, 78; and ESG, 101–4, 154
China, 1959–61 agricultural crisis, 31, 42, 68–9, 199n20
Club of Rome, discredited positions of, 156
collective intelligence, economics as the study of, xvi–xvii
compensation: celebrities in the arts and sports, 124; CEO, xviii, 122–5; exceptional prizes, 124–5; fair and reasonable, 13; inequalities of, 124; priority factors, 19–22, 58
competencies, specific, 7, 12, 31, 33, 36, 84
competition: dynamics of, 49; protection of, 79. *See also* anti-competitive practices

competition-based social democracy (CSD): challenges and pitfalls, 168–71; education (K–12), 175–80; foundations, 35–8; generic policies, 48–56; and health care, 171–5
competitive mechanisms/processes, 8, 31–7, 43–4, 49–50, 87, 92, 158, 168–73; challenges of adopting, 115–17; contestable markets, 44; right to economic contestation, 35, 39, 44–5, 85, 173; supply management, 155
competitive prices: agricultural, 87; in CSD, 50; Lindahl, 93; supply management, 155
competitive-sector organizations, 46–7
copyright boards and pools: 15, 89, 93
core competencies: public vs competitive, 48
corporate income tax, abolishing, 75–7
corporate social responsibility. *See* ESG
creative destruction, 24–6, 49–51, 64–5, 79, 129
crony capitalism, 59–61, 71, 76–80, 83, 138, 154

Deaton Review (IFS), 126
dependence, culture of, 52

easy credit, 9, 61
economic contestation, right to, 35, 39, 44–5, 85, 173
employment dynamics, 24–5
enterprise, different forms of: capitalist, 20, 57, 67, 99; co-operative, 20, 33, 36, 48, 67; EllisDon, 21; IP, 22; mission statement, 72; prime stakeholder, 22; residual value, 19–22; shareholder value/welfare maximization, 99; state capitalism, 58; workers' enterprise, 21, 67
entrepreneurs, role of, 19. *See also* CEO, role of
entry, barriers to, 4, 60, 63
environment: Montreal Protocol, 108, 204n3; value and protection of, 5, 37, 70, 73–8, 98–100, 105–12. *See also* extended liability
environmental security, 156
equity, 6, 94, 133
ESG: corporate social responsibility, 99, 104, 136, 139, 196, 201, 207, 214; definition of, 72; ESG capitalism, 199n1; as mainstream economics, 100–1; principles and policies, 94–103; as public-sector responsibility, 98
ethics, 60; economic and environmental, 94
extended liability, 75, 114–15
externalities, 99–100. *See also* environment

Fannie Mae and Freddie Mac: 10, 17, 60, 184–6
financial crisis (2007–10), 9, 16–18, 166, 184, 186
food security and sovereignty, 155–6
FRAND: access to networks, digital platforms, and essential patents, 81; global price cap, 81; principles of, 203n7; real options, 81

free trade, 76, 78; alliances for development, 55; buy-local protectionism, 78; comparative advantage, 153, 157–60; dynamics of, 157–60; exchange rate, 160–5; as foreign aid, 56; foreign investments, 157, 160–5; win-win, 18, 43, 134, 164

GAFAM, and taxes, 76–7
globalization of markets, 5, 36, 62, 86, 125, 131, 153, 168
governmental-competitive dichotomy. *See* public-private dichotomy
government operations control (GOC), 142, 146
growth: "fab four" factors of, 85–93; quantity and quality, 39

holdup situation, 42, 143, 146
human capital, 6, 19, 20, 50, 67, 85–8, 131, 171

immigration vs outsourcing, 56
incentive contracts, 47
incentives, the power of, 41–2, 89, 170
income-support policies: direct and transparent, 52
inequalities: income, wealth, consumption, 125–9; intergenerational issues, 132–5; social role of, xiii–xiv, 9, 60, 129, 131–2
inventions/innovations, 3, 28, 43, 49, 51, 85–9, 149–51

job creation. *See* creative destruction

liability. *See* extended liability

manipulation: of incentives, 12, 17, 82, 184; of information, 4, 17, 48; of prices, 50–2, 72, 97–8
mergers and acquisitions, 80
modularity: and innovation, 148–52; promotion of, 51; value of, 44
multi-source procurement. *See* modularity

new competition-based capitalism (NCC): challenges and pitfalls, 168–71; generic policies, 71–84

organizational challenges, 11
organizations, economic understanding of, 12

patent pools, 93, 150
performance: evaluation of, 187; pervasive lack of, 4
petrochemical resources, value of, 73–4
price controls, 28, 92–8. *See also* manipulation
profit: supra-competitive profit, 8, 23, 59. *See also* value, profit, and trust
provision of public and social goods and services (PSGS), definition of, ix
public assistance programs, auctioning of, 79–80, 92, 139–40
public funds management, 140–2
public-private dichotomy, 30, 33, 35, 45–6, 170
public-private partnerships (PPP), 60, 142–7
public programs evaluation, 53. *See also* public funds management; public projects

public projects: evaluation and governance of, 142–8

rationality, 40–1
real option valuation, 81–3
regulation and competition, 70–1
responsibility. *See* extended liability
risk: known vs unknown, 144; risk sharing, 147–8

Securities and Exchange Commission, 77, 122
shareholder value/welfare maximization, 66, 70, 99–100
social cohesion and inclusion, 35, 38–9, 54, 59, 85, 168
social democracy: challenges of, 7–9; as dare, 3–6. *See also* competition-based social democracy
social democratic reform proposals: Australian Labour Party, xviii; Blair-Schröder manifesto, 35; Rogernomics, xviii; third way, 35. *See also* competition-based social democracy
social discount rate (SDR), 138–9; cost of public capital/funds, 104, 136–9, 196, 201, 207, 214
social justice, 35–6
social objectives vs means, xi–xii, 46
social partnership, 9
social transfers in kind (STiK), 127–30
stakeholder capitalism, 199n1
status quo, power of, 26–8

taxation: corporate, 75–7; tax reform, 54
Thunberg, Greta, 132–5
tragedy of the anticommons, 29–31, 73
tragedy of the commons, 29–31, 73; institutional challenges, 170–2
trust. *See* value, profit, and trust

value, profit, and trust, 13–19, 38, 58

water: as commodity, 73–4, 114; as human right, 47, 117–20; pricing and trading, 98, 107, 119–20